THINKING THINGS THROUGH: ESSAYS IN PHILOSOPHY AND CHRISTIAN FAITH

Andrew Murray SM

The Marist Series
Through the Marist Series the Society of Mary (Marist Fathers) shares projects by Marists in the field of theology and history and works about the role of the Marists in the church, in particular in the Pacific.

Series Editor: Alois Greiler SM

1. *Catholic Beginninigs Perspectives in Oceania: Marist Missionary Perspectives*, 2009, edited by Alois Greiler SM

2. *A Mission Too Far ... Pacific Commitment and the Missions 1835–1841*, 2012, Jan Snijders SM

THINKING THINGS THROUGH: ESSAYS IN PHILOSOPHY AND CHRISTIAN FAITH

Andrew Murray SM

ATF Theology
Adelaide

2012

National Library of Australia Cataloguing-in-Publication entry (pbk)

Title: Thinking Things Through: Essays in philosophy and Christian Faith
            Andrew Peter Murray

ISBN: 9781921817649 (pbk.)

Series: Marist series.

Notes: Includes index.

Subjects: Christian philosophy
            Christianity

Authors   Murray, Andrew Peter

Dewey Number: 211

Cover design by Astrid Sengkey. Original artwork by Yvonne Ashby.
Layout by Anna Dimasi:
Font Minion Pro 11pt

Published by

An imprint of the ATF Ltd
PO Box 504
Hindmarsh, SA 5007
ABN 90 116 359 963
www.atfpress.com

In memory of
Elizabeth and Michael
Peter and Helen

Contents

Philosophical Reflection

Aboriginal Reconciliation

Preface

These essays first appeared in the Australian Catholic newspaper, *The Catholic Weekly*, in a regular column, which I wrote at first fortnightly and later weekly during the 1990's and early 2000's. They are written by a philosopher as a philosopher but also by a committed Christian, writing in a Christian context. They therefore endeavour to bring light to the issues they address from twin sources – faith and reason.

The life of a philosopher is foremost the life of thinking but it is also the life of imagination that dreams of and investigates possibilities that might not otherwise have been raised. The life of a Christian is the life of faith, hope and charity, and so it both looks to things beyond this world and regards this world with compassion. The two can work together. Faith softens reason, and reason sharpens faith. Imagination finds new ways to articulate in concrete circumstances what has belonged to long traditions of thought.

These essays cover a wide range of topics either by way of simple reflection on life or in response to issues that arose around the time of writing. The period of writing was a varied one. Life looked so stable in the mid-nineties that we contemplated Australia becoming a republic and sought Aboriginal reconciliation. It remained uncomplicated at the time of the Sydney Olympic Games in 2000 but became troubled by political events and by the terrorist attacks of 2001. The essays respond to this time. Four essays not published in the *Weekly* have been added to take note of more recent changes that have taken place in the Church and in our world. Some essays have been updated.

I am grateful to the editor of *The Catholic Weekly* at the time, Donna Wedesweiler, firstly for the way in which she inducted me into writing for the *Weekly*. Tightly written essays do not fare well if cut in the ways that newspaper editors often do when faced with issues of space. Donna was very generous when dealing with such matters. She also offered helpful suggestions and corrections when they were needed. Secondly, I would like to thank her for her encouragement when I first thought of republishing the essays in this form.

I would like to thank two other people for consistent help and encouragement in writing. Gerard Kelly, a friend and colleague, was always ready to talk about issues and gave me the benefits of a prudent and subtle mind. Mary Roddy, a friend of many years, is always interested in what is happening in the world and in the Church and contributed to the project of writing with both enthusiasm for what is and care for how others might respond. Both were always available to talk over a difficult sentence or paragraph.

Special thanks are due to Neil Brown, who, in his time as President of Catholic Institute of Sydney, made the opportunity to write available after first persuading me that writing is a good thing.

xiv   *Thinking Things Through: Essays in Philosophy and Christian Faith*

Finally, I would like to thank Hilary Regan and the staff of AFT Press for their excellent work in bringing the essays to publication in this form and for the enthusiasm and ease with which they did it.

The essays have been grouped into sections of broad subject areas, which show up in the table of contents. Within those sections they appear in order of publication. An index is provided to give access to discussion of particular topics.

Andrew Murray SM
Catholic Institute of Sydney
15 August 2012

ETHICS AND SPIRITUALITY

What Constitutes a Happy Life?

Moral debate rages around us all the time. It tends to focus on issues that are either difficult or controversial or both, such as euthanasia or abortion. Within the Church things such as the publication of a new encyclical or the disclosure of wrong-doing by someone in authority generate similar discussions.

Necessary though they are, these debates tend to obscure the most fundamental question of morals. It is a question that is unremarkable at first glance. Yet it is also one that precedes all these others and one that ought be asked every day.

The question is this. What constitutes a happy life? What makes up a happy life? How do I live a life that is happy? It is a general question in so far as it can be asked of human nature in general. But it is also a particular question and must be asked within the context and circumstances of a particular life. It is about life, and hence for the question to be asked there must be a life, and it must be lived. In this sense the question does not lose its vitality until life is over.

It is not an easy question to answer for two reasons. First, it has to be answered without first determining what happiness and the good are. Rather, what they are will emerge once our question begins to become clear. Second, the answer will be complex because it covers life and every aspect of the activities that go to make up life.

There are, of course, other very basic questions, for instance, how are we to live together? The believer must ask, how do I relate to God? The Christian must ask, how do I follow Christ? The dispensation of grace raises its own issues. However, I believe that the question, what constitutes a happy life?, remains fundamental. It is philosophical rather than religious, and the believer may well have a richer answer. But, if moral questions are separated from this fundamental question, they will become vacuous and nonsensical.

The question is particularly relevant today. I am sure that it troubles the young and even that it is probably only vaguely formulated by them. In former ages it was not a big issue. How one lived was determined to a large extent by the village in which one lived and by who one's parents were. Today the young are faced not only with a bewildering array of possibilities for what they might do with their lives but also with a bewildering array of ways to think about it.

We can assist the young by helping them to focus on this question. When the latest advertisement moves their desires towards a new product, or when the suggestions of a music video catch their attention, or when they are negotiating the complexities of relationships in their lives, or when they just want to know what to do, we can bring them back to the question of how all these things fit into a whole life and a happy life. We can deal in similar fashion with the issues of our own lives.

What is Moral Reasoning?

At the beginning of his *Ethics*, Aristotle tells us that the investigation 'will be adequate if it achieves such clarity as the subject-matter allows'. He goes on to indicate that ethics is not an exact science and advises that 'it is a mark of the trained mind never to expect more precision in the treatment of any subject than the nature of the subject permits'.

All of this reads a bit strangely to us today. We are used to regarding the physical sciences as the prime instance of good reasoning. Even what we call the social sciences attempt to take on their methodologies. By means of idealisation, measurement and mathematics, these sciences provide us with very precise answers to the questions we put. These answers, moreover, are said to transcend the contexts of particular individuals, cultures and languages. If Aristotle was right, ethics does not belong here.

Australian, Sydney based, philosophers, Damian Grace and Stephen Cohen, provide a contemporary account of moral reasoning in the first chapter of their book, *Business Ethics*. They distinguish a top-down approach and a bottom-up approach. In the first, we take general principles and apply them to specific situations. In the second, we start with the judgments based on intuition and feeling that people actually make in particular situations and see these as statements of first principle. Grace and Cohen combine these two in a third approach, in which 'neither particular judgments nor general principles are pre-eminent'. Rather, the two are kept in 'reflective equilibrium'. 'Moral reasoning is a matter of bringing into harmony, or consistency, various particular judgments with each other and with the principles which we hold.'

In more traditional language, we can say that moral reasoning combines both the ability to draw out the implications of moral principles, such as the commandments, and the sensibility or moral feeling to perceive good and evil in particular situations and contexts. Each presents its own problems. The difficulty of finding general moral principles is the basis of the many ethical systems around us. Sound moral feeling, on the other hand, is dependent on well-developed character. Further, we fail when our thinking becomes either too cerebral or purely a matter of sentiment.

Such a way of thinking and reasoning is quite different from the ways in which we think about other things. We cannot measure or calculate moral outcomes. Nor can we ever eliminate the need for judgement of particular cases. Since it is a special way of reasoning, we need to learn how to do it. One of the difficulties of the major ethical debates of our time is that often the proponents, while sophisticated in their own disciplines, lack similar training in moral reasoning.

Reference: Damian Grace and Stephen Cohen, *Business Ethics: Australian Problems and Cases* (Melbourne: Oxford University Press Australia, 1995).

Excellence Rather Than Prohibition

While talking about moral activity in his *Ethics* (II, 6, 1107a9), Aristotle makes the following statement.

> Not every action nor every passion admits of a mean; for some have names that already imply badness, e.g. spite, shamelessness, envy, and in the case of actions adultery, theft, murder; for all of these and suchlike things imply by their names that they are themselves bad, and not the excesses or deficiencies of them.

For Aristotle, these kinds of things are simply bad and there is not much else to be said about them. Indeed, outside the paragraph in which this sentence appears, Aristotle says very little about them at all. Instead, he talks about happiness, about human excellence and about friendship. He clearly finds these things far more interesting and important.

For Aristotle, the human excellences that lead to happiness are a matter of balance. They involve finding the balance, or what he calls the mean, between the extremes of possibility in feeling, thought and action. When that balance is achieved a human being functions at its best and, says Aristotle, is most assuredly happy.

A good example is what he calls friendliness, which has to do with the kind of pleasantness that smooths the social interactions of people. To be truly friendly one has to find the balance between two pairs of opposites: between contentiousness, in which one opposes everybody, and obsequiousness, in which one praises all; and between churlishness, in which one is disagreeable simply out of meanness, and flattery, in which one is agreeable but only in hope of gain. Friendly people have the knack of finding the balance between agreement and disagreement and between praise and opposition in the situations and circumstances in which they find themselves.

The point of balance differs according to differences in individuals, in groups of people, in time and in circumstance. This is what Aristotle finds interesting in ethics—the ability to suit thought, feeling and action to the circumstances of the moment and therefore to live successfully individually and in relation to other people.

This gives us a clue to why Aristotle has so little interest in those other moral issues. As he says, 'goodness or badness with regard to such things [does not] depend on committing adultery with the right woman, at the right time, and in the right way, but simply to do any of them is to do wrong'.

Catholic moral discussion has probably spent too much time focusing on the simply bad. This may give us the advantage of being mostly right, but it also makes us terribly boring and perhaps authoritarian and even lazy. Our tradition, on the other hand, contains wonderful things about love, about friendship, about reconciliation, about destiny, about the meaning of life, about the finest things in life. Were we to offer these to the world, we might find there a far more favourable reaction to our message.

References: Aristotle, *Ethics* II, 6; II, 7 (Princeton: Princeton University Press, 1984).

Ethics in Journalism

A number of years ago, by a strange irony of fate, at the very time that Earl Spencer was castigating the press for the destructive roles it played in the life and death of his sister, Princess Diana, the Ethics Review Committee of the Australian Journalists' Association Section of the Media, Entertainment and Arts Alliance was preparing to publish its report, which proposes a new code of ethics for Australian journalists.

The proposed code itself takes up just over two pages. It consists of twenty standards that journalists will be expected to apply to their activities. The standards are preceded by statements that set out the ethical aspirations and values of journalists and followed by a guidance clause that assists in interpretation of difficult cases.

The report, however, is a full-length book of 186 pages. It includes an introduction that explains how the committee went about its work and the issues that were raised for it and provides an extensive discussion of what a code is and of how one might work. A detailed commentary discusses the meaning and relevance of each of the standards. There is a significant section on enforcement of the code and a number of useful appendices that fill out the context of the study.

It is interesting to compare standards in the code with Earl Spencer's accusations against the press. He said, 'It would appear that every proprietor of every publication that has paid for intrusive and exploitative photographs of her, encouraging greedy and ruthless individuals to risk everything in pursuit of Diana's image, has blood on their hands today'. Standard 4, on use of 'fair and honest means to obtain material'; and 8, on disclosure of payments cover this.

The Earl said, 'I always believed the press would kill her in the end'. Standard 16 states, 'Never knowingly endanger the life or safety of a person . . .'

The Earl called his sister, 'the most hunted person of the modern age'. Standard 13 says, 'Accept the right to privacy of every person . . .', and the commentary discusses the issue of privacy for public figures. Standard 14 says, 'At times of grief or trauma, always act with sensitivity and discretion. Never harass'.

Finally, the Earl asked why the media would treat his sister in this way and concluded, 'My own and only explanation is that genuine goodness is threatening to those at the opposite end of the moral spectrum'. The whole code and the commentary is an answer to this accusation, because its purpose is to help engender an ethical culture among Australian journalists. Its intent is serious.

Ethical issues are often difficult, but within a short time it will be a fair challenge to any Australian journalist to ask, 'Do you have a copy of *Ethics in Journalism* (Melbourne University Press, 1997) and have you read it?' The report is meant to be educational and failure to consider it on the part of journalists or of the interested public will, indeed, be a moral failing.

References: Media, Entertainment and Arts Alliance. Ethics Review Committee. *Ethics in Journalism*. Melbourne University Press, 1997.

Pro-life Means Pro Life

In an address during his Pontificate the Holy Father, Pope John Paul II urged Catholic families 'to show the world that it is possible to be faithful, responsible and generous in loving'.

It is important to keep this kind of instruction in mind when we think about what it is to be pro-life. It is easy to think of pro-life issues as relating only to the time between conception and birth with, perhaps, an extension to the final moment of death. Life, however, is most manifest in the time between birth and death, and it is something to be lived. It is what we can show about the possibilities of this time that will be the strongest argument for life at its beginning and end.

The world has for some time been shocked by the ugliness of the extreme wing of the anti-abortion movement in the United States. They have shown a readiness to engage in violence against persons to support their cause. While we can appreciate the distress that has lead them to act the way they do, their actions destroy the very case they are trying to make. As well, the bitterness of their public statements repels rather than attracts people, who might want to deal seriously with the issue.

Within the public discourse of the Catholic Church there has appeared to be a tendency to equate the gravity of contraception with the gravity of abortion. Anyone who thinks about it for a moment must realise that these are vastly different kinds of things. It would be tragically ironic if their identification were unwittingly to support the growing practice in which abortion is used simply as a form of contraception. That such practice has become common in Australia is immensely regrettable.

If we are to support life seriously, we have to address all the issues that impinge on life. At the social level these include those issues to do with the effects of population stress and with the causes and conditions of hunger and poverty in the world. We have to tackle injustice even in those places where this is uncomfortable for the Church, such as in South America where the Church appears to have been in collusion with unjust regimes for some time.

Above all we need to find a way of showing the world that life can be lived lovingly and well. To do this in the world in which we in the West find ourselves is not easy, but it is the significant challenge that the Holy Father has issued to us. The difficulty is seen in the chaos experienced by many families during the decades since the Second World War; the ideal is one of harmony, human achievement and meaningful life. The serious moral question is: how does one live well in the time and under the circumstances in which it is given to one to live?

Euthanasia: A Question?

One of the strangest things about the euthanasia debate is that it is debated at all. Although suicide has always been with us, it is recognised as an act of desperation in which a person's mind is so disturbed that death appears as the only alternative. The notion, on the other hand, of persons fully in control of their faculties calmly and rationally deciding to end life neatly and clinically seems all-wrong. One of the fundamental inclinations of ordered life is to preserve life, that is, to live.

Why is it then that in our time society should be debating a question that ordinarily would not even be asked? One way of answering this question is to recognise that before euthanasia could become a problem many other things had to go wrong. As a moral issue, it is parasitic on a host of other issues that are being dealt with badly in our time. It is worth raising some of them.

How does one live old age? There have been times when few people survived long beyond the years of child bearing and raising and certainly beyond the time of economic necessity. Today the average life span of both men and women has crept into the seventies and many live into their eighties. Medicine and good food keep them alive and economic planning makes them independent. It should be a time of grace and choice, a time of richness of life, a time of healing, but is it?

How does one die? Much is being published about inadequacies in the practice of palliative care, and specialists are telling us that few need die in dreadful pain. But deeper issues are at stake. We live in a culture in which the processes of death are shunned. People seem to want either to hold death at bay or to hasten it. We need to learn how to die and how to face death.

What is wrong with physical pain? Our culture recoils from physical pain at the same time as we subject ourselves to all sorts of other distress—substance abuse, stress, destructive relationships, emotional violence. Why is it that we should find physical pain so objectionable? Are there not circumstances in which pain might be a tolerable consequence of some greater gain?

What is medicine for? Medicine has advanced enormously during this century. Its practice is often based on the premises that health is the primary good of life and that life ought to be extended as long as possible. Are these premises true? Or is something more subtle needed?

How does one live a happy life? A happy life demands thoughtfulness and discipline, yet how rarely do we ask how one goes about it. Do all the things that we seek to have, to be and to do make our lives better?

Whom is a life for? Is it for just the one living it, or do others have claims too?

The euthanasia debate is important. While the Church is firm in its opposition, it is not enough to keep repeating the argument 'life is sacred'. We need to find new arguments that will persuade the people of our time. We also need to examine and address the conditions that allow the question to arise. Until we manage to do that, it will not go away.

Protecting Choice: Against the Legalisation of Euthanasia

Persons suffering a terminal disease do not come to what might be called the final moment instantaneously. Rather they go through stages of diagnosis and treatment, which are accompanied by moments of challenging readjustment to the situation and by complex renegotiation of familial and other relationships. This process is not normally completed even at the beginning of the final medical phase, when treatment becomes palliative rather than curative.

In all of this there are many choices to be made. Early on, decisions may be made largely in terms of medical benefits and side effects, but, as the situation worsens, other factors such as the person's age and commitments, relationships, wishes for their final days, hopes, fears and spiritual goals become far more significant. These are matters calling for personal choice.

Choices have to be made about who to tell about what is believed to be a likely outcome of a disease and when to tell them. Neither an early fatalism nor adamant denial to the last minute on the part of either the sick person or members of a family are helpful, yet the middle ground is found only by careful negotiation of feelings and understandings as the overall situation develops. Doing this well demands careful and enlightened judgement, so that the sick need to feel that they have freedom to choose carefully.

In a liberal society, a fundament role of law is the protection of people's freedom. This is often expressed in terms of rights—the right to free speech, the right of assembly, the right to representation in government. These freedoms can also be expressed in terms of choices—choices about career, children's education, where to live and so on.

In the simplest case this protection is envisaged as protection from the activities of the state itself. However, it is generally extended to protection from other individuals as in the case of security of person and property, and to protection from society as such, as when we insist on allowing minorities to be different. In an egalitarian society the pressure to conform to common opinion can be enormous, so that the state has a role in protecting even those who want to be different as long as that difference is not disruptive of other people's rights or of harmonious living.

The problem with legalising euthanasia is that euthanasia is such an apparently easy solution to a very difficult situation that it obliterates not only all other choices but the very structure of choice itself. In the face of such an easy option, a patient will not be able to find his or her way into those many issues that call for resolution at the end of a life. Yet this will have denied the person the possibility of a much richer process of choice and adjustment. Families, too, will have had to adjust not to a gradual process of coming to terms with death and separation but to the stark reality of a *fait accompli*. Although legalised euthanasia may seem at first sight to increase personal freedom, when examined more carefully it is seen, in fact, to diminish freedom.

The state does have a significant role in protecting people's freedom and choice in the event of terminal illness and death. Part of that role is to legislate against euthanasia so that the complex structure of choice at this most difficult time remains intact.

A Spirituality for Ageing

In an article called 'Ageing, Faith and Spirituality', Father Laurence McNamara CM set out some fundamental principles for a vision about ageing and being old that would see the elderly both valued in themselves and appreciated for the significant roles they play in society.

In our culture, ageing is often experienced as something very negative both by those who are ageing and by those not yet ageing. It is something that a culture that pursues youthfulness and activity finds hard to even mention. Ageing itself is often experienced as something foreign, coming upon one from outside, a relentless and unwelcome visitor.

Father McNamara points to three aspects of the experience of ageing, which can be understood in ways different from how our culture usually understands them.

Ageing brings with it a sense of slowing down. Gone is the rapid metabolism of youth and the fast-paced life wherein one experience follows another in rapid succession. Does this leave life meaningless? Perhaps it is, instead, an opportunity to experience situations and persons with more attentiveness and care. Time then can be measured not in its duration but in its depth.

The bravado of youth denies destructibility until tragedy forces itself into consciousness only to be denied again. The experience, however, of frailty in old age is enduring and keeps before our minds the unalterable fact of human existence that we live with the possibility of injury and destruction. It reminds us to care for our bodies and for our souls as precious gifts and to care for others similarly.

In old age, death is foreseen. It ceases to be just a speculative concern and becomes part of the fabric of one's own existence. This need not be greeted with horror. Rather, in grasping at last that life is truly finite, one can better realise the significance of the infinite. The very un-speakability of the being of God stands in awesome contrast to our own being.

In the Scriptures, many great figures, such as Abraham or Anna, led insignificant lives until they experienced God more profoundly later in life. Their very weakness enabled them to experience themselves, others and God in new ways, and so to become instruments of Divine mercy.

By viewing old age with renewed senses of time, dependence, need and leisure, we can see it as a period of life full of meaning in itself and as generative of great good for others. Though no longer youthful, it is not discontinuous with youth. The experiences of a lifetime can be reintegrated as not simply linear but as richly related.

Without the pressure of the desperate rush to get on to the next thing, the elderly have the opportunity to lay open the meaning of the present moment. There is not a greater gift that could be given to the young.

Reference: Laurence McNamara, 'Ageing, Faith and Spirituality', in *The Australasian Catholic Record* 76/1 (January, 1999): 40–53.

Ethics and Heroin Addiction

A major division of ethical theories through the ages distinguishes those that are law-based and those that are virtue-based. Most moral theories tend to be more one than the other. It was given to Thomas Aquinas to bring them together by distinguishing law as an extrinsic guide to moral behaviour and virtue as an intrinsic guide.

When assessing the moral condition of ourselves or others we tend to use the categories of good and bad. In virtue-based ethics, we speak about virtue and vice.

It was Aristotle who realised that this categorisation is too narrow. It does not even suit most people. He proposed four further categories. (*Ethics* VII) Above the virtuous he proposed those *super-human* in virtue. This is not of concern to most of us.

Between virtue and vice he proposed two categories. Those who are *self-controlled* act rightly, but, unlike the virtuous, they are pulled by desire towards wrong-doing. Those who are weak do the wrong thing but against their better judgement. Desire pulls them to action, but they do not engage in it with the willingness of the vicious.

Below viciousness, he proposed a condition of *brutishness*. This could be a result of a physiological defect in a human being or could come about through damage or morbidity. It takes a human being beyond the sphere of the truly moral.

It is my suggestion that heroin addicts are mostly in this last condition. The extreme addictiveness of the drug has taken them beyond a condition of choice, understanding or even of perception of law, whether moral or civil. This holds irrespective of what responsibility they might have for becoming addicts in the first place. Morally speaking they are in a condition of morbidity, generally without resources to get beyond that condition.

The question for the rest of us is, What do we do about this? We could leave them to die, and some arguments presented in the drug debate imply, though they do not state, this position. We can, and we do imprison them. While this may be necessary for the protection of the general population, it seems more usually to make their overall condition worse.

A fair attitude for those working with addicts is to recognise and value them as human beings while admitting the morbidity of their condition. It may be a Christian or a humanitarian thing to sit with them and comfort them, but a fair goal for those who work with addicts is the reconstitution of a moral person, that is bringing them back to a condition where choice and right, good and bad, are at work.

Strategies like the proposed injection room at Saint Vincent's are of limited value, if all they do is keep people alive. They do need to do that, but one would expect that their goal be the reconstitution of the persons they serve, difficult though it might be.

A Consistent Ethic of Life

A little booklet written a few years ago by Dr Elizabeth Hepburn IBVM and published by the Queensland Bioethics Centre adopted as its title the phrase 'A Consistent Ethic of Life'. This phrase was taken from a book by the late Cardinal Bernadin of Chicago and is an attempt to capture the sense of the Church's teaching on life in all its aspects 'in accessible language fit for use in a postmodern pluralist society'.

It is easy during conflict over some of the questions of life to get lost in the conflict and to forget the whole picture. We might, for instance, take positions on the distribution of wealth or on euthanasia and yet forget in our actions the respect that is due to all persons or even to the environment in which we live. This little booklet attempts to face the major questions about life and to do it in a way that is consistent and easily accessible. It does it well.

Sections deal with the beginnings of life, protecting and promoting human life, respecting the world around us, sharing the wealth of the earth, understanding human dignity, evaluating technology, and diminishment and death. The booklet does not only explain a position, but it also shows ways in which our lives on this earth can be improved by adopting practical measures to put these positions into effect.

In discussing the protection and promotion of life, the booklet raises the questions of capital punishment and of war. Can we, for instance, support the widespread use of land mines in conflicts around the globe, and what responsibility remains for those who laid them and, indeed, for the whole world to remove them? It is, after all, the poor who continue to be maimed by them. In like fashion, can we be morally justified in investing in the arms industry?

Technology marks all our lives and, in these days, seems to be racing past us. It could almost seem to have a life of its own, yet how often do we ask, what good will it do? Or, how will it affect those least likely to benefit from it? Or, how will it change our understanding of what it means to be human? Or, how will it affect the lives of those walking on this earth seven generations hence? Some of these questions are beginning to be asked as ethics committees and environmental impact studies begin to raise more than simply technological questions.

And, when we get old or sick and approach death, how will we go? Even Jesus was afraid of death and suffering and asked that the experience pass him by. Medical and pastoral development in palliative care can make the lot of the dying easier and make the parting less brutal for both the dying and the living.

Reference: Hepburn, Elizabeth, *A Consistent Ethic of Life* (Brisbane: Queensland Bioethics Centre, 2000).

Can Virtue be Taught?

The question, can virtue be taught?, rebounded around Athens in the later part of the fifth century BC. The Athenians were aware of how much their greatness and prosperity had depended on men of great quality. Pericles as leader of the democracy had held it together while the arts, trade and diplomacy flourished. Themistocles, a general of enormous stature, had masterminded the defeat of the invading Persian army in a daring sea battle in the Straight of Salamis.

Yet the sons of neither of these men turned out well. How could this be? Why did they not have a similar measure of sound character to their fathers? Was not something conveyed through blood? Could not such great men have taught their own sons well? Where did virtue or excellence come from? Was it natural or a gift of the gods or something taught?

The question was of great practical import because the Athenians were aware that Athens had become prosperous and great because it had had men with the right political and military skills available when they were most needed. Was this just luck? Was there a way in which the city could ensure that it would have leaders of the necessary quality in future?

The question quickly became involved with other questions. What is teaching? Is it just telling or is it some more complex kind of instruction? Does it involve some kind of practice such as is done in learning a musical instrument?

At another level, people like Socrates raised the question of whether virtue is one? This question has important philosophical and logical implications, but it also has practical implications. Is there some one thing we have in mind when we wish to teach virtue or, in other words, to form human character? Experience seems to say that the issue is far more complex than this.

To start with, when we investigate virtue, we find that there are many virtues—courage, temperance, justice, holiness, friendliness, and so on. Can one have any one of these without the others? If so, can such a person be said to have good character? On the other hand, if character is marked by such multiplicity, how could one ever specify it sufficiently so as to be able to engage in the development of character?

At another level, there are difficulties about the virtues themselves. What is the difference between rashness and courage? A man who readily approaches dangerous situations might be called brave in war but foolish in the daily political life of the city. Can human beings readily change how they feel and act in different situations or will it forever be that some do well in one situation and others in other situations?

Character is complex, and in order to do well, particularly in difficult times, we need a vast array of fine qualities and the right balance among them.

For Parents of Homosexual Children

At different times during the last few years, parents have asked me to talk with them and sometimes with their families after one of their children had announced his or her homosexuality and had begun to work out what it meant. I am not sure why I was asked, but the experiences taught me a great deal, not the least about my own intolerance.

Two parameters guide discussion on this matter. The first is that for the most part homosexual orientation is not a matter of choice but rather a matter of how someone is. There are mediating causes such as traumatic response to assault or the effects of sexual experimentation, but by and large awareness of this orientation is a matter of discovery rather than of choice or invention. The process of discovery is commonly painful and chaotic.

The second is that the life of a homosexual person as such is not a great life. The exasperated cry of a young woman was relayed to me. 'Mum', she cried, 'do you think that I would choose this kind of life?' It is here that I part company with many gay activists, who, in my view, have not matched their demands for acceptance with frankness about their condition of life.

Whatever else happens, parents faced with this situation can expect turmoil and usually a long period of adjustment. The reality of the situation will not be clear at first to parents or to the child or to siblings. It will become clearer in different ways and at different rates to different members of the family, and this will cause tensions. Fathers typically find it very hard to accept that the situation is real. Mothers are often torn by their love of the child they bore and the tensions evoked in the family.

If a way of accommodating one another is to be worked out, and this will take a lot of time, there is going to have to be love and tolerance on all sides. Love is natural to parents and children. It is also at the heart of the Gospel. Tolerance allows us to respect others despite important differences of attitude, belief and practice. It is valued in the modern world. Both are likely to be challenged by feelings and opinions.

Whatever the outcome of efforts to come to terms with a child's homosexual orientation, life is never going to be what it had been thought to be or what it had been hoped to be. Child and parents have to learn new boundaries and to find ways of meeting that allow love to be exercised without distraction or tension.

The Church is not without compassionate voices. The bishops of the United States showed this in their 'Pastoral Message to Parents of Homosexual Children and Pastoral Ministers' (*Origins* 27/17 [October 9, 1997]: 286–291). It contains much that is helpful.

Blessed are the Gentle

'Blessed are the meek, for they will inherit the earth'. Thus we read in Saint Matthew's rendering of the Beatitudes. Meekness is not something we prize today, and the word has a history that carries negative connotations of tameness and softness. 'Gentleness' is a perhaps a better term for today, but in an age when rage is seen as an expression of individuality or as a necessary impetus to action, argument still needs to be given for the claim that gentleness is an important virtue or quality of character.

Thomas Aquinas treats gentleness together with clemency, and distinguishes them in so far as clemency has to do with action and gentleness with feeling or emotion. He defines clemency as a virtue, which moderates the infliction of punishment according to what is reasonable with respect both to the fact of punishment and to the degree of punishment. Its opposite is cruelty, an excess, which flows from hardness of heart.

Gentleness, on the other hand, moderates the anger that consists in a desire for inflicting punishment or revenge. It does not get rid of anger altogether but tempers it both so as to direct it to a wrong rather than to a person and so as to moderate its intensity, so that any action flowing from the emotion will be of reasonable degree.

Thomas places clemency and gentleness under temperance because they have to do with restraint of feeling and action. In so far as they affect how we react to other people, they also relate to justice. It is here that we see how important it is to link the two together. Many kinds of external constraint such as law or custom can limit what we might inflict on other people. We can, therefore, seem to act fairly, while at the same time we seethe with anger underneath.

These feelings and actions affect our relationships with other people deeply. Most people deal well with actions that they judge to be just, even when these actions take the form of retribution or punishment. Cruelty, however, whether it is verbal or physical or whether it applies constraints on movement or on feeling, brings only resentment. Even where an action is just, contrary feelings are often communicated, and these cause breakdowns in relationships between people.

We live in a time when there is a lot of anger around. It is present in responses to recent world events, but it was there even before they occurred. To some degree, our politics is guided by anger as people experience frustration in dealing with changes in our society or with the difficulties of modern economic life.

To be gentle is not to turn our backs on our problems. It is rather to calm our passions so that we can use our minds to improve our conditions and so that our own passions do not excite those of others in a hopeless spiral.

Understanding our own Behaviour

In his *Letter to the Romans* (7: 15–16), Saint Paul complained in the following way. 'I cannot understand my own behaviour. I fail to carry out the things I want to do, and I find myself doing the very things I hate.' One can sense his disappointment. His complaint, however, is not unique. It is one with which the philosophers have also had to deal.

Socrates brought the question to a head by claiming that to know what is good is to do good or, in other words, to know virtue is to be virtuous. Socrates' claim is extraordinary. Does anybody really think that simply knowing the right thing to do will ensure that we do it? Paul certainly did not, and the experience of most of us probably runs closer to what Paul describes than what Socrates claims.

Scholars find solutions to Socrates' position, but these are not our interest here. What Socrates did was highlight the problem of a human world that is divided only into virtue and vice or excellence and wickedness or good and evil. It is a very harsh world, a very black and white world. While we might hear this kind of world preached even with the sting of a preacher's own disappointment, it hardly fits with our experience.

Aristotle (*Ethics* VII) resolved this dilemma by recognising the complexity of the human make up. Firstly, he recognises the reality of virtue or of character that enables human beings to do the right thing easily and pleasantly in the different circumstances that they meet. Conversely, vicious persons engage in wrongdoing without compunction. Through habituation they readily and easily engage in what we might call evil lives or practices.

Secondly, he acknowledges that this is not the whole story. Experience tells us that sometimes we are torn. We may engage in wrong actions against our best instincts and contrary to our wishes but pulled by desire or slow to act. This might be called weakness. Alternatively, we sometimes find ourselves doing the right thing but at considerable cost. We have to strain against our inclinations. This can be called self-control.

By inserting self-control and weakness as conditions of character between virtue and vice, Aristotle recognises that many of us work out our lives being neither extremely good nor terribly bad yet for the most part wanting to do what is good. We take joy at our successes and strive to remedy our failures.

At a more systematic level, by taking account of this complexity in human character and action, Aristotle avoids some of the epistemological extremes that we find in the world around us. On the one hand, he asserts without compromise that there is objectivity to good and evil. Relativism is not an option. On the other hand, he rejects a dogmatism that views human action and life in terms that are merely black and white.

LITURGY AND SACRAMENTS

Christmas and Meaning

Preaching at Christmas has always struck me as a somewhat difficult task. It is instructive to reflect on why this might be so.

Liturgical principles call for a homily that is connected to both the feast and the readings set down for the Mass. The readings are in fact designed to span four Masses. The first reading in each is from the Old Testament and speaks of the messianic hopes of Israel. The gospel readings cover the whole event from the genealogy of Jesus in Matthew, through Luke's account of Jesus' birth and the visit by the shepherds to John's highly theological account of Jesus' coming. The second readings are excerpts that express New Testament awareness of the significance of the Christ event.

Part of my perplexity is removed when we ask what we are expecting from a re-flection on Christmas. Are we looking for knowledge, or for truth, or for meaning?

What we might want to know about Christmas is very simple. A child was born. His birth was accompanied by some unusual events seen by a few but unrecognised by most. He was to grow up in Nazareth in the care of his parents and later to do marvellous things. Most of us have known this for a long time, so that little is likely to be added to our knowledge.

Are we then looking for truth? This is not very likely either. Parts of the Christmas story have been challenged from time to time on historical or other grounds. These challenges have been answered in various ways and are unlikely to trouble any of us who are committed to the celebration of the feast.

What I believe we are seeking is meaning. What is the significance of the birth of this child so long ago? What is added when we realise he was to go on to make extraordinary claims, to teach us wonderful things and to die and to rise for us. What is our response when we realise that this birth had something to do with us and with hopes that we entertain?

It is not easy to find the meaning of things. Meanings somehow stand behind what we see and experience. Parents of a new-born child can rarely express what the birth means to them although they readily show their feelings of joy and gratitude, and they are able to tell the story and show the photographs again and again. We can spend our lives penetrating the meaning of the Christmas event, and it was so also with Mary, who "pondered all these things in her heart".

What we do at Christmas time is tell the story again. We re-enact it in plays. We sing about it. We decorate our houses to make the time special. We give gifts as an expression of our joy. While all of these have an element of response to what we already believe, they also make the simple event present to us again so that we attempt to penetrate its meaning afresh.

What should I say? I would like to read the gospels from all four masses so as to get 'the whole story'. Then I would like to sit quietly and to ponder it all in my heart.

A Feast for Strangers

It was some three hundred years before the Church began to celebrate the Feast of Christmas. Its first mention is in the *Depositio Martyrum* in the Roman chronograph of 354. It is noticeably absent from a list of feasts given by Origen in his work *Contra Celsum* in about 250. Once it was celebrated, it was celebrated simply as the memorial of Christ's birth. It was not until about 450 that Leo the Great recognised it as a mystery feast—as a liturgical celebration of the mystery of the incarnation.

What this tells us is that it took the Church all this time to come to a general appreciation of the meaning of Christmas. It had given much time and energy to understanding the implications of the death and resurrection of Jesus, but it had been slow to penetrate the wonder of the human beginnings of God made man in the world.

The first celebration of Christmas happened around the time of Constantine, who was the first Roman Emperor to become a Christian. As Christianity spread throughout the empire, it was a feast with which the new Christians could identify and in which they contemplated the marvellous things that God had done and in which they could now share.

It takes time for each of us to penetrate the meanings of events that are important in our lives. In the same way, a culture takes time to come to terms with the most important things in its history. On the other hand, meanings for both individuals and cultures linger on long after the details of the original experiences have been forgotten.

We live in a time that is very different from that of the early Church. It is not a time of expansion but rather a time of contraction when meanings linger on without any real connection to the experiences that first brought them to light. This is so in our culture with Christmas. Many celebrate it, but few either believe in Jesus or know much about him.

We can have different attitudes to this. Perhaps the best is to see it as an opportunity to re-evangelise our culture. If people come into our churches or speak to us as Christians because they are attracted by a glimmer of light, surely we should welcome them and hope that they might find their way to knowledge and belief in Jesus.

Such an attitude makes sense not only at Christmas but also at Easter. Both are feasts that the public world in which we live still recognises. It also makes sense in the celebration of the ritual passages of life—birth, death and marriage—when people turn to a liturgy that may be very unfamiliar to them, so as to bring dignity and understanding to the things that are affecting them.

Among the first to visit Jesus were strangers, the wise men from the East. Today the strangers are among us, and they are our own flesh and blood. It will be a great thing if our celebrations of the important moments of life can draw them back to a recognition of Jesus, on whom depends the meaning of what we all celebrate.

A Time for Reconciliation

Both the season of Advent and the mood of the country call for reconciliation. Advent, which is a time of preparation for the birth of Jesus, takes its tone from Jesus' herald, John the Baptist, who preached in the wilderness, 'Repent, for the kingdom of heaven is close at hand'.

Nationally, barely a day goes by without mention of Aboriginal reconciliation, and in many places, both before and since the Reconciliation Convention, groups of Australians have got together in acts of ritual reconciliation so as to begin to heal the relationships between indigenous peoples and later immigrants. Beyond this, if we listen carefully, we notice that the word 'reconciliation' is gathering momentum and is gradually being found in more and more contexts in our language.

Globally, too, there is a shift, though yet barely discernible in the language. The end of the cold war has removed excuses for the kind of international brutality in which both sides revelled. Recognition of how closely national economies are related, of how much activities in one country affect the lives of people in another and of how small the world really is has forced on nations the realisation that we all have to get on in this little village. No longer is imperialism plausible, nor does 'might is right' carry any credence.

As Church, we are well placed to bring life and action to this new mood. Reconciliation has long been part of our sacramental practice, and the renewal of the Council has seen new emphasis on the communal aspects of reconciliation.

The Rite of Penance, revised by decree of the Second Vatican Council and published by Authority of Pope Paul VI in 1975, endorses three forms of sacramental celebration: reconciliation of individual penitents, reconciliation of several penitents with individual confession and absolution, and reconciliation of penitents with general confession and absolution. The first is what we have long known, the second is in common practice in Lent and Advent, but it is the third that will surely speak to the mood of our age.

At present authorities in the Vatican restrict the third rite to situations in which sufficient priests are not available for the second rite.

But these situations are increasing daily as a diminishing and ageing body of clergy finds itself unable to rush frantically from parish to parish so as to sustain the second rite. What has been truly remarkable has been the enthusiastic response of parish communities in different parts of the country where necessity has established use of the third rite.

It is to be hoped that the authorities will soon cease merely to bend to necessity and instead embrace the desire of peoples for communal reconciliation by endorsing a ritual and sacramental practice that holds profound meaning for our time. An ancient practice, in which the Church celebrated one penitential day during each of the four seasons, would provide a suitable framework.

Christmas: Essentials and non-Essentials

A recent poll in the United States examined the way people prepare for Christmas and sought to compare the amount of time they spent in prayer with the amount of time they spent shopping. To everybody's surprise, on average the amount of time spent on each turned out to be about the same and was said to be approximately sixteen hours.

This finding was greeted with some surprise, and, of course, many wanted to challenge it. Do polls really work? Journalists suggested that it might have been taken in a monastery or that people had counted the time they had spent driving around shopping malls praying for somewhere to park. Australians might simply point out that Americans seem to be more religious than they are.

What this story does for us is remind us to think about what is essential to the experience of Christmas and of Christianity and about how the things that surround essentials are related to them.

The essence of Christianity consists in knowing, loving and trusting Jesus in such a way and to the extent that we begin to live as he lived. The history of Christianity is about Christians doing this more or less well and more or less radically.

We find Jesus in the Gospels. They are not very long. Despite two millennia of theological writing and Church teaching, we find that what God has told us is very little and very simple. At the same time it is very important. We come to know, love and trust Jesus by reflecting in prayer on his life, actions and words. At Christmas time we start again with the birth of Jesus.

All the other things—holidays, gatherings, parties, decorations, cards, gifts and shopping–are for the sake of what is essential. They remind us that there is something we prize. They help us all to think about the same thing at the same time. They do for us in action what otherwise might be only in intention. They prevent us from slipping into lethargy because life seems always the same.

When these things get out of hand, we find Christmas a burden. When they seem to be driven by business, we call it commercialisation. Who leaves shopping to the last minute or the worst time? Is dinner such a production that we cannot enjoy it? Do we send cards to people whose faces we no longer remember? Do we make ourselves do things that were once enjoyable rather than find the best ways to celebrate now?

The sixteen—sixteen plan is not a bad one: some time shopping, some time celebrating, some time in prayer. We can use the celebrations to remind us that there is here something worth living for. We can use the time in prayer to think of Jesus anew - now as an infant and as such infinitely approachable.

Who Needs More Than a Stable?

Jesus was lucky to be born in a stable.

I had always imagined the stable as a typical Australian barn--large and somewhat ugly, bails of hay piled high in the middle, feeding troughs at one end, miscellaneous farm machinery parked at the other, and a broken pitch-fork or two poking out of loose straw on the floor--not a good place to be born.

I realised that this was a wrong image when I went to Quebec in Canada and saw how during the winter snow lay on the ground for months on end and temperatures hovered around -25°C. There animals are kept in a barn, and next to it stand silos that hold sufficient food for the whole winter. The barn is often not heated, but the body warmth of the animals keeps it at around 20 degrees centigrade. Such, indeed, is a good place to be in December in the northern hemisphere.

Scripture scholars tell us that around Bethlehem people lived in caves in front of which they built a part of a house--something like the underground houses at Coober Pedy in Central Australia. The inn of the gospel was not the local Travelodge nor even a Shakespearian travellers' rest, but rather the front room where guests could be entertained and also accommodated overnight. Animals were kept back in the cave and were like a furnace that kept the whole house warm.

So Jesus was born in a good place—not in the front of the house where all the guests were, but back in the cave. It was private. It was quiet. It was warm. It was populated only by the resting farm animals. Safe in the care of Mary and Joseph, he had all that he needed.

This might beckon us to reflect on how much we need. The answer to such a question implicit in our actions is often 'as much as we can get'. In Australia, as the number of people living in houses gets smaller, the houses seem to get bigger. Similarly, our city roads are clogged with vehicles that are capable of handling the worst of outback conditions yet which have never been on a dirt road. Every second shopping trolley seems to have a mobile phone in it.

We find all kinds of justifications for this. 'The family might visit'. 'It is a safer car for the children.' 'Someone might need to contact me.' The more likely reason is that we have the money, and so we buy the goods.

There is no call for us to live in stables, but there is good reason to ask ourselves about what we really need. At the same time we can ask about what others need. Inequities in our own society mean that for some life is a constant battle. In other parts of the world, people starve.

Speaking at a Funeral

In another essay in this volume, I have discussed how religious culture is handed on by way of symbols, rituals and roles and the difficulties we are now facing renewing them in Catholic life in response to our new understanding of the Church, which was generated by the Council.

One area, in which I believe we have had outstanding success, is in the reform of the funeral liturgy and of the rituals that surround it. Although we do not even use all that is available yet and although some emendation may yet be necessary, it seems to me that Catholic funerals are able to stand out as moments in which the Church has got it right. The consolation that can flow from the funeral liturgy is there for all and makes the liturgy a marvellous evangelical moment.

Here, in this essay, I will consider just a narrow aspect of this liturgy, namely, the speeches that might be made at a funeral and, in particular, those that might be made by lay people. I addressed this in more detail in 1994 in an essay called 'The Rhetorical Form of a Christian Funeral Oration', see *Australasian Catholic Record*, 71 (July, 1994): 352–259.

Speech has a most significant place in the funeral liturgy. It reminds us of the love of God and of our hope of resurrection. Equally, it brings the life of the deceased person to mind and acknowledges the sadness of those left behind. It will do other things such as expressing joy at a person's life or bringing into common understanding the things that might be most difficult about a particular death.

It is wonderful that lay-people have a role in speaking in this liturgy. No one, for instance, can fail to be moved while hearing parents speak together about a child they have lost. Further, while he will always shed the light of the Gospel on the moment, the priest is not always best able to call the deceased to mind.

Again, we are gradually learning how to do this well. There are three moments when someone might speak: at the rite of symbols, when the person is brought to mind; in conjunction with the homily, when someone other than the homilist might recall the life of the person before the homilist reflects on it in the light of faith; at the final commendation, which always carries a note of farewell. Not all of these need generally be used.

An important principle is that speeches are for the purposes of the liturgy, not simply because someone wants to speak. Should many people want to speak, that can be best done at a vigil service or at a wake before or after the funeral.

Two rules will save discomfort and embarrassment. First, none of the addresses at a funeral should be long. It does not suit our Australian culture. Secondly, due to both the sensitivity of the moment and to the deep feelings it brings, an address ought always be written out beforehand.

What Can we Make of Lent?

Those of us that have been around for long enough can remember Lent as a rather austere time marked by obligatory fasting. For some, especially for those involved in heavy work, the fasting was severe. It did, however, make it easy to know what Lent was about and what we should do. With fasting came penance for our sins, self-denial and preparation for the celebration of Christ's death and resurrection at Easter.

Much of this is still valid, though we may sometimes feel that it has become a little disjointed. In some quarters, not much is said about Lent, and even the *Catechism of the Catholic Church* is almost silent about it. The reason for the changes was to allow us to engage in deeper personal conversion, but that leaves us the challenge of how we might go about it.

Lent is modelled on the forty days that Jesus spent in the desert fasting and dealing with temptation. The older words that go with the signing with ashes on the forehead call us to sober examination of ourselves: 'Remember, man, that you are dust and unto dust you shall return.' The whole season stands in preparation for the passion of Christ, so that it is a time of sober reflection rather than of exuberance and joy, a stark contrast with but an excellent preparation for Easter.

When we are faced with seeking a way of making such a season practical in our own lives, two questions can be helpful.

The first is, 'About what do I want or need to be reminded?' Each of us will have our own answer to this question, and it will relate to our life's story and to how things are with us at the moment. We might want to remember God's kindness and care, or our own failure and need of forgiveness, or the frailty of human life, or the hope that God's love offers us. Whatever it is, it will be something that bears on our lives at the moment but to which we have not recently given much attention. Daily reflection on it during Lent will enable in us a change of heart.

The second question is, 'What habit would I like to develop by the end of Lent?'. Forty days is a long time, so that something new that we do for each of those forty days, though difficult at first may well be habitual and pleasurable by the end of that time. Again, what each of us might choose will be personal and chosen in the light of our own self-knowledge. If we want to be more generous, we will give regularly. If we want to be more controlled in some respect, we will exercise such control regularly.

By making Lent practical, not only will we enter more fully into the season, but we will also live better lives because of the season.

How Shall we Pray?

In another essay in this volume, I address the issue of the thanks we give to God and of the confusion that certain modern conceptions can raise about this religious activity. We can just as well ask what we are doing when in prayer we ask God for the things we need.

The Gospel of Luke (11:1–4) presents the prayer we know as the Lord's Prayer as a response by Jesus to his disciples' request, 'Lord, teach us to pray'. In Matthew's account (6:7–15), it occurs as part of a longer discourse by Jesus and with some interesting advice.

'Do not babble as the pagans do,' says Jesus. He goes on, 'your Father knows what you need before you ask him'. The prayer itself is very general. After praising the Father we ask that his Kingdom come, and this is linked to his will being done on earth. For ourselves, we ask simply for our daily needs, for forgiveness and for protection from evil. In response, we pledge forgiveness to those who have offended us.

This prayer avoids both the superstitions of the ancients, who tried to control God with various kinds of magic, and the presuppositions of the moderns, who all too readily expect that prayer ought be a tool for getting just what we want. It leaves the detail to God, who knows what we need, and avoids the babble of pagans, ancient or modern, who with a stream of words would like to conform God's will to their own.

Prayer is an act of religion. Its most important outcome is the strengthening of our relationship with God. This is an unequal relationship and one that is dependent on the love of God. For our part, prayer is an expression of our dependence on God, and its outpouring is the natural response of any person who glimpses what God has done for us or how we stand in relation to God.

This does not mean that we do not pray for particular things. Indeed we do, because the particular needs of ourselves and of those who are near to us are very concrete expressions of our condition of dependence. In so praying, we act in tune with the relationship in which we stand with God. What we expect from these prayers is not that we will control God but that God's will may be done and that our relationship with God will be sound.

The way in which God's will works is beautifully put by the prophet Isaiah (55:10–11), who has the Lord say:

> as the rain and snow come down from the heavens and do not return without watering the earth, making it yield and giving growth to provide seed for the sower and bread for eating, so the word that goes from my mouth does not return to me empty, without carrying out my will and succeeding in what it was sent to do.

On Enjoying a Pilgrimage

A few years ago in the Christian Churches in Australia we heard a lot about pilgrimage as the leaders of the Australian Churches joined in a pilgrimage of Reconciliation from Government House in Canberra to Uluru. The concept of pilgrimage is a little strange to us, because, despite numerous advertisements for fly-away pilgrimages, we do not have a place of pilgrimage in our own land. As well, being part of the 'New World', our religious traditions have often been cleansed of some of their more human dimensions during translation.

My own experience of pilgrimage was several years ago in England, when with a confrere I joined two thousand pilgrims from the Diocese of Birmingham on pilgrimage to the medieval shrine of Our Lady of Walsingham in Norfolk, a devotion that had begun in 1061 after access to the Holy Land had been cut off. The original shrine, which represented the house at Nazareth and next to which was built an Augustinian Abbey and church, had been destroyed by Henry VIII, himself once a pilgrim, but the site has remained sacred.

The pilgrimage began with a Mass in the Chapel of Reconciliation one mile from the shrine. The day was sunny and warm, and Mass was followed by picnic lunch on an area of lawn surrounded by fields spotted with cows and summer flowers.

At 3.30 pm, we all assembled and began the one mile walk to the shrine, which some, in ancient fashion, did barefoot. The route followed a narrow country lane that ran parallel to a small but swiftly flowing river. The different parish groups said the rosary or sang hymns. As people moved around, old friends caught up for a chat. Our group got a bit mixed up when a strong-voiced Irish girl in the group behind us started the rosary out of time with ours. We changed to a hymn and drowned out the distraction. There were periods of silence and a chance to say 'hullo' to a group of bike riders that had become stranded by the procession. At times, I thought of Chaucer and of the fun it must have been on a long pilgrimage to stop at night in inns and barns. As we came into the village of Great Walsingham, the locals appeared at their doors and waved.

Benediction and other prayers took place on the site of the original shrine in amongst the ruins of the abbey church. In a moment of special devotion, the Bishop of Birmingham prayed for the intentions of the pilgrims.

Afterwards, we all fell in around the pubs of the small village looking for refreshments. My confrere and I had a pint each and were just leaving, when he was recognised as 'the priest' by an Irishman. We soon found what might have been fourth or fifth cousins, and as they dashed for their bus each ordered a pint to keep us going.

Why did Jesus Come into the World?

As we celebrate the event of Jesus' entry into the world and our belief that he is the Son of God, it is fair to ask the question, why did Jesus come into the world?

The question can, of course, be answered in different ways, which might see us using words like salvation and redemption. Jesus, however, answered the question himself in far more concrete terms, when he visited the town of his up-bringing at the beginning of his public ministry and read from Isaiah (61:1–2).

'The spirit of the Lord has been given to me, for he has anointed me. He has sent me to bring the good news to the poor, to proclaim liberty to captives and to the blind new sight, to set the downtrodden free, to proclaim the Lord's year of favour.' (Luke 4:16–22)

His commentary was brief. 'This text is being fulfilled today even as you listen.' With this he proclaimed his own mission, which was to show the way to the Father, to heal, to reconcile, to teach and to introduce a change into human affairs.

A little later at the beginning of his great sermon, he filled this out in what we have come to call the Beatitudes. 'How happy are you who are poor: yours is the kingdom of God' (Luke 6:20–26; Mt 5:1–12).

This kingdom has some peculiar characteristics. It is one in which those who rule serve, 'just as the Son of Man came not to be served but to serve, and to give his life as a ransom for many' (Mt. 20:28). It is a kingdom that will see its fulfilment only in heaven but which, nevertheless, is already among us (Lk 17:20-21), although it may have overtaken us without our awareness (Lk 11:20).

The point of the Beatitudes is not that it is great to be poor but that in the kingdom, in so far as it is present and active, the poor, who in the ordinary run of human affairs are ignored and exploited, are heard, and more than heard: the kingdom is theirs. And so it is with all those whom Jesus came to free: the poor, captives, the blind and ailing, the downtrodden.

To be Christian is to continue the mission of Jesus. 'As the Father sent me, so am I sending you' (Jn 20:21). The practicalities of this mission have been envisaged in different ways in different times, but it can never be valid unless it takes up the core of Jesus' mission—'to bring the good news to the poor, to proclaim liberty to captives and to the blind new sight, to set the downtrodden free, to proclaim the Lord's year of favour' (Isa 61:1–2). This is why the pursuit of justice, particularly on behalf of the least advantaged, is essential to the Christian life.

Thoughts on the Baptism of Jesus

A question that must come to mind when we contemplate the occasion of the baptism of Jesus by John the Baptist is why did Jesus submit to baptism? The question is present in one way or another in each of the synoptic gospels. John proclaimed that he baptised with water but that one would come after him who would baptise with the Spirit. Again, John recognised Jesus and protested that Jesus should baptise him, but Jesus insisted that the normal pattern be kept.

Part of the answer is that Jesus, though he was God, came to be one like us. Change and salvation came into the world not in the person of a mighty god, a powerful king or a fierce warrior but in the person of one who, until he began to act, was little distinguishable from the rest of us. As he took on full human form with all its weakness, so he accepted baptism from John. His ministry began quietly, though from the beginning recognised by the Father.

In Isaiah 42, the Song of the Servant of Yahweh takes up this theme. 'He does not cry out or shout aloud, or make his voice heard in the streets. He does not break the crushed reed, nor quench the wavering flame.' Then, however, it takes a different turn. 'Faithfully he brings true justice; he will neither waver, nor be crushed until true justice is established on earth, for the islands are awaiting his law.'

How is it that one so mild could bring justice to the world? If he was meant to bring justice, how is it that two thousand years later people still go hungry and nations are ravished by wars? Would not a powerful king or a fierce warrior have been more successful?

To answer these questions, we have to recognise that there are many kinds of justice. There is the justice according to which we expect to be paid when we are employed to do work. There is the justice according to which we expect that all human beings will have enough to eat. There is the justice according to which we expect that nations will live at peace with one another. Beneath all of these, however, there is a more profound form of justice according to which every human being can expect to be recognised as a human being and as loveable by other human beings. It is this last, I believe, that Jesus primarily came to establish.

This is the justice that exists wherever that love that regards each human being as outstandingly precious exists. Even in the direst of situations it exists where Christians live as Christians and where noble souls minister to those that suffer.

We continue to fight for all forms of justice, but this form, which underpins all others, can exist wherever the law of love exists.

A Lenten Reminder of Limitation

On Ash Wednesday as we are signed on the forehead with ashes, we are also reminded of the spirit of the season we are entering. 'Remember, man, you are dust and to dust you will return', or in an older more poetic form, "remember, man, that thou art dust and unto dust though shalt return'. Unfortunately, this form of words does not survive a move to inclusive language very well. This is a pity, because the message is old and profound.

The exclamation comes from Genesis (3:19) and from God's words to Adam after the fall. It is a reminder of a fundamental aspect of the human condition, the reason why suffering and limitation is part of our lives.

Modern science has distracted us from a primitive understanding of dust or dirt that would help us make sense of the passage from Genesis. For us, dirt is matter, and matter can be analysed into chemicals, broken down into energy or recombined into more complex and useful chemicals. From a more primitive and a more closely human perspective, dirt is what is all around us. It is inert and almost featureless, and, while we depend on it as something on which we walk or in which we grow crops, in contrast to the marvel of living things, there is not much to it.

Yet, God reminds Adam and through Adam all of us that despite our pretensions we are made from dust or dirt or matter. This is the reason why we suffer, why life is a battle, why at the end of life we will decay back into dust. It is a stark reminder of the limitations of the human condition, of human existence.

We are not, however, just dirt. God's injunction to remember makes this clear. Dirt does not remember, but human beings are able to be aware not only of things around them but also of things that are past, of things whose presence to them is no longer physical. It is only for human beings that the question of where we came from and where we will go has meaning.

Modern existentialism has made much of the ability of human beings to question their origins and end, but its conclusions have been rather dreary and negative. Our Faith is much richer, because we believe that God breathed Spirit into the dust and that we are made in the image of God. This complexity in our being is what makes the vast gap between our aspirations and our experience of limitation possible.

Lent, then, is a time to remind ourselves of our limitations—that pain touches us; that we have to labour for our sustenance; that we cannot know all we would like to know; that distractions draw us away from what we value most—not so that we despair but so that we might turn humbly to our God.

FAITH AND THE GOSPEL

Fides et Ratio: An Encouragement to Scholarship

It is over a decade since the publication of Pope John Paul II's encyclical, *Faith and Reason (Fides et Ratio)*. It was signed by the Pope on 14 September 1998, and was launched on 20 October of the same year, the twentieth anniversary of his pontificate, by press releases to the world media channels and by placement on the Vatican web site.

The encyclical is a formidable piece of work on a difficult and long-lived topic—the relationship between revealed truth and the truth of natural reason. It brings the fruits of John Paul II's long reflection as a Christian thinker and religious leader carried out in consultative collaboration with leading Catholic scholars around the world.

The encyclical covers many issues, among them the relationship of faith and reason; the nature of truth and meaning; the role of culture in human and religious experience; the interpretation of texts; the Church's tradition of engagement with philosophy in Christian reflection; the relationship between magisterial statements and autonomous learning. Each of these and others will be the topic of serious study in the months and years ahead.

An appropriate response is to remark on the encouragement that John Paul II gave to learning and scholarship in this work. He called on the sciences, and particularly on philosophy, to address those questions and issues that give meaning to human life. Does life have a meaning? Where is it going? How do we understand suffering and confront death? These questions all have an answer in faith, but in this encyclical John Paul II asked us to find answers through reason in ways appropriate to our times.

It is outstanding that in this encyclical John Paul II did not answer these questions himself in the name of philosophy. He issued the challenge and he stated criteria for a solution such as the unity of human thought and a firm grasp of first principles. He also raised issue with certain tenets of modern thinking such as eclecticism, historicism and nihilism. To philosophy, however, he left its autonomy intact.

Similarly, while he endorsed the long tradition of Western philosophy and theology and the work of people like Augustine, Anselm, Aquinas and Bonaventure and modern writers like Newman and Gilson, Pope John Paul repeatedly stated that the Church has no particular philosophy of its own. He praised some of the findings of modernity. He looked to philosophies of the East, especially those of India. He valued science. He respected cultures other than his own.

What this amounts to is a call to scholarship, a call to wrestle with the issues of our time in language consistent with our time. This is a serious call meant for the betterment of human life.

Is God Good?

Is God good? 'Of course!', we will all say. Perhaps, though, we should reflect for a moment. How do we know what 'good' is? How did we learn about it in the first place? Maybe when words started to form for us we realised that Mum was good and that that is what good is like. Maybe we just learnt that ice-cream is good. Are we then saying that God is like Mum or that God is like ice-cream?

Before we answer this, we might think about some of the other things we say about God. In the Psalms, we hear, 'God alone is my rock, my stronghold, my fortress'.

Sometimes we get more grand, and then we say that God is infinite or all-powerful or immutable or eternal. These words are comforting because they seem to tell us what God is like and that nothing else is like God. But, if these words can be applied to nothing apart from God, how do we know what they mean?

These are all problems that confront us when we start to think about the words we use about God. How will we resolve this?

In another section of this volume I dealt with the issue of analogy. We use words analogically when we extend their meanings to senses like but different from their original or primary meaning, for instance, when we get 'computer menu' from 'restaurant menu'. This is part of the answer to our questions.

When we say 'God is good', we use analogy. We have learnt what good is in the ordinary way of earthly things and we apply the word to God in a way, however, that is different, because for God to be good is much more than it is for ice-cream or anything else to be good. In fact, there is a twist to it. We learn about goodness from the things around us, but goodness itself belongs primarily to God.

This is not the only way we use words about God. In the examples from the Psalms, we use metaphor. In metaphor, we call something by the name of some other thing. The meaning is conveyed not because the things are very much like each other as in analogy but because the word conveys an image that helps us grasp a meaning. Hence, to say God is a rock or a fortress is to use the image to convey something of what God is to us.

The grand words belong to another tradition, which says that we can only know what God is not. Hence, to say that God is infinite means simply that God is not finite and so not like the things we know. Similarly, to say that God is all-powerful means that there is no limit to God's power or to what God can do.

Each of these ways of dealing with meaning helps us speak of a God, who, though beyond our understanding, has revealed the Word to us.

References: Psalm 61; Thomas Aquinas, *Summae Theologiae* I qq. 1–13.

At the Heart of being Christian

A few years ago I set out on a camping trip to find the Macquarie Marshes, an important wildlife habitat in the western New South Wales of Australia. The marshes are easy to locate on a map, because they sit between two parallel roads running north from Warren to Carinda, but they are harder to reach, because they are at the backs of farms, which front onto the two roads.

Eventually I called into the pub in Quambone, a tiny town about half way between these two towns. The barman did not know where the marshes were and referred me to a couple of locals, who did not know either but who suggested that I ask (let us call him) George over in the corner, because he knew everything around there. As George could not tell me where to go, I asked him whether I would see anything if I took a road that seemed to me to cut across where I expected the marshes to be. George said, 'All you'll see down there, mate, is a heap of bulrushes'. That was good enough for me, but I left feeling that George had missed the point.

More recently, I was talking with a friend of many years. She has been a wonderful Catholic wife and mother and for a long time has been vigorously involved in church and community activities. When she confided that she felt she believed less now than when she had been young, I asked her what she did believe. She said that she believed that love was the main thing.

It seems to me that she had hit the point and that she is at one with Jesus, who gave us only two commandments, to love God and to love our neighbour as ourselves.

In recent years we have seen that love is not everywhere in the Catholic Church. Revelations that Catholics have travelled around parishes not to worship but to spy and to take notes have shocked many of us. There have been reports of Curial officials in Rome colluding with these people in activities which will only drive a wedge between the pope and the Australian Catholic bishops. We might refer to all of this as beating around the bulrushes, but, if it affects communion in the Catholic Church, it is far more serious.

A recent discussion on possibilities for evangelisation concluded: 'Jesus assures us that people would be startled into admiration, which would lead to belief, if they experienced a community of believers in that loving unity which is the reflection of the unity of the Trinity.'

That surely is what we believe and also what most Catholics are trying to do, difficult though it may be in a pressured and changing world and in a Church that for the moment has lost some of its energy. Love, indeed, is what it is all about and little else counts.

Reference: Bishop John Heaps, *A Love that Dares to Question: A Bishop Challenges His Church* (Melbourne: Aurora Books, 1998), 34.

Sin, Reconciliation and New Life

One of the criticisms that Australian Catholics have been labouring under in recent days is that we have lost a sense of sin. It was listed specifically in the *Statement of Conclusions*, and one suspects that fear of such a state of affairs arising is one of the issues behind conflict about use of the third rite of reconciliation. It seems to me, however, that the truth of the matter lies in a contrary direction. Evidence of this is the frequency with which the term 'reconciliation' now appears in daily discourse. It is worth listening for it.

In Australia, one of the most significant movements of our time is the movement towards Aboriginal Reconciliation. The movement implies past wrongdoing and, for the God-fearing, sin. Whatever the complications of history, a people have been wronged and healing will not be effected until there is an acknowledgment of wrong-doing, a call for reconciliation and forgiveness.

Similar movements abound in Australia and around the world. The movement for reconciliation with the earth and with the environment recognises that we have lived in ways that are not sustainable and that damage the earth on which we depend.

Reconciliation is still being sought for the wrongs of the Second World War, and governments are being forced to say "sorry" more than fifty years after the conflict, because the suffering of people who live with the effects of various forms of brutality has not yet been recognised.

Even governments are changing. The arrest of General Pinochet in Chile showed that civil law is recognising that some crimes are so great that they attain world status and that irrespective of the stance of the state in which they were committed, the world community cannot rest until justice has been enacted. Similarly, the War Crimes Tribunal has been active even as the conflict, in which the crimes that they were investigating were committed, has been raging.

In the Catholic Church, the pope has for some time been urging the Roman Curia to examine how the Holy See might apologise for the wrongs of the Inquisition.

There are here competing senses of sin and reconciliation. Reconciliation takes forms appropriate to the life and times of those who seek it, but seek it we must, because failure, wrong-doing and sin touch all our lives.

For us Christians, the point of reconciliation is twofold. First, it restores a world in which love is active. Peoples who have been divided and who have hurt one another begin again to live together in the love of God. Second, it opens us to the redemptive activity of Christ, which we celebrate this Easter, an activity that is to renew the whole earth. It was for the sinful that Christ came, but he came that we might have life.

Reference: Luigi Accattoli, *When a Pope Asks Forgiveness: The Mea Culpas of John Paul II* (New York: Alba House, 1998).

Marist Project Continues Mary's Work

The canonisation of Marcellin Champagnat, in 1999, was a great moment for the Marist Brothers, who recognise him as their founder. It was also celebrated by the various Marist congregations, all of whom share in what has sometimes been called the Marist Project.

On the 23rd of July 1816, a group of about twelve seminarians and newly ordained priests including Champagnat went on pilgrimage to the much venerated shrine of Our Lady at Fourviere high on a hilltop overlooking Lyon in France. There they made a pledge to found a religious congregation that would be dedicated to Mary, the mother of God, something they had been discussing for four or five years.

The plan was to found a single congregation called the Society of Mary, which would consist of four branches—brothers, sisters, priests and lay associates. Founding a new congregation proved not to be easy, and, in fact, in time four different congregations were founded.

By the 2nd of January 1817 Champagnat had brought two young men together and later that year opened a school.

In 1817, Jeanne-Marie Chavoin took the first step in forming a group of Marist Sisters, who took the religious habit for the first time on the 8th of December 1824.

On the 11th of March 1836 the Marist Fathers received approbation from Rome following a long series of representations by Jean Claude Colin and quickly took on the new mission of Oceania.

In 1845, a daring French lay-woman, Franciose Perroton, boarded a ship on her own accord to go to the Pacific to work with the women of Wallis alongside the priests. What she began became the third order Regular of Mary in 1881 and the Marist Missionary Sisters in 1931.

Different lay groups have been associated with all these branches.

Central to the early plan was the idea that through a congregation dedicated to her name, Mary would continue to work in the Catholic Church. She who had been present at the inception of the Church would be there until its end. Such a congregation would think, work and act like Mary, quietly 'pondering these things in her heart'.

The need that the congregation set out to meet was that of the country districts of post-revolutionary France where in many senses the Church had collapsed and modernity was beginning to be felt. Children were not being educated in the faith, and the pastors that were left often could not communicate well with the people of the villages and towns. A new way of speaking was needed.

Prior to the French Revolution the Catholic Church had acted very much in the mode of the Church triumphant. Though in some respects it would continue to do so, the original Marists realised that this way of action would only alienate people from the faith and from returning to the faith. Like Mary, they wanted to act as 'instruments of Divine mercy', and so were to live in the world 'hidden and as if unknown'.

References: Luke 2, 19; Jan Snijders, *The Age of Mary*, Maristica 1 (Rome: Centre for Marist Studies, 1988); Jean Claude Colin, *Constitutions of the Society of Mary*, 1872 (Rome, 1992), no 50.

Church Unity: An Imperative for Today

By chance a few years ago now I came across some statistics that prompted thought about the urgency of church unity.

In the parish of Gladstone, Queensland, in 28.5% (576) of 2,020 families with at least one Catholic parent, and children living at home, the other parent is also Catholic. In 58.1% (1,174), one parent is Catholic and the other belongs to another Christian denomination. And in 13.4% (270), one parent is Catholic and the other is either non-Christian, of no religion or stated no religion in the 1996 Australian census.

The same census recorded the following levels of religious affiliation for Gladstone: Catholic—22%; other Christian denominations—51%; non-Christian, etc—27%. While the percentage of Catholics in Gladstone is below the national average, these statistics tell a story.

Briefly it is this. Fewer Catholics (10.4%) are married to non-Christians than would be the case if marriage partners were chosen by random. In other words, Catholics tend to marry Christians. Roughly twice as many Catholics (44.2%) are married to Catholics than would be the case if marriage partners were chosen by random. In other words, there is still a tendency for Catholics to marry Catholics, though it is not as strong as it used to be. On the other hand, 45.2% of Catholics married with children at home are married to non-Catholic Christians, which amounts to over half of the marriages in this group.

If the family is the Domestic Church founded on a sacramental union, and assuming that the figures are some indication of conditions Australia-wide, these conclusions have enormous significance for how the Catholic Church in Australia should think about itself and how it should conduct itself. At the domestic level, church unity is a fact. When Australian families pray together or when they make decisions based on religious belief or when they share in any way their religious convictions, ecumenism is at work.

This was not always the case. In the 1950's, Catholics tended to marry Catholics. 'Mixed marriage' was frowned upon and the different denominations tended to live in separate communities in towns and suburbs. At times there was hostility between groups, and those of us who grew up in that time can remember stories of strange doings. Non-Catholics who married Catholics often have bitter memories of their weddings being relegated to the sacristy.

The change has been good, though not without its difficulties. We believe that Christ instituted one Church and that its division is a scandal. Greater accommodation between Christians has been a move towards being better Christians and specifically toward better showing the love of Christ to the world. This has happened at the level of formal dialogue between Churches, but as these figures show even more quickly at the domestic level.

The change makes it imperative that, at the level of parish communities, ways be found to welcome and respect spouses of Catholics. Exclusionary practices can only damage the Church. At the level of Church leadership further advances towards unity are absolutely necessary.

Reference: Australian Catholic Bishops Conference, *National Catholic Census Project: Parish Tables from the 1996 Australian Census–Gladstone* (Pastoral Research Projects Officer, PO Box 1209, Clayton South, Victoria 3169).

Whatever Happened to Hell?

Occasionally someone asks the question, 'Where has hell gone these days?' The strict answer is that hell is not the kind of thing that can go anywhere, but that is not what people mean when they inquire in this way.

Usually people who ask this kind of question were alive and active at least in the 1950's and possibly before that. They remember strong sermons given often by fiery missioners that left the clear impression that if one did not perform to standard the sub-terrestrial flames would eagerly scorch their next victim.

Changes in theological opinion have some relevance to the issue, but when we ask why hell is not preached to us so much any more, the fundamental answer is that nobody would listen. That is very interesting.

When we wish to bring a person to change, either to act differently or to think differently, there are three basic ways of doing it. We can use compulsion or coercion or consent.

Under compulsion people are made to act in a certain way by force. It may be physical or emotional—a clever bit of manipulation or the use of physical strength. In any case people do not act freely, and we regard this kind of thing as violent and unacceptable.

Coercion, on the other hand, is a normal part of life. Persons with authority indicate that if we do not act in a particular way certain penalties will follow. We remain free, but we have to live with the consequences. Many people obey speed limits on the roads for just this reason.

Consent is at work when people agree to act in a certain way because they have come to recognise that it is the best way to act. For this to happen speech and persuasion have to be at work.

Most groups work on a mix of coercion and consent. Life is richest when most actions are performed by consent, but usually some degree of coercion is present. In our time the Road Traffic Authority does its best to persuade people to drive safely, but coercion remains for those for whom consent is lacking. On the other hand, groups will tolerate only so much coercion and when it stands alone it is usually ineffective.

Hell was for many years the tool of the Church's coercive approach to moral and spiritual life. That it was overdone is without doubt when we consider the stories of people who grew up in those years. Once overused, coercive power is weakened especially when, as now, reaction against any form of coercion is strong in society at large.

What the Church has now to do is to persuade people. It needs to show them the person of Jesus and the attractiveness of a life lived in Jesus. This is something we have yet to learn to do well, but it can be done.

A Significant Step Towards Unity

On the 12th of May 1999, The Anglican-Roman Catholic International Commission (ARCIC) issued a statement called 'The Gift of Authority'. The Commission was set up in 1970 by both Churches following the visit of the Archbishop of Canterbury, Dr Michael Ramsey, to Pope Paul VI in Rome in 1966. It is composed of scholars from both denominations and its task has been to formulate statements on doctrine to which both Churches could agree. A number of these have already been published.

The 1999 statement is on authority and was written in response to questions raised by the 1998 Lambeth Conference of the Anglican Communion on the issue of universal authority in the Church and by Pope John Paul II in his encyclical, *Ut unum sint*, on the ministry of unity of the Bishop of Rome.

What is extraordinary about this document is that the Commission concludes that the Churches are 'in sufficient agreement on universal primacy as a gift to be shared, for [it] to propose that . . . primacy could be offered and received even before our churches are in full communion'. In other words, on the basis of the understanding of authority developed in the document, there is no obstacle to the Anglicans accepting the pope as primate of the universal Church or of the pope exercising that role.

It is, of course, not quite as simple as that. The Anglicans say that it would have to be under certain clear conditions, and it is clear from the document that both Churches would have to engage in new learning and that both would have to re-receive aspects of the Church's tradition that have been 'rejected, forgotten or not fully understood'. On the other hand, nothing of the document's discussion of authority in the Church stands out as contrary to Catholic teaching or even as exceptional. The issues relate more to how that teaching sees its way into practice.

In recent years there has been some stagnation in the exercise of authority in the Catholic Church. This may have a variety of causes such as the crisis of authority following the encyclical, *Humanae vitae*, or the consolidation of Roman Curial power under an unusually long papacy. The ARCIC document, on the other hand, makes much of the *sensus fidelium*, the notion that authoritative teaching must take place in dialogue with the Faithful, and we could well accept this reminder. On the positive side, post-Conciliar experimentation with Synodal consultation can be seen as a worthwhile development.

'The Gift of Authority' is a response to questions raised by Church leaders of both denominations. It will also be a further challenge to them. It specifically lists issues facing Anglicans and issues facing Roman Catholics. Among those facing Catholics are: the effectiveness of lay and clerical participation in emerging synodal bodies; implementation of Vatican II's teaching on the collegiality of bishops; consultation of local Churches before decisions are made affecting them.

Reference: ARCIC, *The Gift of Authority: Authority in the Church III* (London: Anglican Book Centre and Catholic Truth Society, 1999).

Do we Know What the Church Teaches?

Some time ago I was teaching a section on ethics in an introductory course. A student intervened and asked, 'Why study this at all? Couldn't we just do what the Church teaches?' I replied that we might neither know nor understand what the Church teaches.

A few weeks later, the point of my answer was amplified when we read an essay from Thomas Aquinas's *Commentary on Boethius' De Trinitate* (question 2, article 4). There Thomas asked the question, 'Whether Divine truths ought to be concealed by new and obscure words?' His answer is enlightening.

Contrary to our expectations and to our experience of the clarity of his own writing, Thomas made it clear that, under certain conditions, sacred truths ought to be discussed in obscure language that hides the meaning of these truths from the majority of people. Further, he cites Saint Augustine (*On Christian Doctrine*, Part IV) as saying that even more care ought to be taken in writing, because books can come into the hands of anybody.

To us in the modern world, this is likely to be surprising. We have grown used to universal education, to making our own decisions in matters of ethical and religious belief, and to the expectation that knowledge, once achieved, will be given the widest publicity. We ought, however, take note of Thomas's reasons.

Thomas uses the principle 'that the words of a teacher ought to be so moderated that they result to the profit and not to the detriment of the one hearing him'. He concedes that some teachings need to be known by everybody and that they ought to be widely disseminated but that there are other truths that could cause harm and that these ought not be openly presented.

He has in mind two kinds of harm. Firstly, should unbelievers learn about some sacred teaching, they might deride it, and that ought to be avoided. Secondly, if some of the more subtle nuances of sacred teaching are presented to those who are not well educated in the faith, they will fall into error due to their inability to cope with fine distinctions.

The point that I wish to draw from this reflection is that continuing education in the faith is extremely important for us all. Two things militate against such continuing education. Firstly, the Magisterium of the Church itself has, over a number of centuries, got used to speaking to uneducated people, so that its teaching has taken the form of telling. Secondly, a modern kind of fundamentalism has put its faith in a few formulations that it repeats over and over again with or without meaning.

As we continue the reform of the Church begun in the Council, an essential part of the practice of the faith remains education in that faith not only as children but as adults and according to our own capacities.

Abandonment to the Will of God

I remember as a young boy wondering why, when the angel announced to her that she was to have a child, Mary asked for a Fiat. It did not trouble me that she should have a small car, but I knew that Joseph could afford only a donkey and that Mary's desire seemed out of keeping with her husband's means. It was some years before I learnt that there was something odd even about Mary speaking Latin.

These reflections must have been occasioned by a sermon from our parish priest, a tough Irishman with a loud voice and great determination. The sermon, I assume, was occasioned by the Annunciation and focussed on Mary's reply to the angel, 'Let it be done unto me', or, in Latin, 'Fiat', something known in a kind of shorthand as 'Mary's fiat'.

The sermon, then, must have been on that great theme of our spiritual tradition, abandonment to the will of God. It is exemplified in Mary, who, confronted by the angel's extraordinary proclamation, accepted something that she could not possibly make much sense of, yet which she believed was what God was calling her to. She was, she said, 'the handmaid of the Lord'.

In abandoning ourselves to God, we acknowledge both God's greatness and our own limitation. God, as creator, not only knows the world and each of us intimately but also loves what that creative act has brought into being. We, who, more often than not, would like to control every facet of our lives, recognise that we cannot even understand all that happens to us and so we cast ourselves into the loving hands of God.

This does not mean that the course of life becomes easy to discern. What if the angel visiting Mary had been unconvincing? Where would God's plan have been then? At the time of my early religious training, it was commonplace that the will of God for a religious was what a superior told him or her to do. The difficulties that might arise with a sick or a difficult or even an insane superior were not discussed. Perhaps we were too young, but it seemed that they were not discussed elsewhere either.

We have come a long way since then. The point of abandoning ourselves to the will God is not that someone else will lay a clear path for us and enable us to live without concern about whether we should turn in this direction or that. Nor will cleverness allow us to discern just what that will is so that we can follow a firm and fixed course.

Rather, we will continue to use all our God-given gifts to live in the best way we can. In so doing, however, we will remember that we do not understand everything, and when adversity strikes we will remain confident of the love of God around us.

Living in a Diminishing Church

It is now commonplace to say that we are living in a diminishing Church. A few years ago we could deny it, but now the signs are all too obvious. Falling Mass attendance and the ageing of those who do attend tell a story. Serious decrease in the numbers of young people joining the priesthood and religious life is presenting its own problems. What are we to make of this?

Australian Catholic theologian, John Thornhill SM has addressed this situation in a very helpful essay called, 'Understanding the Church's Present Difficulties, and the Reaction they are Producing', in the *Australasian Catholic Record* 76/1 (January 1999): 3–14.

His first question is about the Second Vatican Council. Should we have had it? Did it go wrong? Indeed, one sometimes hears people suggest that we should not have had the Council or propose programs that seem directed at restoring the pre-conciliar condition of the Church. Thornhill's response is unequivocal.

By the time of the Council, the Church was in serious need of reform. The crises provoked by such historical events as the emergence of the culture of modernity and as the Protestant Reformation had developed a strong reactionary character in the Church. 'The Church saw itself as living *in a world apart*, no longer sharing fully in the struggles and hopes of humanity and its history'. Such a Church had become rigid and institutionalised and looked for life to canonical discipline rather than to the Scriptures, the Sacraments and to its own heritage, particularly the teaching and practice of the early Church. It was, indeed, in need of reform.

Nor did the Council fail in any serious way in its program of reform. It recognised its mission to the contemporary world and recognised that the Church had to rediscover itself immersed in the Paschal Mystery of Christ. This was confirmed by the Synod of Bishops, called to evaluate the Council, in 1985, when it stated that it was 'unanimously in agreement that the Second Vatican Council was a legitimate and valid expression and interpretation of the deposit of faith'.

From where, then, have our current difficulties come? Thornhill suggests that what was not understood at the time of the Council was what it would take to see the program of renewal through and the radical dislocation that this would cause. Change of this nature could not be brought about simply by decree. It affected the whole culture of Catholic life, and the ways in which that culture is lived and passed on would themselves have to be developed anew.

The faith is passed on, not so much through ideas and doctrines as by the symbols, rituals and roles through which it is lived and communicated.

Symbols, Rituals and Roles in Church Life

In a previous essay I used John Thornhill's article, 'Understanding the Church's Present Difficulties, and the Reaction they are Producing', in the *Australasian Catholic Record* 76/1 (January 1999): 3–14, to show how the difficulties we are experiencing in the Church at the present time are an understandable outcome of the reform of the Council. In this essay I will continue with his analysis of how religious culture is passed on by means of symbols, rituals and roles.

When he convoked the Council, John XXIII said, 'The substance of the ancient doctrine of the deposit of faith is one thing, and the way in which it is presented is another'. While staying true to the ancient faith, the Council embarked on a rigorous program of reform of the way this faith is lived and presented. The extent of this reform was made even greater because the Church had been so static for so long.

Living the faith happens through symbols, rituals and roles. *Symbols* are the images and language that we use. They may be the sacred images we place in Churches and homes, or the language with which we surround the sacraments. *Rituals* are the devotional practices, prayer forms and formal rites of the Church. Roles are positions that people exercise in the daily life of the Church.

Not only are symbols, rituals and roles intimate to the way we live, they are also at the core of how we hand on the faith. In my childhood, were someone to ask why I did not eat meat on Friday, I would have said, 'because I am a Catholic'. I became a Catholic by doing the things Catholics do.

Many of these symbols, rituals and roles had to change because the Church's understanding of itself and of its place in the world changed. No longer are all ministerial roles reserved to the clergy. We use symbols that emphasise our common Christian heritage rather than our differences from other Christian denominations. We have worked hard to make the rituals surrounding important moments of life like birth, death and marriage, more transparent and meaningful.

The problem with a program like this is that it cannot happen over night. It may take some generations to develop the forms of life and practice that are consistent with faith lived in the world. In the meantime, as John Thornhill says, '[t]he process by which our way of life is transmitted to future generations has been radically dislocated'.

What should we do about all of this? First, let us not despair or take on guilt that does not belong to us. Second, let us be realistic about the situation in which we find ourselves. Many of us were educated before the Council, but we can work to bring about a Church which is spiritual rather than administrative and to develop new symbols, rituals and roles, which will carry the faith into the future.

Symbols, Rituals and Roles in the Eucharist

In a previous essay I looked both at how symbols, rituals and roles allow us to live and to pass on our faith and at the dislocation that we are experiencing in their regard as we find our way towards the full implementation of the reforms of the Second Vatican Council.

It ought be no surprise that many difficulties should centre around the Eucharist, for it, in symbol and in reality, is at the heart of our living together as Christians. When the Mass was first said in English in the 1960s, some people awaited the new 'big missal', which would have every possible celebration in it and which would last them for the rest of their lives.

There was, of course, no such 'big missal', although attempts were made to publish one. Things have, in fact, kept changing as surely they must, because the finer details of our rituals and practices can be worked out only by doing. We are still learning how new ministries such as the ministry of communion to the sick are best carried out and who is best at doing them. Hymns that we thought were great just ten years ago have sunken into oblivion.

The development we are undergoing is illustrated when we think about the language we use around the Eucharist. Take, for instance, the words with which we refer to the consecrated bread and wine.

Before the Council, we were most familiar with terms like 'Blessed Sacrament', 'Host', 'Real Presence' or even 'Consecrated Species'. These came out of a culture in which affirmation of the reality of Christ's presence in the Eucharist was of paramount concern. It generated attitudes that saw the words of consecration and the elevation of the Host as the singularly important moment of the Eucharistic liturgy.

Since the Council, we have had a fresh openness to other terms, which we have found in the Scriptures and in the Fathers. We more readily talk about 'the Bread of Life and the Cup of Salvation', and, when we speak of 'breaking bread', we refer not just to the bread before the consecration, but to the whole Eucharistic action. In one of our hymns, we sing, 'wine for us all shed'.

The shift in our language signals an attempt to become more conscious of the sacramental dimensions of the Eucharist. Our mysterious relationship with God is experienced only through signs and symbols. Even the twisting of the metaphor in my last example challenges us to come face to face with the extraordinary nature of the action in which we participate so often.

We need not be troubled by change in language. In fact, a language that is alive is always in change. We can, however, have moments of difficulty when we attempt to choose the best words to pass on our faith, particularly to children. My own preference is to make better use of scriptural language.

Fundamentalism in the Catholic Church

One of the greater though less noted woes to beset the Catholic Church during the last two centuries has been the manner in which the Roman Magisterium has acted swiftly to condemn various forms of relativism while at the same time turning a blind eye to complementary forms of doctrinal fundamentalism. It has meant that it has been unable to cope with some of the Church's best thinkers, who have laboriously kept away from either of these extremes as they investigated the things that concern us.

This happened at the time of the modernist crises of last century. It happened in the middle of this century, when scholars like the French Dominicans, Dominique Chenu and Yves Congar, who later became significant thinkers for the Council, were silenced.

There is a reason that it happens this way, because, although, as I have outlined in this volume, relativism and fundamentalism are opposed aspects of the same mistake, fundamentalism tends to be more congenial to authority. The error in both lies in the failure to acknowledge and live with the complexity of nature, revelation and human affairs. While relativism tends to say that we cannot really know anything with certainty, fundamentalism takes simplistic formulations as all there is to be said. An authority that is primarily interested in control finds support in the latter but is undermined by the former.

Doctrinal fundamentalism is alive and well in the Australian Church today. Ready examples can be found among articles in magazines like *Fidelity and AD 2000*. It can be understood psychologically as a response to disappointment both at the general state of the Church and at failure to keep some form of control on things. In this guise, one can have some sympathy for the distress that people are feeling and for their attempts to do something about it.

In itself, however, this form of fundamentalism is extremely destructive, because it blocks all attempts to grapple thoughtfully with a situation. We saw this at the time of the furore over the Third Rite of Reconciliation. With few exceptions, what discussion there was was not about how to evangelise Australians in the late 1990s, nor about how to find symbols and rituals that would both carry our ancient traditions and speak to Catholic life today. It was, rather, about Church law and in its most legalistic interpretation.

In 1954, writing about the divisions in the French Church that followed from the *Syllabus of Errors* of 1864, the Dominican Yves Congar wrote:

> That division still persists although the proportion of the two parties has undergone a fundamental change; and indubitably it is accompanied by a certain *malaise* among many owing to the fact that those who are *contra* make considerable use of secret delation [OED: 'informing against'] to Rome, a veritable disease, in its widespread use, and a disease which is specifically French.

There is no longer any reason to think of it as a particularly French disease.

What Jesus Would Have us Do?

As we live again the experience of the birth of Jesus Christ, which, though it occurred in humble circumstances, was to mark time so profoundly that much of the world still measures its time from that moment, it can be fruitful to think about the kind of lives that Jesus would have us lead.

In doing so, we turn readily to Jesus' response to a challenge from the Pharisees and Sadducees, 'You must love the Lord your God with all your heart, with all your soul, and with all your mind. This is the greatest and first commandment. The second resembles it: You must love your neighbour as yourself' (Matt 22: 37–39).

Jesus took these commandments from the Old Testament (Deut 6:5 and Lev 19:18), but made them the central focus of the life of a Christian, so much so that St Paul could say that all the commandments of the Old Testament are summed up in the one commandment, "You must love your neighbour as yourself' (Rom 13: 10). The radical nature of this command is conveyed by the parable of the Good Samaritan (Luke 10: 29–37). Our 'neighbour' consists not of those we like or favour but of all human beings, especially 'outsiders'.

Lest this seem easy, and sometimes it does, because we have got used to it, let us contrast it with another saying of Jesus. 'If any man comes to me without hating his father, mother, wife, children, brothers, sisters, yes and his own life too, he cannot be my disciple' (Luke 14:26).

The power of Jesus' commandment was brought home to me recently by someone who said, 'I cannot feel affection for all those people whom Jesus would have us love'.

Affection is something that we feel for people who are close to us. Because it is a feeling it has a physiological base and is, therefore, something that we share to some degree with animals. It is a natural instinct.

The truly radical nature of Jesus' call is that the love he asks is a love that transcends affection. It is, therefore, not just a natural response to our families and friends, hence the need to 'hate' or be detached from our families. It is rather a response that comes from our intellects and wills, a human rather than an animal response, and one that touches the divine.

The basis of this kind of love is that "the life and death of each of us has its influence on others' (Rom 14:7). This is an awesome responsibility, and it takes us beyond tribal loyalties and ties to careful consideration of the lot of all human beings.

It may not even be possible to feel affection for, say, a drug addict in the worst condition imaginable, yet, if we follow Christ, we will transcend our instincts and deal with that person as one made, like us, in the image of God.

Why do we Thank God?

In an article in Australian based *The Sydney Morning Herald*, a journalist once took issue with sportsmen and women who have thanked God publicly after success in their particular events. He did it with clumsy humour, and, although he claimed that he did not want 'to be gratuitously offensive to all those with sincerely held religious beliefs', the article may have seemed offensive to some Christians.

He did, however, pose a real issue, about which the Christian tradition has been very thoughtful. He said, 'the real problem is [that] when you draw attention to the notion that all glory belongs to God for helping you come first, the inherent assumption must be that he wasn't with the one who came second'. He conceded that 'it might possibly work when you've just won the Nobel Peace Prize or something'.

Faced with these kinds of issues, I generally turn to the Dominican theologian Thomas Aquinas. Saint Augustine would also be most worthwhile, but it is a bit harder to find one's way through his works. Thomas deals with these issues in a section of his *Summa Theologiae* (II-II qq 81–83) on the virtue of religion. Question 83 deals with prayer, which Thomas divides in article 17 into prayer, intercession, supplication and thanksgiving.

Thomas places religion under the virtue of justice, which consists of one person giving to another what is due to that other. Religion differs from justice itself in that we can never adequately render all that we owe to God, who has given being to us and to the world around us and who calls us into loving and everlasting union. When we give God thanks or praise, we are recognising that in justice we owe God thanks and praise, but we know at the same time that our response can never supply all that we owe.

The virtue of religion, therefore, denotes a relationship with God to whom we ought always be directed.

The mistake that modern and non-religious thinkers make, when they look at intercession or thanksgiving, is to view them in an instrumental way. The dominant question then is, 'How do we make things happen?' This mistake would not have been made by a Christian or by an ancient thinker. Religion and prayer are not about working out how we can put a rather powerful resource somewhere in the sky to effective use in order to meet the goals that we have established.

Seen in this way, the example of an athlete thanking God for a win is rather trivial, although it might seem sharp. What the religious athlete is doing is giving the thanks that is always due to God and that can never be finally and adequately given. Its appropriateness to the time, though not necessarily to a non-religious public, is that it is being given in a moment of humanly outstanding achievement and exhilaration in the athlete's own life.

A Church Seeking Purification

The expression of failure and request for forgiveness by Pope John Paul II during his Pontificate, expressed in the year 2000, and the similar act of the Australian Catholic Bishops Conference will stand as extraordinary events for a long time.

The research of the International Theological Commission, published in its document 'Memory and Reconciliation: The Church and the Faults of the Past', did not find in Scripture or in the history of the Church any exact precedent for the Pope's action.

The people of the Old Testament were aware of the sins of their forebears, but although in confessing the sins of the present generation they would link them with those of their forebears, they did not confess those sins as belonging to the present. In the Church of the New Testament the Commission finds that there was 'no explicit call addressed to the first Christians to confess the faults of the past'.

During the life of the Church, the Catholic Magisterium has on many occasions condemned the actions of Church authorities. It has even acknowledged past abuses such as when, in a message to the Diet of Nuremberg in 1522, Pope Adrian VI acknowledged, in reference to Leo X's reign, '"the abomination, the abuses . . . and the lies" of which the "Roman court" of his time was guilty.' He did not, however, request pardon.

The Church has long held that it is holy because of its incorporation into Christ. Since in its oneness with Christ it is indefectible, the Magisterium has never before seen grounds for an apology for actions of past generations. What has changed this is a distinction that was made by the Second Vatican Council. In *Lumen Gentium* 8 it said the following.

> Christ, 'holy, innocent, and undefiled' (Heb 7:26), knew no sin (cf 2 Cor 5:21), but came only to expiate the sins of the people (cf Heb 2:17). The Church, however, embracing sinners in her bosom, is at the same time holy and always in need of purification and incessantly pursues the path of penance and renewal.

Although holy in Christ, the Church also carries the sins of those who are part of it through baptism.

We might ask why this has come now. We know that the Holy Father has been very sensitive to divisions in the Church stemming from the Reformation and earlier schisms. He has come to recognise that any healing will demand recognition of error where wrong was done.

We might also recognise the power of written history, which takes memory far beyond a few generations. The Church has been a stable institution for twenty centuries, which have been centuries in which the written record has been developed to degrees unimaginable in even the Greek and Roman worlds. Sooner or later the weight of this had to tell. It is not only the Church that has changed. The call to say 'sorry' is, indeed, a sign of our times.

Glad to be a Marist

My call to become a Marist came early in my life and was nourished by many influences most of which I do not really remember and many of which I may not have been specifically conscious at the time. Two I do remember, however. One was reading the missionary letters of Fr Emmet McHardy sm, written from the Solomon Islands during an early part of the twentieth century and published as *Blazing the Trail*. The other was spending time on holidays with a large number of Marists—brothers, priests and students—with whom I found a common spirit. My dream was to one day preach the Gospel on coral sand under the shade of coconut palms.

That was during the years of the Council. By the time I was in the seminary, profound and rapid change had brought chaos and everything seemed to be falling apart. By the time I was ordained as a Catholic priest, Oceania was Christian and vibrant, and the pagan was here in Australia. I stayed in a land without coconut palms.

The ensuing years have been most interesting but have also carried their own specific difficulties. In common with all other religious congregations, the Marists were forced to deal with enormous change brought on by the developments of the Council, by directives of Roman authorities and by the vast changes in our own culture. In contrast to other periods of great change, such as the period of missionary expansion, change in this period was wrought in a time of weak authority, strong differences of view and pressure from the effects of diminishing numbers and ageing population.

Although some in the Church, who continue to resist change, argue that the change was too great and that it happened too quickly, it seems to me that the change was momentous only because the Church had been unable to change for several centuries due, in part, to the shock of the Reformation and to its reaction to the rise of the modern world.

During the two millennia of the Church's life various kinds of religious life have arisen. Each has attempted to live afresh the radical call of the Gospel in ways that addressed the most serious needs of the time and in forms of association that were consonant with these goals and with the culture of the time and place. As conditions have changed, many religious groups have passed out of existence. The challenge of our time has been to adapt to new needs and changed culture.

For Marist Fathers in Australia, the response to this challenge has been mapped by Assemblies held periodically over the last thirty years. Many have been painful, but, in my judgment, at an Assembly a few years ago, we finally allowed one another to be individuals in a way consonant with the modern world. It was only a beginning, but it was a real beginning and one that gives hope.

Why Bother About Salvation?

An ordinary question for people who are not religious but to whom the practice of religion is recommended is 'What would religion offer me?' A first answer to this question is likely to be 'salvation'. Indeed, our religious language is full of talk about salvation. 'God saves us.' 'Christ is our Saviour.' 'The Gospel brings salvation to all.' Salvation is what most religions, and certainly our Christian religion, offer.

A fair response to this answer is likely to be 'Why should I bother?' Therein, I suspect, lies a significant part of the difficulty that the Church faces today. What Christianity has to offer in the first instance, namely salvation, seems meaningless and unattractive to many people.

The experience of salvation for the people of the Old Testament was very concrete. They faced all manners of danger—war, sickness, oppression, famine, disruption. God saved them either by bringing together a range of circumstances that fended off the danger or by providing them with leaders like Moses or David, who brought them deliverance. In time, it was recognised that in bringing salvation God made a judgement setting apart the just and sinners.

Similarly, Jesus revealed himself as Saviour by concrete actions—curing the sick, calming the storm, feeding the multitude. Moving beyond the physical, he forgave sins, saving people from destruction in the order of the spirit. After the death and resurrection of Jesus, the Church understood that salvation would be finally realised in the transformation effected by the second coming of Christ.

It seems to me that in offering the promise of salvation to the people around us we Catholics have in recent times often begun with the more abstract and forgotten the concrete. What value is heaven to people who have little understanding of it or who think that it is probably alright to live in this world? Those who have found themselves on the mailing lists of some of the extreme Fatima devotions will recognise a kind of twentieth century religious pathology that was totally caught up with damnation. Little of this will be attractive to a person who is without religious experience and whose needs are very concrete.

If, then, we are to offer salvation to the people of our time as something attractive, we will have to begin with the concrete crises they face. These are unlikely to be simply the same as those faced by people of the Old Testament. In the West, for instance, famine is not the problem it was, nor, in the presence of modern medicine, is illness likely to be viewed in quite the same way.

Yet problems do beset us—the loss of a sense of meaning to life, the illusive nature of justice, the difficulty of finding an ethics that begins from concrete experience, the impact of a world that so often acts without compassion.

How Shall we Show them Salvation?

A committed young male teacher engaged with me once about the issues of salvation addressed in a previous essay. He asked, 'How can I teach my students about salvation?'

This is not an easy question to answer. I suspect that, if we had a cogent answer to it, our Churches would be packed with people of all ages and dispositions. In fact, they are not.

In some respects, we are our own worst enemies. For centuries, the Roman Catholic Church acted as if it were an empire in a permanently stable world, and for some reason this attracted people to it. That will no longer happen. In Australia, if the letters to the editor of Catholic newspapers are any gauge, we are becoming a grumpy old Church that would lay down burdens for people but give little relief. This is hardly salvific.

If we are to offer salvation and to teach about it, we must learn again to act and to speak as Jesus acted and spoke.

In the first instance, Jesus reached out to the concrete needs of the people around him. He healed the sick, cured the lame, and so on. While he praised their faith, the faith that he praised had initially been not much more than willingness to seek help in desperation. It grew as they came to understand this Jesus, who had helped them in their moment of need.

Today, we are hardly likely to perform miracles, but there are two questions that we must ask. What are the concrete needs of people today? How can we can meet them? These are, in fact, the same questions that Jesus had to answer in his ministry. He was able to answer them, because he walked among the people and because, as the Gospel says so often, he had compassion.

Another aspect of Jesus' ministry is that he reached out to the poor and to the dispossessed. To these he promised not riches but that they would be blessed. 'Blessed are the poor' did not suggest that poverty was a great way to live but that, in the Kingdom, the poor would be heard—a way of salvation till then outside their experience. It seems to me that the growth of the kingdom is intimately connected to the entry into it of the poor and the marginated.

Perhaps, then, the 'miracle' that we can offer lies in touching the lives of those who are hurting with a little kindness and with a listening ear. The miracle will not lie in the material help that is given but in the fact that someone cares.

I think all Catholics and all Christians should look at the question of how to speak of salvation.

The Question of Salvation Remains

In response to a challenge to address the question of how to speak of salvation, I received a number of responses. One, from a parish discussion group, was particularly challenging.

In one respect, what they wished to be saved from was the Church itself and specifically from aspects of its teaching on original sin, which seem to denigrate human life. Why, they asked, does a child become a child of God only at baptism? Are we not all children children of God from birth? Do we have to be fallen before Jesus has something to offer us? When science answers so much, why do we have to maintain a sense of mystery?

These are significant questions. They have to do with how our experience of and thinking about life and the world have changed, and they raise questions about whether the Church's thinking has kept up with this change. It is not necessarily the case that the Church has kept up, because it is possible that it has not been prompted to think afresh about these issues or that it has been so busy rethinking other areas of belief and practice that it has not had the opportunity.

So the questions remain. Can we see creation as beautiful and a new-born babe as even more beautiful without having to posit some dreadful fault before being able to say that Jesus might have something to offer to this person? If science has taken the mystery out of why sometimes it floods and why at other times we face drought, are there not other things to which we need to look to God for resolution? Perhaps the question of the moment is, can we live with a certain ambiguity in our understanding and still recognise a need for God?

These questions take us beyond philosophy and call for a theological response. I will, however, suggest some ways in which I suspect we do look for salvation, even if we do not see it as salvation.

Father John Hill suggested in article in *The Australasian Catholic Record*, in April, 2000, page 236, that the salvation we seek is related to fear we feel and that in our age what we fear most is meaninglessness. The search for meaning, often spoken, can be seen as a way of seeking salvation. Many people are turning to New Age religion to answer this need, but should not we in the Church be able to offer something?

What about the interest of our society in personal development or its interest in life-long education? Do not these two phenomena indicate that we believe that for all the good in us there is still more that we could become?

And So, into the New Millennium

As we moved into the start of the new millennium there was a hope for refreshment of body, mind and spirit that so often accompanies the change of calendar and season. In the southern hemisphere, that refreshment is always helped by summer, when the world around us warms up and plants thrive. It is helped also by being a time of holidays, when rest and new activities lift our spirits.

A new year may also feel a little anticlimactic. A new year begins with its new opportunities and its challenges, but some of the old is still present.

What, then, we wondered will this third millennium be like? That, of course, is not something we could answer beforehand except in the most general terms. It would and has of course taken its own course as people responded to events and to each other. In many respects, we could expect that patterns of history would be repeated, but it would carry its own surprises also.

Perhaps the question that dogged us then and still dogs us is one about hope. What could and what can we hope for? In what would and in what will our expectations be grounded?

The Feast of the Epiphany gives two answers to all these questions of hope and expectation.

In the first place, the birth of new human beings gives hope, because this is how society renews itself, as does nature. Fresh minds and bodies with youthful energy and interest learn how to live in the conditions in which they find themselves. This energy is superabundant, so that although in the long term much of it might seem wasted, life will go on and good things are possible.

The particular birth that we celebrate in the Epiphany, the birth of Jesus in Bethlehem, also gives us hope. This singular event at the beginning of the first millennium marked the entry of God into human affairs in a new way that will remain living and active until the end of time.

Those who first recognised Jesus were strangers and the poor. The wise men came from the east guided by a sign (Matt 2:1–12). The shepherds came from close by, alerted by angels (Luke 2:1–20). The powerful in the person of Herod tried to destroy any opposition to themselves, and the religious authorities let the opportunity to enter into God's salvific action pass by them.

So, perhaps what the new millennium calls us to is to understand the Gospel anew, not only with our minds but also with our hearts so that it informs our lives fully and guides all that we do. In so acting, we will welcome strangers and listen to the poor, because unless this is done, the Kingdom of God cannot be among us.

A Short Response to Bishop Spong

John Selby Spong's visit to Australia created considerable interest across a broad spectrum of people. Spong sympathises with those Christians who have found belief unfruitful. He identifies a crisis in the Christian Church and tenders his own response to it. It seems to me that there are three claims that underlie much of what Spong says.

The first is the claim that Christians expect a literal interpretation of Scripture. Finding this impossible, he rejects what he calls the mythical explanations of Scripture, though he does want to keep the experience of God that gave rise to them. He casts aside such stories as the creation, the birth of Jesus, miracles and the Ascension.

At the philosophical level, Spong confuses myths or stories with explanations. Myths are not explanations but rather stories that carry primitive experiences and meanings that need ever to be understood anew. As a Catholic, I have never expected to rest in a simple literal interpretation of Scripture.

The second claim involves modern science. Modern science narrowed its epistemology to exclude spiritual things so as to achieve a greater penetration of matter. It has been most successful in the latter but leaves untouched questions about the former. Spong does not recognise this. Science also tends to reductionism, and Spong's reduction of spirituality to psychology leaves nothing of the Spirit with which to engage.

The third claim entails recognition and criticism of the Church's failure to deal with new learning and of its slowness to engage in structural change. On this matter, I have more sympathy with Spong, though there is some ambiguity in his use of the term 'Church'.

The question that Spong's position raises is, 'who will do the hard yards?' In other words, who will work out an understanding of Christian origins that both does justice to Christian tradition and takes full account of contemporary learning and attitudes? What do we make of Christ's claim to be one with the Father? What does the story of Christ's Ascension really mean? Why do we engage in petitionary prayer, if it is not to prod God into changing the course of history?

Spong is not going to do the hard work but seems rather to prefer to drop the difficult questions. He imagines himself instead as the instigator of a New Reformation. Nor, however, is the Catholic Church doing particularly well. The recent investigation of Father Dupuis has made theologians wary of testing new waters and the official Church seems to have wearied of the effort of learning how to speak to people who are educated but who are not erudite in esoteric theologies.

John Spong will appeal to many. Among them will be those who desire change and those who are anxious about the state of the Church. Others, who no longer bother with religion, will find in him easy justification of their stance.

Why Catholic Teaching Must Change

There are still parts of the Church where the suggestion that Catholic teaching, doctrine or belief might change creates consternation, rejection and, at times, outbursts of indignation. The causes of the attitudes that underlie these reactions are multiple but include a post-Tridentine mythology that held, in reaction to the Protestant Reformation, that the Catholic position had never changed.

To the contrary, Catholic teaching has generally been open to change despite its principle of commitment to previous determinations of what is doctrine. The term that we use is 'development of doctrine'. Development is a species of change that implies not an overturning of past definitions but rather the continuing clarification of our understanding of the divine and human realities that were first articulated in the Scriptures.

In an essay titled 'Rahner's Theology of the Priesthood and the Development of Doctrine', in *Philosophy and Theology* 12/1 (2000): 155–185, Richard Lennan spelt out among other things Karl Rahner's understanding of the necessity for the development of Catholic doctrine.

According to Rahner, the truth that we know can only ever be a beginning both because of the nature of divine truth and because of the nature of human knowledge. Since it is a beginning we live always with the possibility that greater understanding might emerge and that the knowledge we possess in this world has not the status of a final conclusion.

As Lennan explains it, Rahner identified divine truth with God's self-revelation, which took place through the Spirit, who 'enabled the church to appropriate and articulate the truth of God's revelation'. The Spirit is the animator and enabler of all that we know of divine things but is not the direct object of our knowledge and so cannot be possessed definitively. Put simply, despite the wonder of all that we do know about God, the reality that is God will always be greater.

On the side of human knowledge, Rahner insisted that the Church's knowledge of God is not different from other forms of human knowledge. In so far as it was 'acquired within history, it reflected the priorities and questions of its cultural context, and was expressed in the concepts and language of its own time'. When, therefore, doctrines are defined, they are defined in the context of the difficulties, obscurities and debates of their time. Difficulties that might arise in a later time due to new circumstances or knowledge may well call for further penetration of and increased clarity about what was first known.

The kind of change that is meant, then, is change in continuity. The Spirit was given to us at Pentecost, so that when the Church does achieve a deeper understanding of God, it is grasping something that was there from the beginning. It is, nevertheless, 'a pilgrim body which [has] to remain open to being moved more deeply into the truth of God who [is] always greater.'

At the Heart of the Christian Life

Each of the synoptic Gospels recounts the incident during Jesus' ministry when a learned Jew asked Jesus which was the greatest commandment (Mark 12:28–34; Matt 22:34–40; Luke 10:25–28). The story has slightly different tone and context in each of the accounts, and some of the details vary, but Jesus' answer is constant.

We can use Matthew's account. 'Jesus said, "You must love the Lord your God with all your heart, with all your soul, and with all your mind. This is the greatest and the first commandment. The second resembles it: You must love your neighbour as yourself. On these two commandments hang the whole Law, and the Prophets also."'

The question was not an unusual one in Jesus' time. People recognised 613 precepts of Old Testament law, and in its ordinary context, the point of the question was to try to bring some coherence and simplicity to this mass of law. Jewish teachers often gave clever and sometimes even witty replies.

At first sight, Jesus' answer was not much out of the ordinary. His first commandment came straight from Deuteronomy 6:4–5 and was one of the texts that pious Jews recited every day. His second commandment was less central to Jewish practice but also well known and came from Leviticus 19:18. Mark's Gospel makes it clear that those speaking with Jesus recognised a good answer and one that was in full harmony with their tradition. Jesus had, in fact, cut right to the core of things.

What is original to Jesus is that in response to a question seeking one answer he gave two and that it was these two that he gave. They are joined by love, love of God and love of neighbour, so that love becomes central to the whole of the Christian life and takes precedence over all other forms of observance, such as knowledge of the law or ritual activities, which are part of such a life.

A consequence of Jesus' two-in-one answer and of the way in which the evangelists record it is that within the Christian life the two cannot be separated. To proclaim that we love God without actually loving those near us is to convict ourselves of empty words. To love those around us without basing this love in our love of God is to do less than we can as Christians.

Luke takes the story further with the parable of the Good Samaritan. That the lawyer's question, 'who is my neighbour', is mischievous is shown by the statement to which it corresponds, 'my neighbour is one who lives near me'. It is a tautology. Jesus uses this to expand the law of love. Now, it becomes available as a way of life to all human beings, Jew and gentile. In turn, love is to be given not just to those near us - our tribe or clan - but to all human beings.

An Opportunity for Faith

An act of faith is a choice to assent to things that we know neither through perception and experience nor through demonstration and argument. In our religious context, we give such assent both to things that could never be seen or demonstrated and to things that are beyond demonstration for any one of us because of lack of ability or of opportunity to study in a certain way. What we call the Christian faith is confident trust in God on the basis of the life and teaching of Jesus Christ.

The closing decades of the last millennium were a time in which people in our society and culture became less and less inclined to make acts of faith that implied the acceptance of Christian faith. It was most evident in the disinclination of many people to act in ways consistent with strongly held religious beliefs. Many explanations might be given for this phenomenon, and it is unlikely that anyone yet understands it fully, but I would like to explore one explanation.

These decades were decades of great certainty about what we could see and about what science could secure for us. Television brought images of events around the world, often in real time, so that we could work out what was going on at the same time as or even on occasion ahead of the commentary. Science and technology seemed capable of answering all our inquiries and of solving all our problems. We expected, for instance, that medicine would cure all our pains and discomforts. We were used to economies that for the most part ran smoothly. The disruptions of war or famine were hardly remembered.

All of this changed when the towers of the World Trade Centre came crashing to the ground. They were meant to be able to sustain the impact of an airliner, yet they turned to little more than dust. Aeroplanes on scheduled routes became potential bombs. The institutions of state security were left speechless. We have yet to learn the full implications of this event.

What I want to suggest is that we have a moment when the certainties of seeing and reasoning are shaken. It is a moment that could lead to profound nihilism, but it is also a moment when a search for understanding might lead to preparedness to act in faith. In this there is a challenge to religion to present its beliefs in ways that are meaningful to those who are searching.

The Catholic Church has like everybody else been caught on the hop. A measure of our health will be the speed with which we can adjust to the issues that now face the world. Our faith has much to say, but agendas of the days prior to September 11 are now obsolete. The opportunity of the moment is also the challenge to engage faith thoughtfully with a world that is significantly changed.

Questions Requiring Religious Answers

In a previous essay I wrote about how the shaking of certainties that we have experienced following terrorist attacks in New York and Washington provides an opportunity for faith. I believe this to be the case both because that shaking may free people for other forms of knowing and because some of the questions that the events have raised will require religious answers.

What was and is still being called the War on Terrorism does, however, raise significant questions about religion itself and about the practice of religion, which we can also expect to reverberate through the world during the next decade. Intense discussion about religion in the media focussed on Islam, but the questions will sooner or later raise issues with which Christianity will have to come to terms.

Although this war is not a religious war in the way that these have been understood in the past, it has significant religious dimensions, and as public discussion suggests, it cannot be understood without grappling with religious issues. The outcomes of the discussion will affect how generations of people think about the place of religion and God in their lives.

After the terrorist attacks in the USA in 2001 Osama Bin Laden's statement of October 7 was couched in religious language and sentiment and gave religious justification for the events of September 11. We might be struck by the way in which he gave first place to God and expects every Muslim to 'rise to defend his religion'. He implied that religious belief should govern every aspect of a person's private and public life. His violence was not hard to understand, for it is a consequence of his single-mindedness and of a fundamentalism that dares to claim that the ways of God are easily understood and that Bin Laden himself knew them with such clarity that he could easily judge other human beings.

In the West, we do things differently. As a consequence of the religious wars that raged in Europe following the Reformation we have invented arrangements for living that separate political affairs and religious affairs. No longer is our civic life thought to be subject to the control of religious authorities. This secularisation has enabled peoples of different churches and faiths to live peacefully together. Not all, however, have accepted it easily, and questions are often raised about whether our religious convictions inform our public life. Christianity has seen its own forms of fundamentalism rise in opposition to modernity. The Catholic Church has had its battles.

If the Church is to remain relevant, it will need to engage thoughtfully with the questions that people raise. Repetition of old formulae and engagement in old issues will not work, because people will be asking questions with a new slant. While we can insist that God is central to the life of every human being, its mere assertion will sound empty. Our answers need to be expressed in ways appropriate to the questions that are asked.

Marriage for the Kingdom

The Sermon on the Mount is about the Kingdom of God. Jesus' mission in the world was to bring the Kingdom of God into being. In its fullest sense, the Kingdom of God belongs to the life we will share after life in this world, but it has to be prepared for and worked for in this world. Jesus was also confident that even in this life it is possible for us to have intimations or glimpses of what life in the Kingdom can be. The mission that Jesus handed on to his followers was to bring the Kingdom into being.

The Beatitudes (Matthew 5: 1 – 12) begin the sermon and divide into three parts. The first part consists of four beatitudes, in which Jesus declares the poor, the weak, the distressed and those seeking justice to be happy. This is strange. How can it be that the poor and the distressed are happy? The answer is that here Jesus is telling us about the conditions that will be present in the Kingdom. If we attain the Kingdom, the poor will indeed be heard. Their belonging will be evidence of the presence of the Kingdom.

The second part consists of the second four beatitudes, which spell out the virtues of those who work for the Kingdom. They will be merciful, pure in heart, peacemakers and enduring. The third part consists of the last beatitude, which announces the joy of those who live for the Kingdom despite opposition.

The goal of bringing the Kingdom into being can be lived in marriage. We all know that men and women are different. That is a good part of what makes marriage so worthwhile and so interesting. But it also makes misunderstanding possible. Women and men sense differently and bring different feelings to their perception of the world around them. These different sensibilities lead to differences of understanding. It is here that disagreement can break out that is not just disagreement between two headstrong people but rather real difference between two people who see and understand the situations in which they are involved differently.

We deal with these differences in different ways, sometimes by telling jokes, oftentimes by knowing when to be quiet, at other times by tolerating one another. There is a deeper way. In love we can come to accept that the vision and understanding of the one we love are valid, even if we cannot get to them directly ourselves. In trust, we can learn to grasp the world through four eyes not two, with two hearts not one and with understanding that goes beyond what we could achieve alone.

When couples understand in this way, they bring the Kingdom of God into being in the world around them. The poor are heard, and the sorrowful are comforted. The richness of seeing, hearing and feeling that develops within the marriage spreads out to those they meet. As the Gospel says, at times they will be rejected, but often enough the Kingdom will be glimpsed.

PHILOSOPHICAL REFLECTION

The Banality of Evil

During the Gulf War the US Government went to extraordinary lengths to show what an evil person Saddam Hussein was. Members of the ruling order in exile from Kuwait hired one of the top American advertising firms to do the same thing. All sorts of rumours, later found to be false, were put around. Placards appeared in the United States clearly identifying Saddam with Adolf Hitler.

There were reasons for all of this. For whatever purpose, a war was to be waged. Its success would be dependent on public support, since American soldiers would be involved. To have a clearly identified enemy who was without doubt grossly evil would make it easier to generate public opinion favouring the war.

It would be foolishness to try to promote Saddam as a good person. He is responsible for grave abuses of human rights. However, we ought to be critical of our own tendency to look for people whom we see as the impersonation of the grossest evil and we ought to be aware of how this might obscure our ability to sort out real evil in the world.

In 1961 the political philosopher, Hannah Arendt, herself a German Jew and refugee from the Nazis, went to Jerusalem as a reporter for the *New Yorker* to attend the trial of Adolf Eichmann. Eichmann had been a middle ranking officer responsible for communicating between the Nazi leadership and those who were responsible for deporting and exterminating millions of Jews. He had been kidnapped from Argentina by the Israelis and was standing trial for crimes against humanity.

The world expected a display of monumental evil in one person. When Arendt's report appeared it was called 'Eichmann in Jerusalem: A Report on the Banality of Evil'. The evil that she found was something trite or commonplace, something weak and meaningless.

In the book published later Arendt described how in prison in Israel Eichmann poured out his heart to his interrogator, a policeman and himself a German and a Jew, and talked often about his great disappointment at only reaching the rank of Lieutenant-Colonel. He seemed to see no disproportion between concerns about his own career and the magnitude of the death and destruction for which he had been responsible. He was without imagination or thought. She said 'he never realised what he was doing'.

Lacking imagination Eichmann was unable to view alternatives, to see the implications of what he was doing, to look at events from a point of view other than his own. Lacking thought he was unable to judge between what was good or evil and what was true or false. In this weakness and in this failure to realise full human potential Arendt found the core of the evil that was displayed at the trial.

The root of evil around us, whether it be in the Church, in our own society, or in other lands, is more likely to be like that of Eichmann than that proposed for Saddam. Evil springs from weakness, from lack of imagination, thought and sensibility, even when it leads to consequences of enormous significance. The fight against evil is a matter of fully actualising ourselves and the institutions and organisations in which we act rather than of tilting at gigantic windmills.

Reference: Hannah Arendt, *Eichmann in Jerusalem: A Report on the Banality of Evil* (New York: Penguin, 1977).

Literacy in Higher Education

In the late summer of each year, the academic year is about to begin. Not long after that essays will be due, and a senior academic or two will bemoan the fact that students are no longer as literate as they once were. This may even extend to criticism of primary and secondary schooling for not producing university students who are ready to write coherently about the new learning in which they engage in the university.

Considerable educational research has focused on these claims during the twenty years since they became accepted as commonplace. Serious studies have been unable to discern any deterioration over an extended period. Other results are even more telling.

Students rarely make the same grammatical mistake consistently throughout an essay. In general, they use correct grammar most of the time, so that errors in the use of a particular form occur in the minority of cases of the use of that form.

It has also been shown that students will frequently write well in one subject and badly in another. They are even seen to write well in the first year of their tertiary studies and badly in later years.

The conclusion drawn by these studies is that the problem is not a matter of literacy at all but rather of difficulty in thinking about the issues. Linguistic errors arise whenever a writer is not fully in control of the discipline being exercised. Students, therefore, who do not fully understand the topic of an essay, will generally make grammatical errors in the area of their confusion.

This result conforms with findings of the philosophy of language, where it is recognised that grasping a thought and generating language about that thought are two aspects of the one activity. Most thinking begins in a kind of vagueness. As it becomes more distinct, it is expressed in more appropriate words, correct grammar and well-formed syntax.

Two mistakes often underlie the claims of illiteracy. The first is a rather primitive understanding of language, in which it is viewed as a kind of tool, which is kept in readiness for manipulating any particular body of knowledge. The second is a view of knowledge that sees it as a rather large mass of data that can be down loaded or dumped onto the students' 'hard disks'.

The task of any educator is to assist students to perceive and to think the matters at hand. This cannot be achieved in an instant but is the product of extended attempts to come to terms with what is to be known. As learning progresses communication becomes more refined. It may begin with something as basic as pointing; the goal is polished speech and writing.

Many of the claims about illiteracy can be viewed as symptomatic of other problems. They can also be viewed as a challenge to tertiary educators themselves. A philosopher once said that 'a person has not spoken until he has been understood'. If student essays constitute evidence that the professor has not spoken, the professor has more work to do.

References: Gordon Taylor, Leo HT West & Peggy Nightingale. *The Writing of First Year History Undergraduates in 1974 and 1984* (Monash University: Higher Education Advisory and Research Unit; University of New South Wales: Tertiary Education Research Centre, 1987); Gordon Taylor and Peggy Nightingale, 'Not Mechanics but Meaning: Error in Tertiary Students' Writing' in *Higher Education Research and Development*, 9/2 (1990): 161–175.

Dealing with Absence

While walking to work one morning, I passed the local primary school. It was the first day of school and all the new students were milling around in their fresh uniforms. Mums and some dads were standing in groups or along the perimeter of the playground. The scene would have appeared tranquil were it not for the intensity of some of the parents as they watched the new scholars make their first moves towards independence.

It took me back to a scene some years ago when I was for some reason on school duty on the first day of school. As parents departed some children wailed; others were already distracted by the exciting new things on offer. One particular scene caught my attention.

The village policeman's son, the eldest of a small tribe, had been conveyed by his mother to his new school. When it came time to part, he walked out of the kindergarten room with his mother and stood at the top of the playground while she travelled the long lonely path to the car park. She paused at the bottom of the playground and looked back hesitantly, half-expecting, half-hoping to see her son in tears. He stood dry-eyed and imperturbable. Chest out, he gave his mother a seemingly casual wave.

We will never know what the young man felt. He was probably filled with a range of feelings. A response of courage would surely have been a part of the mix. What we do know is the stance he took. It was a parting, and he did what was decent by way of farewell, but it was an important stage of life. He was five and ready to take responsibility for what had to be done.

Dealing with absence is an important part of growing up, but it is also philosophically interesting.

The emotional development of young children involves their learning to be alone. The expectation that mother will come back after the door is shut and the light is turned off is an early act of trust that lays the foundation for many further kinds of learning.

In similar fashion, young lovers are often unable to be without each other. To the casual observer, they seem to be smothering one another. Maturation of relationship does not come until they are able to be apart so as to experience and relish love in the absence of the beloved. Even the reality of love does not firm up until it is appreciated apart from the driving immediacy of physical presence.

Without absence, we cannot think. Thinking comes into its own when we achieve distance from the reverberations of singular perceptions. Our grasp of essences is dependent on our learning what is constant in the coming and going of things. A primitive sound becomes a word only when it can be uttered in the absence of the object to which it refers and which it makes present in a new way.

Parting is hard especially when it is for the first time or at the start of something new and big, but it also provides varieties of presence and absence that allow us to tap into the richness of human existence.

Ways in Which Words Fail

Robert Sokolowski in his book, *Presence and Absence*, on the philosophy of language explains two of the ways in which words fail.

Underlying his explanation is the recognition that all words carry feeling. This is obvious in cries or exclamations, which are immediate responses to perceptions that generate feeling—alarm at the sound of a fierce animal, joy at the sight of a new-born baby, pleasure at the taste of an ice-cream on a hot day.

Language, however, develops beyond mere cries and exclamations to reports about things that are absent. In doing so it makes claim to some objectivity. The affective or feeling dimension moves into the background and becomes less strong. Sokolowski's point is that even so, feeling remains significant. Everything has its pleasures and pains, and unless we can respond to them we cannot contribute to what is said about a thing.

Words fail when they do not maintain the balance between objectivity and feeling. At one extreme, words are overwhelmed by the pleasure or pain being expressed and regress into being mere symptoms of our feelings. We see this in children who return home after an outing with, say, grandparents and pour out a stream of vocal excitement that objectively is rather jumbled. We are able to read their emotional response to the outing in the flow of words, but just what happened remains somewhat unclear.

At the other extreme, words can fail to carry any affective response to the things that are named. This happens, for instance, when we simply repeat the words of others without enjoying the perceptive experience ourselves. Journalists often fail in this way when they string series of quotations together without themselves ever grasping the matter under consideration. Likewise homilies can fail when they emptily repeat either something that has been said many times before or what was learnt many years ago. In these cases, writing or speech is rigid and wooden and carries no sensitive involvement with the things that are referred to.

Sometimes we can recognise both of these failures of language in the one conversation. For example, in a moment of crisis a couple might find themselves trying to discuss something that carries with it a lot of feeling. A common scenario arises when a woman becomes so emotional that her speech becomes almost completely a symptom of her feeling. A male will often respond to this by withdrawing all feeling whatsoever from his speech and by retiring into apparent objectivity.

After such an exchange, a woman will often feel that her feelings have not been recognised. A man will wonder why something he said so clearly and objectively was not heard. If he challenges the woman about something she said, either she will not remember it or, if she does, she will say that she was just expressing what she felt. In either case, language has failed through being loaded with either too much or too little feeling.

Reference: Robert Sokolowski, *Presence and Absence* (Evanston: Northwestern University Press, 1974).

The Romantic Belief in Progress

The decision by the American Congress not to allow cloning of human beings on ethical grounds was widely publicised a few weeks ago. Some news programs included a statement by a scientist who disagreed with the decision. His argument was, 'you can't stop progress'. We could say that what he meant was that any technological development is progress; that progress is ultimately good; that by it we will achieve happiness; that it is inevitable in any case.

A number of assumptions lie behind the scientist's position, but the one we will examine is called by philosophers simply 'the belief in progress'. It is so much part of our culture that few of us realise that it is not more than four hundred years old. The Greeks were aware of change for the better and of increase in knowledge, but they did not imagine that the world would get better than it was or had been. Times good and bad were simply repeated over and over again. In the Middle Ages something better was envisaged, but it was in the next world.

John Plamenatz suggests that the modern belief in progress is occasioned by four prior claims: that there exists a course of social and cultural change; that there is a future condition infinitely better than the present; 'that human knowledge and power over nature increase indefinitely; and that this knowledge and power bring worldly happiness'. First articulation of the position is attributed to Francis Bacon, who urged that the mastery of nature would bring happiness to all. It would be developed much further in the nineteenth century.

Plamenatz argues against this assurance on the grounds that as knowledge and power increase, they are not held by one person but are spread among many. Even if it were the case that one person who knew everything about how to achieve happiness and who desired it would certainly use that knowledge to achieve happiness, it is not the case that many among whom the knowledge was distributed would do the same. For this to happen knowledge and power and will would have to come together and they rarely do. History seems to show that they are more likely to be at odds with one another.

There is a deeper reason. The knowledge that technological science brings us is knowledge of matter; its method is not amenable to the examination of spirit. For the Greeks, knowledge could bring happiness, but only if it was knowledge of oneself.

During the last few decades great moral effort has gone into dealing with one kind of power over nature—that of atomic physics and the power of nuclear weapons. Things seem better than they were, but it is not clear yet whether the change is a moral and social victory or simply a consequence of fear of an event that is unthinkable for the scope of the destruction it would entail.

Reference: John Plamenatz, 'The Belief in Progress', in *Man and Society: A Critical Examination of Some Important Social and Political Theories from Machiavelli to Marx* (London: Longmans, 1961), 409–457.

From Progress to Disillusionment

The romantic belief in progress holds that human knowledge of and control over nature will increase indefinitely and that consequently humanity is finding its way towards a state of complete worldly happiness. It is an assumption that sits deep in our culture. It finds its home in the precincts of science and technology and of political and social theory, because it is these that are expected to provide life without distress.

One of the consequences of this belief is disillusionment. It often appears as pessimism, but it is different. Sophocles expressed the position of the pessimist: 'Not to be born is best, but having seen the light, the next best is to go whence one came as soon as may be.' Disillusionment, on the other hand, assumes that life ought only be good and is a reaction to hardship and adversity.

Yves Simon, one of this century's finest Catholic philosophers, called those who fall into disillusionment, disillusioned optimists. Writing fifty years ago, he described the condition in the following way.

> When a man calls attention to himself by the bitterness, the snarling tone, of his criticisms of modern errors, the aberrations of his contemporaries, the stupidity of the majority, the increasingly rapid decadence of our civilisations, it is generally easy to observe that his psychology is dominated by the feeling of a scandalous contrast. If he considers it necessary to talk so much about evil, to say nothing at all about good, and to prophesy a continual increase of the evils he denounces, it is because, somewhere in his mind, he has a model of harmony to which, whether consciously or unconsciously, he compares the disorders revealed by his daily experience.

Some generations on it seems that disillusioned optimism is still with us but that it has spawned new attitudes. One of these might well be outright pessimism and certainly a negativity about life that makes self-extinction seem reasonable. Another might be the attitude that sees adversity as unwarranted and unjust, and so demands compensation for every suffering or setback. Yet another might be the desire of a pristine environment altogether free of human presence.

The way around these attitudes is a philosophy of nature and of human life that recognises both the good of the world and the disruptions that are part of it. Nature itself is wasteful as we see in Australia when inland floods encourage furious breeding of birds and animals many of which perish when the waters dry up. Yet nature will also renew itself, when the season turns good again.

In human affairs, people frequently act from malice, ignorance or weakness in ways that affect us seriously. Living well is a matter of negotiating all these things—avoiding what we can and re-establishing ourselves when hurt. The human spirit, unless confused, pulls together the energy that is needed.

References: Yves Simon, *The Community of the Free*, translated by Willard R Trask (Lanham MD: University Press of America, 1984), 84–136; 103. Simon quotes George Sorel, *Reflections on Violence*, 8–9, as his source for the distinction between pessimists and disillusioned optimists. Sophocles, *Oedipus at Colonus*.

The Doom and Gloom of Science

At times we seem to be deluged with predictions of disaster and destruction by people who claim to talk in the name of science. If the millennium bug does not get us, there is certainly an asteroid wheeling around out there waiting to make a big splash. Should we survive these, population explosion, global warming or El Nino will surely make life untenable. What are we to make of all of this?

What is most confusing about it is that it comes to us as the conclusions of science. We live in a time and culture in which science is the dominant locus of certitude, so that, for instance, in the recent discussion about heroin trials, the argument, 'We know nothing, give science a chance to examine the matter', was accepted as a strong argument. That this implied experimentation with human beings or that there might be ethical and political arguments and considerations tended to be obscured.

What is it about a scientific culture that promotes the generation of feelings of doom?

As early as 1637 Descartes recognised that the scientific enterprise would be vast and that it would be so expensive that only governments would have the resources to fund it. Science, therefore, needed a political face that encouraged the populace to support funding not because they appreciated what it was doing but out of a kind of self-interest. This self-interest has to be fostered, and where this is done with fear, the situation that we are addressing arises.

Part of the answer lies in the nature of scientific reporting itself. A scientific report generally provides very precise information on a very narrow topic. This relates to the nature of scientific study, which looks at small parts of reality and rarely or never at the whole. When these reports are picked up by the press and broadcast without consideration of the scope of the study or suggestion of other relevant concerns, misconceptions necessarily arise. Reports in the prestigious journal, *New England Journal of Medicine*, often suffer this fate. Badly misunderstood, they become the source of fears and fads until a new report demonstrates the wastefulness and harmful social consequences of the last.

Yves Simon suggests a third reason. There is a lassitude that springs from an optimistic culture. If we believe that growth in knowledge is relentlessly taking us to a condition of complete worldly happiness, we will not readily engage in passionate action. Often the predictors of gloom and doom are attempting to counter this tendency to inaction. What we see is their passion.

Scientific truths have an important place in our lives and decision making, but we have to take care not to take them as necessarily the whole truth. They have to be placed in broader contexts—the context of other scientific truths and the various contexts of moral and political life and action.

Reference: Yves Simon, *The Community of the Free*, translated by Willard R Trask (Lanham: University Press of America, 1984), 84–136.

What Kind of Argument?

Douglas Walton in his book, *Informal Logic*, distinguishes several kinds of argument in which any of us might find ourselves involved. They are worth consideration because, often when our communication with others goes wrong, it does so because we have engaged in the wrong kind of argument for a given purpose.

A *personal quarrel* is an argument gone wrong and is 'characterised by aggressive personal attack, heightened appeal to the emotions and a desire to win the argument at all costs'.

A *forensic debate* is what generally occurs in the courts where argument is conducted according to rules and judged by a third party. The goal is to win by whatever means are possible within the rules. In *negotiation*, on the other hand, the parties attempt to bargain for their own interests, often successfully creating value to the advantage of both.

In *persuasive dialogue* we attempt to persuade others of a thesis by establishing common premises and by showing how our position follows logically from what both parties hold. *Action-seeking dialogue* aims to draw others to a specific course of action.

In *information seeking* one party attempts to find out something that the other is thought to know by questioning broadly. It differs from an *inquiry* where strict rules of evidence are followed and which develops its conclusions step by step from what is already known to be true.

Each of these kinds of argument operates according to different rules, and things go wrong when we mix them up. The Australian Parliament often makes itself unattractive by engaging in forensic debate when persuasive dialogue would be more enlightening. If we use persuasive dialogue when we really need action-seeking dialogue the discussion can be interminable without ever leading to action. Similarly, somebody wishing to avoid action may move the discussion from action-seeking dialogue to negotiation. Children can be experts at this.

Often, however, we do have to be ready to move from one kind of argument to another. Every used car salesman knows that he has to persuade a potential customer to enter negotiations before engaging in negotiation itself. If we are engaged in persuasive dialogue and realise that we have no common ground with the other person, we may have to switch to information seeking so as to find an adequate starting point.

Current public discussion has raised the issue of whether argument in our courts ought be based on forensic debate or on inquiry. Justice and truth sit in delicate balance with one another especially when the facts are confused or difficult to discern or deliberately hidden or simply unknown. On one hand, we recognise a right to fight for justice; on the other hand, we often wish for less painful ways of ascertaining the truth. At issue is what the court is trying to achieve. In some courts, negotiation has been found to work well.

Reference: Douglas N Walton, *Informal Logic: A Handbook for Critical Argument* (Cambridge University Press, 1989), 3–9.

Stages in Argumentation

Each of us engages in argument whenever we wish to engage in fair means to change another person's thought or action or the way in which they relate to or understand us. In a previous essay I have suggested that there are different kinds of argument. Douglas Walton further distinguishes four different stages of an argument.

In the *opening stage*, the participants agree to enter into argument and determine what kind of argument it will be. It is useful to know that we do not have to enter into argument unless we wish to and that often doing so might be our first mistake. On the other hand, if we wish to persuade someone of something or enter into negotiations with them, we first have to elicit their permission to attempt to do so. We also have to select the right kind of argument. It is no use engaging in a vigorous forensic debate, when what we really wanted was to engage in gentle inquiry.

The *confrontation stage* is where we agree on what the argument or discussion is about. People who just like arguing tend to avoid this stage as it ties them down. They prefer to be able to change their ground when it looks as if the argument might dry up. Interactions with this kind of person can often end in a quarrel.

In the *argumentation stage* the participants make a serious effort to fulfil their goals in the argument. In negotiation this will mean gaining what is wanted while conceding what is not too costly. In persuasive dialogue we find the common ground and develop and shift arguments so as to display the reasonableness of our position. In forensic debate we set out to defend our own position and to demolish that of our opponent.

Arguments do not have to go on until we drop, nor are they ended simply because one party walks off. The *closing stage* of an argument is when we recognise that the purpose of the discussion has been achieved or when we agree that we have done as much as can be done for the moment. Properly concluded, an argument leaves us in peace, whatever the outcome.

In formal meetings, agreed procedures announce each of these stages. In our day-to-day commerce with others we need to find our way through them as best we can. Often we tend to move backwards and forwards between the stages, and we may not be able to clarify one of the early stages fully until we have moved on. However, being aware of them can help us argue more effectively, both from the point of view of achieving our goals and from that of dealing peacefully with others.

Reference: Douglas N Walton, *Informal Logic: A Handbook for Critical Argument* (Cambridge University Press, 1989), 3–9.

Rules of Argument

In the previous essay I suggested that there are different kinds of argument and that each has a different starting point, purpose and rules. Logicians tend to make lists of rules, but most of us do not advert to them until we think someone has outwitted us by cheating, and then we get most indignant, though often for reasons we cannot fully explain. Normally we operate out of a kind of instinct and from experience of what works well.

While most of the rules are best left to the logicians, it is useful for the rest of us to have some idea of what they are like, so that we can modify our behaviour and make our interchanges with people more fruitful. We can do this by looking at the different broad kinds of rules. Douglas Walton offers a useful classification.

Locution rules state the kinds of things we are allowed or not allowed to say. In an inquiry we can say only things we know with certitude. Generally we are limited in the kinds of personal question we might ask.

Dialogue rules set out who can speak and when. We are not usually permitted, for instance, to burst into the middle of somebody else's sentence.

Commitment rules spell out how we are committed to what we say. If we make an assertion early in persuasive dialogue, we are expected to concede it when the other party uses it later in the dialogue. We are not, however, committed to generalisations of our more specific comments.

Win-loss rules determine how an argument is concluded. We all know the irritation of someone reigniting an argument we thought was finished with the mighty "but".

Rules of relevance keep us to the point. Sometimes students fill exam papers with all sorts of things, apparently on the assumption that, if they put in everything they know, at least some of it might answer the question.

Rules of cooperativeness prevent us from just being difficult. We ought, for instance, answer fair questions truthfully.

Rules of informativeness insist that we use arguments that our interlocutor is able to understand. We all know the irritation of being "dazzled with science" especially when it may not have been very relevant anyway.

Our lives can be disrupted when discussions and arguments do not succeed in reaching their goals. We may be left feeling that we had had an important point to make but that we had not been treated seriously. Alternatively, a group we belong to may fail to do something necessary because discussion about it has gone wrong. Similarly, someone may end up taking the blame for something because they were not able to explain themselves adequately.

The rules of informal logic assist us in arguing effectively and in a way that is respectful of all those who are involved. They also help us to identify and deal with people who are simply being difficult.

Reference: Douglas N Walton, *Informal Logic: A Handbook for Critical Argument* (Cambridge University Press, 1989), 3–9.

Becoming all Things

In a short passage in his work *De veritate* (2, 2), Thomas Aquinas talks about two kinds of perfection or completeness. The first is the perfection of being; the second is the perfection of knowing.

The perfection of being belongs to a thing simply because it exists and is measured against the kind of thing that it is. A gum tree, a horse or a human being each bring goodness into the world simply by the fact that they exist. The particular form of goodness relates to the species under consideration.

Thomas points out that among created things there is always limitation to this perfection. A human being cannot live as long as a Sydney Blue Gum nor run as fast as a horse. The perfection that it has is simply the perfection of a small part of the universe. Its lack of the being of other things can be regarded as an imperfection.

There is, however, a remedy for this limitation, and it lies in another form of perfection—the perfection of knowing. Thomas explains that to know something is in some sense to become that thing. What could he mean by this?

When we know a species of tree, for instance, what we do is grasp the what-it-is-to-be-a-tree of that tree. Somehow the what-it-is-to-be-a-tree is in us and becomes part of us, though, of course, in a different way from how it belongs to a particular living tree. We do not become woody or leafy, nor, if we allow our knowledge to accumulate at a manageable rate do we become filled up. Yet something of what-it-is-to-be-a-tree is actualised in us, and, for Thomas, this means that by way of knowing we become in a way the tree.

The point that Thomas wants to make is that this second kind of perfection, the perfection of knowing, makes up for the limitation we experience in our being. Being human, as rich as it is in itself, precludes being many other things, but by knowing we can share the perfection of all that exists.

In modern times, we human beings have had great success in overcoming the limitations of our nature. By inventing machines and breaking open new energy sources, we have been able to fly and to speak across the oceans. This is not what Thomas is talking about.

For Thomas satisfaction lies in contemplation. By knowing and understanding the created universe, we can share in its perfection and reach our own perfection. In holding it present to ourselves, we can see its beauty and love all that God has made. In so doing, we begin the life of the spirit, in which we find satisfaction not in material possessions but in becoming all things.

Ultimately, our happiness will be in the next life, when, seeing God face to face, we will see all things in the One Who made all things.

These Can be Shared without Being Lost

In the Exsultet of the Easter liturgy, we hear these words, 'Accept this Easter candle, a flame divided but undimmed'. The hymn takes up the fact that no matter how many candles are lit from the Easter candle, it will remain undiminished. Rather, by giving its light, light will be increased, just as when Jesus gives his Word, it is not diminished but increases.

This thought is readily applicable to human knowing. Knowledge shared is not diminished in the sharer, but in the sharing of knowledge a community of knowing comes into being, which enriches both the original giver and those drawn into community.

The reason for this is that knowledge is an immaterial or, we might say, spiritual thing. The difference can be seen, if we consider a cake. A cake can be had in two ways. It can be eaten, and then it is all gone and nobody else can eat it. It can be known, and then it can be shared and appreciated by all, and nobody is the poorer. A wedding cake is not made to be eaten. Although usually we all have a tiny bit with too much icing, a wedding cake is made to be seen by all as a symbol of the event being celebrated. Simplicius said in the sixth century:

> Goods of the soul, sciences and virtues are present undivided to those who share them; shared with another they are not diminished in the other but rather increased. For these are awakened and enkindled together in the soul of sharers, and shared they are multiplied many fold.

In our time, another spirit is abroad. From Thomas Hobbes we hear '. . . if all men have it, no man hath it . . . ' From John Locke we hear '. . . it is impossible for anyone to grow rich except at the expense of someone else'. It was Locke who was influential in giving us our modern understanding of property, which is largely exclusive and to which, under the guise of money, there need be no limit.

Boethius had earlier showed the problem of this kind of position when he pointed out in his *Consolations* that wealth is of value to us only when it is being spent, and then it is gone and someone else has it. In his words, 'A voice indeed fills equally the ears of all that hear; but your riches cannot pass to others without being lessened; and when they pass, they make poor those whom they leave'.

The kinds of goods that can be shared without being diminished are those like knowledge, understanding, love, goodness, and virtue. It is in sharing these that we can find true human community. To consider them as material or as property is to misunderstand them.

We can conclude with the words of Shelley, 'True love in this differs from gold and clay, That to divide is not to take away'.

References: Exsultet of Holy Saturday Liturgy; Simplicius, *Epicteti enchiridion* 30; Thomas Hobbes, *De cive* I, I, 2; John Locke, von Leyden 210; Boethius, *The Consolation of Philosophy*, II, prose 5; Shelley, *Epipsychidion*, 160–61. With special recognition of my teacher, Thomas Prufer.

Where Do Words Come from?

Not infrequently we find that we need a word to name something that is new in our experience. In our time, new inventions or technology have tested our ingenuity, but the practice of forming new words is time-honoured. Some examples may help.

The word 'envelope' was brought into English directly from French. When, however, television was invented, we went back to older roots of our language and combined a Greek syllable, *tele*, with a Latin word, *visio*, to convey the sense of seeing from afar. With the advent of computers we discovered a menu that does not have food on it. It looks a bit like a 'real' menu, because it is a list, but the kinds of things on it are certainly not anything one could eat.

There are other ways of forming words, but it is the last-mentioned way that we will examine now. It is interesting because of what it does with meaning. We use the term, 'menu', of the menu on a computer screen because that menu is somewhat like, though different from, the menu in a restaurant. This connection gave us a new meaning that leans on the old meaning. Because of the linkage, we were easily able to grasp the new meaning in its new situation. Philosophers call this process analogy.

Words and meaning can be looked at from another direction. Sometimes we use the same word about different things. When we use the word 'bark' of the sound made by a dog and of the outer layer of a tree, there is no common meaning and we say that the word is used equivocally. When we use the word 'tall' of a man and a tree the meaning in each case is the same and we say that the word is used univocally. Analogy sits between these two.

Interesting things happen when we experiment with these different ways of expressing meaning. The word, 'family', comes from the Latin word for household, which included servants. Today, however, because of how we live, we would probably say that it primarily refers to two parents and their children. We can extend it analogously to an 'extended' family or even more remotely to 'the family of man'. We can also cope with differences, as when, say, one parent or even a child has died, and we speak of 'the family' but with a qualification that expresses the loss.

Another process that sometimes occurs is called equivocation, and it is an age-old trick in argument. Here what happens is that one word is used in an argument with two quite different meanings. Controversy arose several years ago, when it was claimed that any group of people living in a single house was a family. Was this equivocation or analogy? Clearly, the issue is a significant one for both how we live and how we speak.

Reference: Thomas Aquinas, *Summa Theologiae* I qq 12-13, etc.

What Is it to Be?

When I was in second class at primary school, the local curate used to come in once a week for a period during which Sister would go somewhere else. On one visit, he went to the blackboard and wrote 'I am'. I do not know why he did this, but then he asked us what it meant. We shook our arms and suggested all kinds of answers, but none satisfied him. Eventually, he told us that it meant 'I exist'.

I was very excited about this, and, when I got home, I went to my father, who was at his workbench in the garage. I said, 'Dad, do you know what "I am" means?' He looked at me, and his brow furrowed. I could not contain myself and blurted out, 'It means "I exist"'. He stuck out his chin and said, 'I don't know about that'. The question has engaged me ever since.

What is it to be? Can we even think about not-being? Not-being, of course, is different from merely ceasing to be. Alternatively, if I am something, how can I become something else? Perhaps I am sad; do I have to stop being before I can become happy? If I did stop being, how could I start being again? Again, can two things be the same? If I am human, how can anybody else be human, because I am already that?

These are questions that have taxed philosophers for two and a half thousand years. We might sum them all up in one question—the question of being; what is it to be? Everything that is shares being; what can we say about things simply because they are?

We think about kinds of beings. Ancient philosophers considered whole beings to be primary, things like people or dogs or trees. Colours or relationships or circumstances can be said to be, but only in reference to whole beings. A colour, for instance, does not exist by itself; it must be in something. Today, scientists sometimes talk as if quarks and mesons were primary, but what are these? Can they be separated, for instance, from the mathematics that brings them to mind?

An important distinction is that between things that actually are and things that are able to be. If I am sad and nothing else, there is no way for me to become happy. But if I am sad and am at the same time able to be happy, though not happy at the moment, I will be able to change, that is, to cease to be how I am now and actually to become something that I am only potentially at the moment.

This is not how we usually talk about things, certainly not at a workbench and not even in second class at school. It is, however, how we have to talk when we touch on questions that have to do with being.

Embracing Postmodernism

When the issue of postmodernism arises, it comes to many of us in the form of art that we prefer not to look at or of literature that seems barely comprehensible. Much of it seems ugly rather than beautiful. On the intellectual front much talk by postmodernists has seemed negative and destructive. The very claim that we must deconstruct language and meaning gives rise to this, and the results of the inquiry seem often empty.

On a visit to Australia, Nicholas Lash, the Norris-Hulse Professor of Divinity at Cambridge University, suggested a richer understanding of postmodernism in a seminar that he gave at the Catholic Institute of Sydney. He said that the project of postmodernism involves a recovery of the past. Lash, who is the first Catholic to be Professor of Divinity at Cambridge since St John Fisher, who was martyred July 22, 1535, is a significant member of a movement that is trying to do just this.

In order to understand postmodernism, we need to grasp two things: what modernity was and how meaning is lost.

Modernity was a movement, which, despite roots in the fourteenth century, began sharply and earnestly at the beginning of the seventeenth century with such thinkers as René Descartes, Francis Bacon, and Thomas Hobbes. They were concerned about many things, but chief among them were the fostering of the new science, which we call modern science, and the invention of new political forms that would promote freedom and do away with the kinds of conflict that ravaged Europe in those years. Implicit in the movement was dissatisfaction with late medieval life.

This movement took the form of a new beginning. It looked to a time that was past, which it called the classical period, as simply past, and tried to step over the medieval period as if it had never been there. In other words, it attempted to remove from Western civilisation both its Greek heritage and the influence of the Christian centuries. It wanted a distinctly new start.

When we attempt to express meaning, either to ourselves or to others, we use words. These words have generally been in our language for centuries and have over that time undergone changes in meaning. Similarly, a thought, which we might convey in a sentence, may have first been expressed in response to a question that we no longer remember. In each of these cases, meaning is not so much lost as precipitated into the language that we use. Just as when chemicals precipitate in a solution, transparency is lost.

The first moment of postmodernism has concentrated on breaking down these precipitated meanings. The second, as Lash pointed out, is involved in recovering the meaning of the things we say. In matters of faith, this means going back not to the Council of Trent and what came after it but to the Apostolic Church and the Fathers and to the superb scholarship of the medieval years.

Can we Trust Reason and Argument?

In his dialogue, *Phaedo*, Plato has Socrates look into the problems associated with mistrust of reason and argument.

He begins, however, with hatred of human beings or misanthropy. He points out that when we begin by believing in someone uncritically, we are often disappointed. We 'assume that a person is absolutely truthful and sincere and reliable and a little later [we] find that he is shoddy and unreliable' (89d). After this has happened to us a number of times, he says, we begin to think that there is no sincerity anywhere and that no human being can be trusted.

He goes on to point out that the error in this situation is the underlying belief that people are either very good or very bad. We assume that very bad people are easily identified and that the rest must be very good. He says that the truth of the matter is otherwise, 'there are not many very good or very bad people, but the great majority are something between the two'. Judgement of the character of a person is not easy and demands a lot of care and skill.

Something similar happens when we engage in thinking and reasoning without either enough skill or an awareness of how difficult it is to find the truth about a state of affairs. We soon find that things go wrong either in our own judgements or, if we are a little surer of ourselves, in the judgements of others. In either case, we end up distrusting reason and the very possibility of achieving an understanding of how things are.

Two responses are likely in this situation. One is to suppose that there is no possibility of knowing how things are or even that there cannot be any fixity about things themselves. This kind of position goes by names such as relativism or scepticism. The other is to trust blindly without thought in something we 'know' to be true. This goes by names such as optimism and fundamentalism.

Up until recent times, our society was optimistic. In particular, it trusted in science, which was expected to make life simple by giving us true and certain answers in all matters that affect us. The events of this century have shaken this confidence and the predominant attitude of our society is now one of relativism: 'you can have your truth, but I will have mine'.

These things touch the Churches, too. Moral relativism is something that we often challenge, but the stronger temptation is towards fundamentalism. Biblical fundamentalism is more a Protestant experience, but doctrinal fundamentalism is prevalent in the Catholic Church. It takes the form of rigid adherence to the formulae of authoritative statements irrespective of their actual relevance or of the context in which they were originally made.

With Socrates we ought avoid both these extremes and seek the truth of things, aware that it is there but, nevertheless, that it is not easily grasped.

Is Pleasure Something Wholly Bad?

In the last book of his *Ethics*, Aristotle addresses the question of pleasure. Is it good, or is it bad? What is it, and what place does it play in the moral life? Anyone who has worked through the first nine books knows that pleasure and pain are recurring themes because of their place in human experience and action, but finally Aristotle addresses pleasure directly.

First, he considers a number of views about whether pleasure is good or bad. The one that we will consider is that which holds that pleasure is something wholly bad. Of the people who hold this view, Aristotle says the following:

> Some of its members [hold this] very likely from a conviction that it is really so, and others believing that it is better with a view to the conduct of our lives to represent pleasure as a bad thing, even if it is not; because [they say] most people are inclined towards it and are the slaves of their self-indulgence, so that they need to be urged in the opposite direction; for in this way they may attain to the mean.

Many moralities in our time have adopted this latter position. In fact, while one is learning virtues like temperance or courage or generosity, it is wise to lean away from what is most pleasant until we learn to act in the best way. What this theory has done, however, is turn some wise practical advice into a statement of moral obligation. Behind such a move is often the assumption that those who are being told are ignorant and could never understand the finer points of the moral life themselves.

Aristotle suggests that this is not a good way to go '[f]or, in matters relating to feelings and actions, theories are less reliable than facts; so, when they clash with the evidence of our senses, they provoke contempt and damage the cause of truth as well as their own'.

It seems to me that we find ourselves in this predicament today, especially with young people, who have rejected things that they were taught because these did not make any sense to them. Often they are right, though in being right they are suffering from a lack of a more sophisticated moral education that would have allowed them to see things differently.

Of pleasure, Aristotle says that it accompanies the action of any of our faculties that performs well and in a way that is in harmony with its disposition. This pleasure, he says, is not what the action is directed to but "a sort of supervening perfection, like the bloom that graces the flower of youth".

Of course, Aristotle is assuming here that one has developed all one's faculties in a most excellent way. That is what his book is about. We call it virtue. A moral life, therefore, ought to be exceedingly pleasurable.

Opinions One Cannot Have

Recently I was at a lecture by a competent political theorist, who surprised his audience by referring to a particular statement as the expression of an opinion that one could not have.

A first reaction might be, 'Why not? We all have rights to our opinions!' This right, indeed, is something we each hold dear. As well, we are used to the frequent assertion of a broad range of plausible and implausible opinions.

That is not, however, what the speaker meant. He went on to say that the economic issues under consideration were simply too complex to be matters on which one could form an opinion.

The distinction that he was drawing on can be called that between real opinion and apparent opinion. This is different from the distinction between true opinion and false opinion. Real opinion can be either true or false, but an apparent opinion is not really a candidate for truth or falsity. Opinion itself is different from knowledge, such as science, which carries with it certainty of the truthfulness of what is held and for which certainty springs from sound evidence, valid reasoning and sure testing. Opinions are views that we hold or judgements that we make that do not carry this degree of certainty with them. Real opinions, however, are supported to some degree by facts and arguments. Apparent opinions lack this support for any number of reasons ranging from the availability of evidence to the competence or thoroughness of the one stating them.

As a Sydney person, it is perhaps questionable whether, when people say, for example, at the start of the Australian Rugby League season, 'Penrith is the best team in the competition', that they articulate a real opinion. What could it mean? Does it mean that one team, Penrith, has a team whose players are each the best for their position? Or that the coach has the best record? Or that the players can play best as a team? Or that they will work well with the coach? Usually, the issue is simply too complex.

What people are really saying is probably something like, 'Penrith is my team. I want them to win, and they seem to have a fair chance [which makes me hopeful]'. An opinion is an assertion, but here we find a wish dressed up as an assertion.

The reason that we dress up different forms of thought or speech as opinions is that opinions make things happen. Opinion is the ground of political life, since it is in gathering, harnessing or changing the opinions of those who are free to act that we enable groups of people to do things. Apparent opinions can be attractive because, though easy to generate, they can be powerful tools in the battle for minds and hearts. What is wrong with them is that they act as instruments of influence without taking serious effort to inform people fairly or truly about the states of affairs under consideration.

Spare a Little Sympathy for Pilate

John's account of the passion of Jesus (John 18:28 — 19:11) has Pilate say, 'Truth? What is that?' It is a question that has echoed down through the centuries and which has been dealt with over and over again by philosophers and theologians but which still demands examination and clarification.

Pilate's question, however, was not of a speculative kind but was rather the question of a practical man, a governor, who, if he was not intent on acting justly, at least wanted to maintain a semblance of order in his domain. His question was a response to Jesus' statement, 'I came into the world for this: to bear witness to the truth; and all who are on the side of truth listen to my voice'.

We can have a little sympathy for Pilate. He was confronted by the chief priests and leaders of the people, on the one hand, who were demanding the death of Jesus for reasons not necessarily the same as they were stating. On the other hand, Jesus, the revealer of truth was not, perhaps for reasons to do with why he came on earth, being very helpful to Pilate, whose job it was to sort things out.

Truth is elusive, especially in human affairs where people want to do something with it. In these situations it can become an instrument for getting one's way, for insisting more effectively that other people follow one's own directives. It is for this reason that I prefer to attend to truthfulness, a human virtue, the exercise of which is our greatest hope of achieving truth.

Truthfulness has two parts, truth-seeking and truth-telling. These parts are not what we might call pieces, like parts of a tree such as branches, roots and leaves that might be taken aside and examined on their own. They are, rather, what we might call aspects, like hue and brightness of colour, parts that cannot be found apart from the other even if they can be talked about separately.

We learn from an early age about being truthful, but it comes in the guise of truth-telling, or rather of not lying. It is only later that we learn the importance of truth-seeking, and we also learn, if we are lucky, how difficult it can be to find the truth. It is then that we are ready to learn how intimately these two are connected. Truth-seeking, for instance, may modify truth-telling such as when speaking recklessly would destroy either the possibility of truth emerging from a state of affairs or the ability of participants to grasp it.

One of the vices contrary to truthfulness is the failure to continue to seek the truth. This may be because we are tired of examining the issues or because for some reason it has become important that the truth be what we had thought it to be.

This Strange Thing, 'Intelligence'

The word 'intelligence' is one that we bandy about quite a lot, and sometimes it seems that we do not use it well. One cannot see intelligence, and so we attribute intelligence to people who can do certain things, which we might regard as difficult. Therein lies a trap.

We might call one person intelligent because she writes books and another intelligent because he always beats us in an argument. People do not write books because they are intelligent. They write books because they have a gift for writing. On close examination, some books show evidence of an intelligent author, but many do not. Even more diverse are the reasons why people win arguments. They may be quick witted but they may merely be aggressive or stubborn or loquacious. Yet, we are inclined to call them all 'intelligent'.

This difficulty we have in naming qualities of mind has its roots in early modernity. Descartes, for instance, begins his *Discourse* with the sentence, 'Common sense', which he equates with reason, 'is the best distributed thing in the whole world'. What Descartes was proposing was that with his method or, perhaps, with the method of the new sciences, anybody could achieve understanding, so that differences of intellectual ability were immaterial.

Thomas Hobbes did see differences in intellectual function but reduced them to quickness of imagination and steadiness of direction, both in large measure dependent on the passions. Reasoning he saw merely as a kind of reckoning or calculation, giving the impression that differences between different intellectual activities were quantitative rather than qualitative.

In the pre-modern world, people were more aware of intellectual activities that were qualitatively different, that is, that were not reducible either to one another or to some other thing. They called them intellectual virtues. Different authors may have compiled different lists of such virtues, but the point was not to generate an ultimate list but rather to see differences. To do so is still useful today.

Someone with technical skill understands how things are made and is able to construct them but may not have much interest in speculative matters. A person with the gift of science is able to pursue matters with precision and exactness. Wisdom somehow allows a person to see the larger picture and so to put all kinds of knowledge about things into perspective. A prudent person is able to mediate successfully between matters of principle and their application in particular circumstances.

If we acknowledge these differences, we can better appreciate how different people do different things well. A great scientist, for instance, may, in fact, not be able to grapple successfully with issues of ethical principle but may, on the other hand, be also prudent and able to apply such principles to concrete situations. An astute judge of character will see these differences and not expect of persons more than they can actually do.

What is Philosophy About?

From time to time, I am asked what philosophy is about. The answer never seems satisfactory in the first instance, because philosophy is about everything—the world and all that is in it, human life and its aspirations, things beyond the world in which we live. The conversation out of which the question comes can, however, generally be extended to other questions, whose answers seem more helpful.

It is the assumption behind the question that generates the answer that seems so unfruitful. The assumption is that intellectual disciplines are separated from one another on the basis of the piece of the world that each carves out for its attention. The assumption works for much of our intellectual life. Geologists study rocks; astronomers study stars; sociologists study society.

Philosophy deals rather with the whole world and with whole beings within the world. It distinguishes itself from other disciplines like theology or like science taken as a whole by the aspect from which it views the world. Philosophy takes its character from human reason and wonder about the nature and origin of things. Its tools are logic, which firms up the exercise of reason, and rhetoric, which entices interlocutors to see the point or to grasp the question.

People also ask whether philosophy is useful. This is a particularly important question today, when the intellectual life of our nation is heavily dependent on funding and when funding is often measured in terms of usefulness and specifically economic usefulness.

Again, there is a contemporary bias in the question. In other times, someone might have asked whether it is good or even whether it is pleasurable. Our modern forms of knowledge, however, are so directed to how things work and to how we might do what we wish, that it is often impossible to separate science from technology or pure science from applied science and the former are often justified in terms of the latter. This drive to have reason do things is called the instrumental use of reason, and philosophy will have none of it.

This is not the same as saying that philosophy is useless or even that it is a frivolous activity that wastes time with puzzles and paradoxes. On the contrary, philosophy is a most serious discipline that reflects on what is happening around us and on the assumptions and presuppositions that underlie all that we say and all that we do. This is the famous 'examined life' towards which Socrates drew us.

Where, for instance, a political scientist focuses quickly on mechanisms that will allow something to happen, a political philosopher reflects from a distance on what is happening as people go about making their arrangements or on what is the good that they might seek or on what various goods can be distinguished in what they are doing.

This makes philosophy interesting yet difficult to turn to one's own purposes.

Problems with the Pursuit of Evil

Human evil of the kind that directly damages other persons exists, has always existed and will always exist in the world. There is a certain nobility in efforts that are taken to seek it out and to eradicate it especially when as happens from time to time it grows in undue proportion. Many of us will have imagined ourselves as fighters of evil at some time in our lives.

It is all too easy, however, to imagine that fighting evil is something like the ancient legend of Saint George and the dragon. There the evil was something big and real and dangerous, but it could be clearly identified and destroyed. The slayer could go home happy and proud that something that had intruded into the world had been done away with and that things had returned to normal.

Such a notion is simplistic because it contains a misunderstanding of what evil is, and that misunderstanding is dangerous.

In the tradition of Augustine and Thomas Aquinas, evil is understood not as something positive but as something negative. In other words, it is not something like a dragon but rather something like a hole. Further, it is not like just any hole but rather like a hole that should be filled. It is more like a vacuum in a container than like the emptiness of space.

Put more technically, evil is a privation of due good. It is not something in its own right but rather feeds off something else. This is not to say that it is altogether nothing, because it takes its character from and can act with the power of what it replaces.

Fighting evil is, therefore, dangerous. One can easily get sucked into the vacuum. It is not surprising, for instance, that inquiries in New South Wales and Queensland found corruption among police, though its proportions in those cases were worrying. In fighting evil, police sit on the edge of the hole. As detectives complained at the time, in order to fight crime they had to be in touch with criminals. Sadly, the environment in which they worked was always ready to affect them seriously and badly.

Special strategies are necessary for the care of all of those who do fight evil in ways more dramatic than dealing with the ordinary moral decisions that we all face daily. Two kinds of care seem important. The first is guidance in ethical reflection about the situations they meet. The second is assistance in leading lives that are not dominated by the evil they fight. In earlier times, small communities had their own ways of providing support, but in our big cities more formal support is needed. A few drinks are not enough.

While fights against evil are very necessary, the only thing that can replace evil altogether is good. Without it, different but derivative forms of evil simply feed off one another.

Truth Seeking and Truth Telling

From time to time in the liturgy, we read a passage from the Book of Wisdom (6:12–16), which goes like this:

> Wisdom is bright, and does not grow dim. By those who love her she is readily seen, and found by those who look for her. Quick to anticipate those who desire her, she makes herself known to them. Watch for her early and you will have no trouble; you will find her sitting at your gates.

Although the sacred author is doing more than just this, the text always impresses me as a rich image for the life of truthfulness. Truthfulness has two aspects—truth seeking and truth telling—and, although it seems that it is failure in the latter that is more often criticised, in many ways it is perseverance in the former that presents the greater challenge.

What is encouraging about the passage is the assurance that Wisdom is there to be seen. She makes herself available. Still, she is elusive; she sits not in the house but at the gate to where we must go to find her.

Failure in this life of truth seeking is to rest with 'having the truth', because this is often illusory. To do so is attractive, because it seems to justify us in sitting still and 'being right'. On a darker note it appears to give us power over others, who risk being called wrong, if they fail to accept our assertions and the consequences that flow from them. Yet, even the repetition of time-honoured convictions does not, in itself, assure us of our being truthful. Like a cockatoo, we may simply be repeating sounds that have been made by a trainer.

In religion and in politics, there is a tendency to confuse truthfulness and fealty. By fealty, I mean an obligation to allegiance particularly as it is demanded by those in power. Where it is felt and particularly in times of stress or crisis, the weight of this obligation can deter people even from telling the truth that they know let alone seeking truths that may be inconvenient. What is thought to matter the most is the cohesion of the group.

Truth seeking calls for care and diligence. Often, when an alarming or tragic event on a scale affecting the whole society bursts into our lives, people rush on to television screens or on to radio to tell us what has happened. Wiser people stand back and say that there is more to be learnt yet. They know that events are complex and that things unravel slowly. They stay with their questions and weigh each new piece of evidence. When somebody speaks they ask what does this mean and what could this person know? Even when it seems that it is all over, they continue to gently wonder what it was all about. These are truth seekers.

MEANING AND LIFE

Learning to Die

Recently I sat or perhaps I should say walked with a man who was dying. At first he was not dying, rather he was fighting. He was fighting cancer with which he had battled for twelve months. Then he was dying; then he died; and now he is dead. Not so long ago he was alive and well.

These were an extraordinary series of transformations and one must wonder whether a person could ever expect to learn how to make them and especially how to make them well. Experience is no guide since dying is something that we can do only once. Nor does understanding tell us much since what is beyond that moment of death remains incomprehensible to us.

Yet we are not without direction. In a death like this, one is not alone. One is with family and friends of different ages, who have varied experience of life and death, and with medical staff, who have been through it before. A kind of collective wisdom is available if it can be gathered. As well death is intimately related to life, and how one has lived holds something for how one might die.

In this case the man died well. While there was hope, he fought bravely and entered knowingly into the most harrowing of medical procedures. It was worth it, he thought, if it would allow him a few years to watch his children grow. He knew, however, that the odds were not good.

After the procedure failed it took time to recognise what was happening. At first things did not add up. What was going on did not match what had been predicted. Subtle changes took place in the nursing care. It was terribly confusing. Then the doctor gently informed him that vital organs were not functioning. Later asked whether he understood he was dying, he said 'yes'. There was not much else to be said, but with that simple acknowledgment reality reasserted itself. The world was drastically changed but it was together.

After that there was prayer, prayer together with his family and with it the anticipation of meeting those who had gone before into a new life. There were thanks, always brief but in words that would be remembered and treasured. There were farewells, sometimes a word, sometimes a gesture that harked back to easier times. Finally, there was sleep, and with pain eased by morphine the sleep extended into eternal rest.

For the family there was the experience of oneness: the oneness of moments when only one thing mattered; the oneness of the experience of a common though harsh reality. There was new knowledge of one another gleaned in the most telling of circumstances. In the sorrow of parting there was the certainty that 'we did what we could' and that 'he did it well'.

We live in a culture in which the processes of death are shunned. People seem to want either to hold death at bay or to hasten it. Perhaps one thing we need to do is to learn how to die.

Understanding Why Things Happen

When four school children and a teacher were shot dead in Arkansas, The American Rifle Association announced that guns do not kill people, people do. The announcement came virtually before the facts of the matter had registered across the world. It would have been very boring, because of the numerous utterances of the same statement after similar events, had not the circumstances been so tragic and the statement so predictable.

On another front, argument rages backwards and forwards about whether violence on television or in the movies contributes to violence in human affairs. During the seventies common thought had moved to assume that there was no relation. Now more people are saying that there seems to be a relationship but are generally unable to prove that there is or to show how it might work. Opponents, on the other hand, are adamant that there is no causal relationship.

Each of these discussions and others like them are very important to the quality of life that we live as a society. That the questions seem irresolvable suggests that there is something wrong with the way in which we think about them.

One proposal is that our understanding of causality it too narrow. For a few hundred years our culture has limited its understanding of causality to the notion that one thing acts on another, as when acid dissolves zinc. An older and much longer lived tradition viewed causality as a complex answer to the question, 'why?'. Once one allows this, diverse forms of causality emerge.

One such is the little spoken of dispositive causality. This is the kind of causality that a farmer uses when he sows a crop of wheat. He does not make the wheat grow, it grows itself. What he does do is ensure that the material conditions for germination and growth are as good as possible. This is no inconsiderable contribution to the development of a healthy crop.

Seen in this way, what the movie maker does is provide the conditions for someone who is disturbed or bad to act out their distress against other members of society in ways that they could not otherwise have imagined. Similarly, what the National Rifle Association does is ensure an environment in which instruments of lethal violence are readily available to anybody, including the disturbed. Neither can be said to have done the violence, but both have brought about the conditions necessary for its occurrence.

The National Rifle Association and the maker of violent movies are not liable in law for the consequences of the conditions that they bring about, nor is it probable that the law could make them so. On the other hand, there is good moral argument to say that they are responsible for injury that happens to other people and hence that the law should limit their actions for the protection of all.

Thoughts on Marriage and Anniversaries

Dear Mum and Dad, intuitively we celebrate fifty years of marriage, and we hope to do it well; but what is it that we celebrate?

Is it long life? It is in part, because long life is a gift. It is not so much an achievement as a product of luck and of circumstance with a little help from medical science. It is rare that two people who have married both live that long, and so we give thanks.

Is it hope? Not really. The marriage began with hope, and the golden wedding anniversary is a kind of mirror image of that beginning. Although the marriage will persevere to death and through death in eternal life, a half-century is a good time to pause and to acknowledge the fulfilment of those hopes.

And so, perhaps, that is what we do celebrate on a golden anniversary—the fulfilment of the hopes, promises, commitments and beliefs of fifty years ago. We celebrate not only their fulfilment but also the qualities of character, the learning and the endurance that have enabled that fulfilment. We celebrate, too, as those gathered around the marriage that have been part of its story, and we recognise what we have received from it and take pride in the way we have helped it.

It has not always been easy. You lost two children—one at birth, and one in the prime of life. What might the first have become? How can the second be replaced?

You both worked hard. Peter, your days in the coal mines were long and tough, and your nights were often given to meetings that furthered the causes in which you believed. Helen, you were sometimes like that lady 'who had so many children she did not know what to do', yet there was always room for care for a wandering soul.

When Steve was born, I said to you, Dad, 'Three more and we'll be ahead of the girls'. Years later my god-father told me that I would never understand how alarming my words had been. How could one even feed that many mouths? Yet, when two more did come, they were accepted lovingly as gifts from God.

Perhaps at the heart of our celebration is the recognition that fifty years ago you made a commitment to one another that you would work out your happiness together, and that is what you have done. It is not just the happiness of which the philosophers speak, because they speak of ideals and abstract from the details of individual lives. This is the happiness of two lives lived together; of difficulties surmounted together; of joys shared together; of two characters blended to find their own harmony together.

After all of this, in whom else could you find your peace but in each other and in the God who first blessed your marriage and in whom you have trusted.

Well done, Mum and Dad!

A Little Understanding Will Help

A famous colleague of mine used always tell a joke at the start of a homily. He claims that they were always successful, and I believe him.

Most of us do not have that experience. Sometimes our jokes work, at other times they do not. We even have the experience of hearing a funny joke at which everyone laughs but of finding, when we tell it in almost exactly the same words only a day or so later, that nobody laughs.

Philosophers explain this last phenomenon by talking about micro-rhetoric. A part of language that is not amenable to logical analysis consists of such things as slight differences of word choice, timing and pausing, indicators such as 'Did you here about the . . .' or 'A friend of mine said . . .' and a whole range of body language and facial expression. It is at this level that we prepare people to hear our jokes and then bring them to laugh.

All of this is, of course, very difficult to learn, and we never learn it formally. Rather, as children we imitate our elders and then in easy stages gather a sense of what works and what does not. In time, we accrue the great advantage to life of mastery of our language.

Although my colleague has a fine grasp of the English language, this was not the only advantage he had in his homilies. People always laughed at the incongruity of a rather ordinary joke being told at the time that it was, but they also stayed alert in the expectation that they would find out during the homily why this particular joke had been told. They rarely did find out, but they always remembered the homily.

Immigrants have none of these advantages. Even if their first language is English, they generally find Australian micro-rhetoric incomprehensible, though they may, in time, learn some. For those whose first language is not English, it is very much more difficult. For those whose culture is founded in a civilisation other than western civilisation and who have lived into adulthood in that culture, it is almost impossible to learn the finer detail of Australian English. It is unlikely, therefore, that their jokes will ever succeed in the normal fashion.

How can we help these people? We cannot teach them, because normally we are not able to articulate the finer detail of our language ourselves. It sits just behind the conscious level of speaking and consists of so many shades and differences that we could never list them all.

What we can do, however, is listen with understanding. While a joke-teller normally has to win permission to tell a joke with subtle linguistic manoeuvres, we can simply recognise a joke because we know that someone is telling it. The joke will not have the spontaneity of a native-told joke, but it can be funny, and, more importantly, in listening we will create a space in which our immigrant fellow-citizens can live.

Ought One to Get married?

Xenophon records that a young man once accosted Socrates and asked him, 'Ought one to get married or not?' Socrates replied, 'Do whichever you wish, you will live to regret it in either case'.

As first sight, this might seem a light-hearted response, either funny or not funny, or, if it were taken more seriously, somewhat cynical. On the other hand, like an oracle or many other wise sayings that get passed down to us, it can be read at many levels.

Socrates was not going to tell the young man whether he or anybody else should get married. Those were their decisions to make. He did, however, make clear that whichever choice of life was made, it would have its moments and with its difficulties would come regrets.

Today I will focus on marriage, and so I will leave consideration of the life of solitude to another time. What, then, are the difficulties that might bring one to regret, even if momentarily, having got married? More specifically, what are the difficulties particular to life in Australia today that would bring on this condition?

The kind of society that we live in is called a liberal society. Although there are different kinds of liberal society, common to them all is the idea that the fundamental role of government is the protection of the individual liberties of citizens. The development of the political structures under which we live began in the seventeenth century in response to a cultural movement, which began a century or two earlier, and in which people started to think of themselves as individuals rather than as members of families or clans or tribes.

In our time, this movement has developed even further with full citizenship granted to men and women alike and with, what we have called women's liberation, an even more radical sense of the individuality of each person.

The problem, then, is how do two people who see themselves so fundamentally as individuals, each with their own opinions and wishes, put together a marriage that will endure. Romance is not enough, nor is family a primary necessity for survival. The instinct to procreate is certainly there, but it has to compete with many other desires and demands. This, I believe, is the central issue that meets young people when they decide to marry today.

At times, churches, particularly, lament that we are a liberal society. This is rather futile, because it will not change very quickly. It is also a little dishonest of people who are ever ready to enjoy the benefits of that liberal society.

The challenge is rather to help people learn how to live an enduring and enriching commitment in this kind of world. We have also to look at how our Christian rituals engage and support people who do this. It is new ground, but that makes it interesting.

Making Time to Enjoy the Jubilee

The end of Lent marks an important moment in the Jubilee Year, which is being celebrated by Catholics world-wide at the beginning of the third millennium. As a time of penance and reconciliation, Lent saw the Pope's recognition of fault in the life of the Church and his request for forgiveness. In our country, the Bishops made their Statement of Repentance to mark the 2000th anniversary of Christ's birth. In time, further acts will necessarily flow from these.

This, however, is by no means all that the Jubilee entails. Activities of various kinds are occurring in parishes, schools, dioceses, and states. They might be educational, prayerful, and especially with the Easter season celebratory.

One of the questions that will face us all concerns finding time for this extra activity. The issue itself belongs specifically to modern secular society.

It is part of the human condition that much of our time is given to work. Roughly a third of our time is given to sleep. It has generally been the case in human societies that other times are set aside to be without work. These times are necessary for healthy human life. When, at the beginning of the First World War, Britain introduced Sunday work and longer hours of work, it was found that weekly productivity decreased. When weekly working hours were decreased, productivity increased.

In our society, the usual time off has been the weekend, although now even this is being eroded. It is made up of Sunday, a religious feast going back many centuries, and the more recent innovation of the Saturday day off. We use it both for rest and for seeking diversion.

In former times, the picture was very different. There were always days off, but in societies in which religion was integral to the life of the society itself, the days were generally religious festivals. A Greek view was that the gods had marked out festival days out of pity for burdened human beings. In classical Greece and Rome, between sixty and one hundred and eighty festival days were celebrated each year. Australians in full-time work today have about one hundred and forty days off each year.

The difference, then, is that, in the ancient or, indeed, medieval worlds, time off was more often associated with religious events, which were integrated into the rhythm of life. Activities on these days were varied. Greek religious sites, for instance, often had stadiums for sport, theatres for drama, and shops associated with their temples.

For us, one of the difficulties of a Jubilee Year is that we have to fit its activities into an already busy schedule. It does not come as a festival with the gift of time that is different from ordinary time and which, with the suspension of work and demand, allows space for remembering. We do, however, have other freedoms that allow us to mould jubilee into our lives.

Let's Not Forget Our Stories

One Holy Thursday morning, I was sitting on the beach of the island of Tumleo off the coast of Papua New Guinea near Aitape. Seven small boys playing on the beach had first run away when I arrived. Later they came and laughed as this ungainly large white man went swimming with his hat and glasses on. Now they gathered tentatively around me, and one said, 'Story!'

I told them the story of Noah. They moved close and listened, though they could have understood very little since they seemed to know Pidgin but no English. When it was finished, they asked for another and I told them about Jonah and the whale. Their attention seemed fixed on words they knew little of and on working out what made this stranger tick. Then we swam and played in the water, and afterwards they brought me some green coconuts from which to drink.

At another time, in Greece, I told a man that I was interested in Aristotle. He became very agitated and proclaimed that Aristotle and his pupil, Alexander the Great, both Macedonians, were Greeks and spoke Greek. Then he railed against the former Yugoslav State, which had called itself Macedonia. 'They are stealing our stories,' he said, 'and soon our children will not know who they are'.

Our stories are most important to us, because they tell us who we are and what we do. As Christians, we find our stories in the Scriptures and particularly in the Gospels. We do as Jesus did.

Scripture scholarship during much of the last century focussed on scientific modes of understanding Scripture. This has been true and useful and good, but it ought not let us lose sight of the fact that the Scriptures are our stories and that in their telling and retelling and in their hearing and re-hearing we establish our identity and find coherent ways of acting.

Even our modern scientific culture has its stories. The fable in Descartes' *Discourse on Method* and the myth in Francis Bacon's *New Atlantis*, though distinct from science, are the founding stories on which our scientific culture was built. It is to such as these that we turn when we want to understand the world that we have created for ourselves.

No one has just one story. Stories build on stories, just as often in the Gospel, Jesus picked up a story from the Old Testament and developed or transformed it. We do, however, need to make our many stories coherent, and chaos often falls upon societies when new and powerful stories intrude into their lives or when old stories are forgotten.

In Australia at the present time, Aboriginal peoples are labouring to absorb the massive story of Western civilisation. Immigrant peoples are endeavouring to learn the stories of this land, so that they will know who they are as Australians. We call this reconciliation.

Letter to a Friend in America

Dear Ron,

I hear from those that love you that now your days may be numbered. That is sad, because we will miss you. But it is also not so sad, because you have had a good life and because an even better life awaits you in the next world.

We said our goodbyes when I last visited you in Washington just over two years ago, but now I would like to say a little more. I'll send it by email, because then it will travel as fast as an angel.

You have been a great friend for many years—since about 1980. In Australia, I would say that you are my mate. That is as affectionate as Australian males get with one another. When I look back over the many moments we have had together, I do not know which stands out most.

Perhaps, it was at the beach in the summer, when in the late afternoon we would chat about serious things but in a relaxed way. Often, our conversation would take up from something we had covered on the previous day, but in your hours on the verandah listening to the roar of the surf you would have thought of something new.

Perhaps, it was an evening after the symphony, when with the log fire burning and the dog sleeping we sat and sipped whisky with Jackie and discussed the sad and funny things in the world and what we thought about them.

Perhaps, it was that Christmas, when I walked over from the College through the snow and you opened the door with a great smile and took me into the warmth of your home.

Perhaps, it was after a meal, when we washed up together in silence and let the hubbub go on in the dining room, while we collected our thoughts.

Whatever it was, Ron, you have been a great mate, and I thank you for it.

When you get to heaven say a good word to God for me. Tell Him that you would like to keep a spot for me. While you are waiting for me to come, find out where they keep the whisky.

May your own time of waiting be peaceful, and be sure that you are ever in my prayers.

Love and farewell

Your old mate.

Ron died peacefully on the Monday of Holy Week. His wife and daughter and a palliative care nurse were with him. On the previous day, many of his family had gathered to say farewell and to pray. In the end dying was simple, his breathing became slower and shallower. The time between each breath became longer, until at last there was no breath.

Making Time for Conversation

At Easter time, I visited close and long-standing Bougainvillian friends in Port Moresby. At the same time, one of their uncles was staying with them. He was a teacher, I suspect in his late fifties, and had come to Port Moresby to see the government about his superannuation payment following an accident that prevented him from continuing in his work.

One morning after I had been there for three days, not much was going on, and I sat down next to Uncle on a bench on the veranda. We found our way into conversation, and he started telling me about the clan relationships and customary marriage laws of his own district in Bougainville. It was fascinating, partly because they are so different from our own, partly because of how the complex network of relationships and responsibilities ensured that nobody in a clan was ever without relationship or care.

After a time, we exhausted the topic for the time being and Uncle asked me some questions about life in Australia. Eventually, he stood up and said that it was time for him to go to see the government. He thanked me for talking with him and then said that it was the first time he had ever sat down and talked with a white man. I was deeply moved, because I knew that he had met many white men and women before me.

A conversation, such as this one, which I will remember for the rest of my life, is of a different order to many in which we find ourselves engaged. We can think of some of those semi-public interactions, such as in a staff-room at work or at certain kinds of dinner party, where a lot of sound is made but little is said. Each of us can surely find other examples.

These apparent conversations tend to be guarded so that the participants are able speak at length without revealing much of themselves, while at the same time jockeying for position in a hierarchy of speakers. How often do we fail by telling our story over the top of somebody else's without bothering to explore their experience with questions and affirmations.

The pity of this lies in the fact that speech is the most obvious sign of our being human, of what is in our minds and hearts, of our having things worth saying, of our being able to connect with one another on an immaterial or spiritual plane. Empty speech is a failure to achieve our humanness.

The philosopher, Martin Heidegger, deplored gossip, not because of its destructiveness to the reputations of those on the receiving end, but because of its very emptiness and therefore of its destruction of the speaker as a speaker. To gossip or to speak emptily is to become 'a noisy gong or a clanging cymbal' (1Cor 13: 1). To be truly human calls for something more.

Wise Men Talking About Big Questions

About twelve months ago, a columnist in the Australian newspaper, the *Sydney Morning Herald* complained about the way in which adults on meeting small children often open conversation with, 'And what's your name?'. She thought that this was somehow demeaning and that adults ought to be able to generate better conversation with children.

At the time, I thought that she was wrong and that there was something appropriate about the question. This came together for me when a friend reported a conversation had between two serious young men at the breakfast table.

> They were having a discussion about when Luke starts school. Luke said that he wanted to sit next to James when that happened, and James was busy explaining that he would be in another class room by then. Well, Luke then asked James if he would still be his brother when he was in another room, and James asked his mother whether he would still be James Cooper when he moved into another room.

These are big questions that have to do with personal identity and with identity through change. They have challenged philosophers for centuries. Who am I? What makes me me? Am I the same now as I was when I was younger—the same person, the same character? What has learning and experience done to me? How do I relate to my memories and to the relationships that have been part of my life?

The great thing about small children is that they ask these questions afresh, not out of some form of personal crisis, but because they are discovering the world and themselves and their own place in the world. They are not yet spoilt by theoretical answers that they may or may not understand nor by impatience to get on and to get something done. They can pause and wonder about what the world is like.

It seems to me, then, that to ask children of a certain age range their name on first meeting them is a good thing, because their name is one of the first things of which they are aware that distinguishes them from the people around them. In the cosy little nest of the family, where all seems one, recognising a name that is one's own and that no one else has is an important step in achieving a sense of one's own identity.

Something of this was confirmed for me more recently by another friend, who asked a young boy what his name was. He replied, 'My name is Michael and my Mummy and Daddy love me up to the moon and back again'.

In this lies hope for us all and for human life in general. We are born not knowing very much at all, yet, in each of us having to learn, the human race is given the opportunity with every new generation to see the world afresh.

Life is Generally Hard

Life is generally hard, though for most of us, not in an absolute sense. It is hard, rather, in some respect or other. Nor is life hard for everyone in the same degree. Whatever obstacles we meet, we seem to meet differently. How we each deal with the difficulties that are a normal part of our lives also differs. Some of us are more successful than others. Perhaps all that remains generally true is that we all have to jump hurdles derived from our own being as we plot our courses through life.

Thoughts like these were running through my mind as I watched athletes at the Paralympic Games. The event that most moved me was the men's triple jump for the sight-impaired. In this event, each jumper's coach helped him into the starting position and then moved to a point on the track midway through the jump. From there the coach called repetitively to the jumper, indicating the direction in which he was to run, striking a rhythm for his paces and signalling the moment at which he should commence the jump.

I remembered my own clumsy attempts at school to do what was then called the hop, step and jump. With limbs jarred and tangled, I usually ended up in a pile far short of where I should have been. Eventually, the coach suggested, not unkindly, that I could probably do something better with my life. I also thought of moments of disorientation, when I had tried to find my way around even very familiar places in the dark and had stepped wrongly.

Later, when I recounted my experience to someone more closely associated with the Paralympics, I was told that the athletes would not appreciate my sympathy. In their own eyes they are elite athletes, the best in the world, and their bodies, which we might view as in some way broken, they own as their own. The sporting achievement, for which we praise them, is something that they attribute to the persons they are.

Each of us carries privations that show up in comparison to the ways in which other people can do things. One of us may find it hard to remember names, another to add up numbers. We carry physical ailments and weaknesses as well as emotional ones. Being small has its advantages when moving through crowded spaces but makes carrying heavy suitcases a burden.

Perhaps what the example of the Paralympics offers us is both the opportunity to accept ourselves afresh as we are in our minds and bodies and feelings and the inspiration to strive to do well those things that are important to the way in which we wish to live in the world. The consistency of each of our lives will, however, be different, so that for the most part we will be aiming to do well rather than to be best.

It is Stories that Hold Us Together

Some months ago, I picked up a small book of Aboriginal dreamtime stories. I persevered with them for a while, but eventually put them down, because I could make nothing of them. This was not a new experience to me but one I had had at other times, when I had tried to read other collections of dreamtime stories in the hope that I would thereby better understand Aboriginal culture and meaning.

The temptation I faced at this point was to write the stories off. They were stories about animals and places and about how things came to be as they are. For me with my Western scientific training, any literal interpretation could not make sense, and I failed to register any other kind of sense.

A truer account is that I simply did not understand these stories. I was left, therefore, unable either to interpret them or to judge them. This is not surprising. They come from a culture of which I have little understanding. They fit with many other stories, most of which I have never heard. The crucial stories and meanings, which ultimately give life to the stories I read, are probably not even available to me.

At the same time, I could respect these stories, not because I could see something in them but because I respected the people whose stories they were.

On several occasions since my last attempt to read dreamtime stories, it has struck me while reading the gospels that in some ways the gospels are just like them. If one puts oneself in the shoes of an outsider, many of the gospel stories about events in the life of Jesus such as the cure of the blind man (Luke 18:35–43) are rather simple and, indeed, improbable. Yet, for us, who know them as a part of all the Scriptures and as the source of a long tradition that carries our meaning for us, they are fundamentally important.

It is not my purpose here to compare dreamtime stories and gospel stories. To do so, I would need to know both well, and there may be many ways in which they are not commensurate. What they do have in common, however, is that each forms part of the mythology of a people.

There is a stream of thought in modern Western culture that deals with life only rationally and which would interpret the application of the term 'myth' to a story as a claim that it was not true. The truth of that stream of thought has itself now been challenged. It left out of its account recognition of much of what it is to be human.

Our fundamental stories give us meaning and tell us who we are and what we do. That is why in the liturgy we return to them daily.

Compassion Can be our Strength

Recently, for a variety of reasons, I took to wondering about compassion.

The *English Oxford Dictionary* gives priority to the following meaning: 'the feeling of emotion, when a person is moved by the suffering or distress of another, and by the desire to relieve it.' The etymology of the word is also revealing. Ultimately, it stems from the Latin verb *compatior*, which means 'to suffer or to undergo or to bear together with'. This is closer to what the dictionary says is an obsolete meaning of the word.

Compassion, then, is a feeling, and we might call it fellow feeling. We did in Australia, to the surprise of much of the world, display this feeling publicly during the Olympics and Paralympics to those who came last and to those who did not win but whose efforts moved us. It may be that living in a harsh land we can readily identify with those who persevere in hard things.

Question arises about whether compassion is a virtue. In other words, is it a strength or an excellence that enriches human character? When we say, 'she is a compassionate person', we refer not just to a particular moment of feeling but rather to a stable condition which enables this person to respond to people in different situations with fellow feeling. In acknowledging that this is something good, we recognise a kind of balance between extreme ways of reacting. That is what virtue is.

The extremes can be interesting. A person can be unfeeling, living in relation to others by calculated self-interest or perhaps being themselves damaged and unable to acknowledge feeling. At the other end of the spectrum, people can get so caught up in feeling for others that they become incapable of acting carefully or well because compassion has turned into grief or sorrow.

This balance will be found differently in different people in different circumstances. A teacher without compassion will be brutal, but one with too much feeling will only create chaos. A police officer will exercise compassion differently when rescuing a small child from a drain and when securing a criminal injured in a chase.

A feeling, then, that sometimes appears as weakness, especially when tears come to our eyes, properly honed becomes a strength that enables us to act well in response to others. It is a richly human virtue that consists in the awareness of our common limitations and needs as human beings and in the readiness to find common ground with others when they are affected by those limitations and needs.

It seems to me that God cannot be said to be compassionate in this way, because God is not affected by limitations. The rich biblical metaphor (Ps 103:8), therefore, picks up something that is best in human experience and attributes it to God, who acts in ways just and merciful through knowledge and love that are beyond our comprehension.

The Importance of Luck

Sometime ago I was having dinner with a couple whose marriage I took to be exemplary, when the conversation turned to marriage itself. After a while, the husband turned to his wife and said, 'I don't know how we did so well—just luck, I suppose'. I was somewhat shocked that so much in the fact of this most compatible union could be put down to luck—simply meeting one another, the spark of initial interest, a decision to marry made not without any knowledge at all but certainly without knowledge of how well each would complement the other.

Luck, or we may call it chance or fortune or fate, affects all our lives for good or for ill. Sometimes it is puzzling; at other times we try to get the best of it. A burst of good luck creates surprise and joy in us; consistent bad luck is depressing and often prompts us to deep questions about the nature of life and how we might live it.

Elements of luck deeply affect the human condition. For each of us, our particular genetic make up results from the joining of one sperm and one ovum, when others could have been united instead. Our parents may have had some plans for the time of our birth, but what would happen in the world during our lifetime was beyond their ken. Where life takes us will often be a matter of chance meetings or casual actions, whose consequences far outweigh the gravity of the meetings or actions themselves.

Being affected by events so far beyond our control does put great uncertainty into our lives. While this might not worry us when things are running well, we become anxious when things seem not to go so well for us. We turn to philosophy and theology to try and understand what chance is and how it works. We also turn to magic, religion and science in attempts to get control of fortune and so to turn it to our own good.

In the present age and in our culture, we tend to turn to science for control, and, in many respects, we have been rather successful. Medical science, for instance, has taken it upon itself to restore health, when it has been disrupted by accident or by chance meeting with an agent of disease. On the other hand, interest in cloning raises the spectre of a world peopled with just a few eccentric types, whose boredom in the presence of one another would be immense.

Before relying too much on science we ought to heed the advice of the physician Hippocrates from the late fifth century BC. 'They did not want to look on the naked face of luck, so they turned themselves over to science. As a result, they are released from their dependence on luck; but not from their dependence on science.'

A Man Who Did No Harm

In 2001, Australian Marist Fathers joined the family of one of their finest men to bury him. Father Patrick Reynolds had died in the early hours of Tuesday, March 27, the day after his seventieth birthday, worn out finally by the effort of breathing.

While I was reflecting on his life during the days leading to his death, it occurred to me that, in all the years I had known him, he had never done me any harm, and I marvelled at how remarkable that was. I mean 'harm' in the broadest possible way: hurt, injury, trouble, ill-treatment, wrong.

It is an easy objection to suggest that then perhaps he had not done anything at all or at least not anything to affect my life. That could not be further from the truth. He had been my spiritual director for most of my early life as a Marist and had taken a keen interest in my welfare ever since. I often found myself engaged in some project with him or constructing something that would make his life more convenient.

Nor was I alone in this. At his funeral, the church was over-crowded by people attracted by his goodness, and this despite the fact that he had had multiple sclerosis for forty years, had been wheelchair-bound for thirty years and had lived in a nursing home for fifteen years.

What is remarkable about the lack of hurt flowing from Pat's life is that the normal condition of human life is to the contrary. We live in groups and there we rub up against each other and compete for what we want. We have minds, and we form views, which we insistently press on one another. We have feelings, and, when they get out of kilter, we jar one another.

We do, of course, have ways of dealing with all of this. We recover. We forgive one another. We get ourselves together and perhaps learn from the experiences that shake us. Despite this, however, hurt and injury is not something that we like to see.

The remarkable thing about Pat was that he contacted people, he did things, he formed and expressed views, and he battled with the difficulties that life put in his way without ever having to hurt or bruise those among whom he lived. In this, it seems to me that he lived a part of the Christian mystery in a way that ought to inspire us all. It is the part of that mystery that puts the commandment of love first.

Patrick Reynolds was a saintly man, who lived the Paschal Mystery daily. Strong and healthy as a young man, he was slowly and inexorably rendered physically powerless by disease, yet out of this very suffering his spirit was deepened and filled with a great gentleness. He engendered not sympathy but admiration. He showed us how to live.

Language and the Environment

In a beautifully titled article, 'Selling Pigeons in the Temple: The Danger of Market Metaphors in an Ecosystem', Timothy C Weiskel analysed the problems we are generating for ourselves and the earth by using economic language in our discussions of environmental issues. His article is available on the web at http://ecoethics.net/ops.

A cursory glance at Australian newspapers will show us that we do indeed talk about the environment in this way. We wanted 'environmental credits' in the global warming discussion. The problems of the Murray-Darling system are expressed in terms of future agricultural potential and its market implications. The commercial value of eco-tourism has become a major argument for protection of the Great Barrier Reef.

The problem with this kind of language is that it reduces all value to monetary value. Nature and even human life become little more than parts of an economy. Even more insidiously, an assumption grows that all problems about life and nature will be solved by the 'natural' forces of the market place. This absolves citizens and politicians alike from the responsibility of looking seriously at what we value and at what is good in itself so as to make serious judgements about the right and wrong of our actions.

The kind of nonsense that is built into this use of metaphor becomes apparent in a question like, 'Can we afford a sustainable environment?' If we negate it, the question comes, 'Can we afford an unsustainable environment?' The assumptions behind the question are absurd. We can either say that we are living well in our environment or that we are destroying our environment and will soon have to move.

We now talk about 'the human and economic cost' of traffic accidents. There is good reason for thinking about cost, because making the roads safer and so saving human lives and preventing injury is expensive and politicians need to justify expenditure and in turn taxation. The phrase, however, has its problems. 'Economic cost' is straight forward and worth considering, but what is a 'human cost'. It is a metaphor for death, pain, incapacity, disrupted lives and grief. The phrase, however, suggests even unwittingly that these can all be measured in economic and ultimately financial terms. The question we are driven to ask is, how much should a life cost? Our society tries to do this through its courts, but there we run the risk of reducing life to mere dollars. The same process applies to the environment.

We can, indeed, address the environment as economists, but we also have other ways. As Christians, we can talk about the beauty of creation and of the glimpse it gives us of our Creator. As human beings, we can relate to the environment as 'my place', where we live and where we belong. As scientists, we can marvel at the extraordinary diversity and complexity of life around us.

Pigs and Love Cannot be Bought

Recently in Bougainville, the cost of a pig of a certain size—not too big, not too small—was 900 kina in the official currency of Papua New Guinea or alternatively five strings of traditional shell money, each about a metre long. At the same time, a string of traditional shell money sold for about 25 kina.

Any reasonably perceptive twelve-year-old Australian entrepreneur will recognise that what one should do is fly to Bougainville, borrow lots of kina, buy shell money and purchase pigs with it, sell the pigs back for kina, pay off the loan and return to Australia rich. The trouble with this is that it will not work. The reason that it will not work is that the people of Bougainville would not enter into these kinds of transactions.

If one wishes to buy a pig for food of for commercial purposes in Bougainville, one has to pay kina. On the other hand, shell money is preferred, if the pig is being bought so as to contribute to part of a bride-price. Land can be bought only with shell money but guided also by complex traditions and family relationships.

What the Bougainvillian custom shows us is that there are some things that are not just commodities and that their value cannot be reduced to monetary value. Obvious things of this kind are human beings and the things that pertain to them, the environment including land, ideas and even money itself. Philosophers call this the incommensurability of goods or value.

When we act as human beings and give value to the things that matter to us or perceive the good that lies in things in their own right, we find that many of them cannot be measured against each other. The place that is my home means more to me than it could as the corner of a parking lot or than the money I might accept if forced to sell to developers. The endeavours of young sportsmen and sportswomen in weekly team competitions have a value that is altogether different from the millions of dollars showered on elite athletes by television companies and advertisers. The worth of a new thought is that it is somebody's thought and that it sheds light on the world for everyone that hears it, not that it is that strange thing we call "intellectual property" and out of which we hope to make money. Above all, love is not something that can be bought.

Our modern culture has lost a sense of these differences and in so doing has diminished us as human beings. We have learnt ways of turning everything into money and, in particular, of turning politics and ethics into economics. We would do well to turn to our own Aboriginal peoples and to the Pacific Islanders to learn again something that our civilisation knew five or six centuries ago.

Leadership in Australia Today

By most accounts, Australia is currently facing a crisis in leadership or more fundamentally a crisis in regard to the exercise of authority in the community at large. It is manifest in disillusionment with politicians and with institutions such as government authorities or the banks. It is also present in the Church in such diverse ways as are found on one hand in those who hold authority in careless disregard and on the other in those who forcibly co-opt authority to their own rigidly held views.

Whatever the causes of this situation, it calls for forms of leadership that are appropriate to the times and that will inspire people to see beyond themselves and enable them to achieve measures of unity in thought and action. When formal structures of authority are weak, more is called for from those who exercise authority.

Australia was fortunate in that it has seen in Sir William Deane, a former Governor General in the 1990's, a model of leadership that is appropriate to our times and that did move a wide spectrum of Australians towards better things. It would be a pity if we did not learn from his example. Although it will take a serious biography and publication of his speeches for us to grasp all the dimensions of his kind of leadership and although we have to separate what is imitable from what is temperamental, news commentary around the time of the completion of Sir William's term of office provided some insight.

Perhaps it was his compassion that touched us most, because, in each of the national tragedies during his term, he was there saying with heartfelt emotion the things that we knew had to be said but that we could not say ourselves. He understood the importance of the symbolic gesture, such as when he took sprigs of wattle for the parents of those killed in Switzerland to drop into the stream that had taken their children. He was self-effacing, not grand, and in always saying what he thought was right, he showed us someone who was true and 'real'.

Sir William understood that his authority came from the people, and so in the end he thanked all Australians 'for the immense privilege in being able to serve in this office'. He led not by command but by example, which saw street kids as his last guests at Government House and led him to sit among Aboriginal people to listen. For this reason, he could be, as former Prime Minister, Malcolm Fraser said, 'the conscience of the nation' not as someone judging remotely, but as one looking into himself and in so doing interpreting the nation to itself in success and in failure.

Leaders, civil or ecclesiastical, have a complex role, and must balance its different functions. They can easily become primarily administrators or primarily politicians. What Sir William has shown is a manner of leadership that is primarily pastoral.

Two Modes of Authority

Broadly speaking authority can be said to be grounded in two quite distinct ways.

In the first and more primitive way, authority is won by a person who shows in speech and action that he or she is capable of forming a group of people into a unit and of leading them into action. This basis of authority has long been known, and so we see in Homer's *Iliad* how Achilles was able to galvanise soldiers into action not just because of his strength but because of his ability to inspire with speech and to focus men's minds on a particular course of action.

In the second way, authority is attached to persons who have political power and implies a moral obligation of people within a particular association to obey them. Historically a wide range of explanations has been proposed for this kind of authority: allegiance, consent, divine right, natural law, the common good; but underlying each is the need for a locus of unity and decision, if a group is to act in concert.

These two kinds of authority are often portrayed as opposed to one another. The movie *Braveheart* showed how the commoner, William Wallace, was able by means of a short speech to stir the Scottish army into action against the English. The chieftains, who had become a self-indulgent and insipid lot, had been unable to hold the troops at all. The charismatic man of speech and action was able to bring about what no amount of hereditary authority could achieve.

It is, however, a mistake to separate these two modes of authority. While one has more to do with origins and the other with continuation, beginning and enduring are but two aspects of a single being. Once the speech is made and followers have committed themselves, they must assume an obligation to persevere or the action will cease. On the other hand, in the exercise of traditional authority a leader must recognise that hearts have to be won every time new people join or are born into a society and every time members forget what got them to where they are.

Yet emphases can change from time to time. In times of stability, traditional authority comes to the fore and people are unquestioning in their loyalty. In times of renewal, charismatic leaders who are able to inspire people arise and societies take new directions. In times of decay, neither may appear to be present in a very strong way.

The Church is founded on Jesus, who 'spoke with authority'. He was a charismatic leader, but he also claimed an authority given him by the Father. Through the centuries the Church has taken on stable political forms that have given increasing emphasis to moral authority. From time to time new movements such as the founding of a religious order or a Council have acted to revitalise the life of the Church. In our time traditional authority is weak, so that the kind of leadership that is needed is one that will win minds and hearts and anew.

Two Systems of Finance

One of the earliest surviving detailed accounts of British royal revenues is the pipe roll of 1129–30. At first sight it presents a puzzle in that the king, Henry I, collected only 14% of the revenue due to him under agreements made with nobles and officers of the realm.

The puzzle is resolved when we recognise that these agreements were part of the practice of patronage. In return for favours, subjects agreed to pay the king large amounts of money. However, if the subject proved friendly to the king, much of the agreed sum would be waived. If, on the other hand, a subject was unfriendly to the king, the full amount would be collected, often breaking the person financially.

Political patronage is a natural extension of a discretionary system of finance, in which both the collection of revenues and the disbursement of funds are done solely at the discretion of the person in control. Although records are kept, there is in general no public measure of what is fair and of what is not, nor is all information relating to decisions made public.

The alternative to a discretionary system is an accountability system such as has been adopted in most of the modern western world. In this system, the manner in which revenues are collected is a matter of public record. While specific personal information remains private, the rates at which people are taxed are public and the same for all, whether the rate be based on income, property, use of resources, or transactions.

Similarly, the way in which funds are disbursed is also public, and the rates of disbursement are expected to be in accord with stated policies and to fairly advantage the different sections of the community. In both cases, all members of the community have access to the decision making process.

The chief advantage of a discretionary system is the freedom it gives to the decision maker. A ruler who is wise and prudent and who has a detailed knowledge of the state of the community is able to institute changes for the good quickly and well. History shows examples of this.

The major disadvantage of discretionary systems is that fairness is dependent on the prudence, justice and good judgment of one person. Further, where a ruler regards the funds as personal or deals differently with the favoured and unfavoured, the system soon becomes one of patronage.

In adopting systems of accountability, the modern world has despaired of being always able to find rulers, whether they be individuals or parties, who have the qualities to make judgements that are consistently fair to all members of the community. Its approach is less idealistic and more pragmatic that that of the medieval world, but it attempts through complex procedures to give a measure of fairness to all.

For the most part, the Church still operates according to discretionary systems at all its levels. This is why people who have been trained in and who live in accountability systems are often faced with some confusion about how financial decisions are made when they come to work within the Church.

Reference: Kenneth O Morgan (ed), *The Oxford History of Britain* (Oxford: Oxford University Press, 1988), 165.

Even the Church Must Die

With Holy Week and Easter we have again remembered and re-enacted the passion, death and resurrection of Jesus. What we call the Paschal Mystery is central to the life of every Christian, and our participation in the ceremonies is one way of sharing again in the death and resurrection of Jesus. It is not the only way.

Baptism, whereby we enter sacramentally into the Church, is a Paschal experience. By immersion in water we die to our old selves, and in rising out of the water we put on Christ.

Moral growth and the development of character involve a dying and rising. We die to our old ways of acting and rise to new ways. We leave wilfulness and the pursuit of immediate desires and find lives whose energy is channelled in fruitful ways.

The trials of life and the suffering they bring are a kind of death. If we are able to find our way through them, there is a new kind of life on the other side. In prayer these, too, can be part of our participation in the Paschal Mystery.

With the Paschal Mystery Jesus has sanctified those natural rhythms by which life renews itself—death of old organisms, birth of the new; the cycle of the seasons. It is no accident that Easter is celebrated during what in the northern hemisphere is spring.

A minimal knowledge of history tells us that the church is not always the same. As an organisation made up of human beings it, too, experiences cycles of decline and renewal. It has at different times even disappeared from parts of the world.

At the present time it seems that the Church is dying to an old form and seeking a new form. It is dying at least as a clergy-run organisation and as a social necessity. Signs of new life are the diversification of ministries in the church and the nurturing of faith-based community. As always the vestiges of what was and the first intimations of what is to be exist side by side.

All of this is painful. It is hard to know just what is what. Many of us prefer to cling to old certainties about the way we live. Others of us grasp at fresh hopes often only to see them fail or to see them squashed. If we ask why it is we should be living in a time like this, the answer that a wise old man once gave me suffices. It is because of when we were born.

In my life-time the church has alienated many faith seekers by the ways in which it has spoken and acted or failed to act. This was not the way of Jesus. It is my hope that in finding new ways of being Church we will convey the person and message of Jesus in ways that are much more appealing and welcoming to the people of our time.

The Political Activity of the Church

Politics has a bad name, so bad, in fact, that even politicians apply the term "political" disparagingly. This is a pity because politics is about how we live in the various associations to which we belong. Two political philosophers offer us helpful notions of what political activity is about.

Leo Strauss says that politics is about action and that action is either good or bad. Politics seeks to achieve what is good and so to pursue a good society and establish the structures that allow it to function well.

Michael Oakeshott says that 'politics is the activity of attending to the general arrangements of a collection of people who, in respect of their common recognition of a manner of attending to its arrangements, compose a single community'. He insists that change comes by way of amendment of what already exists and that it follows the tensions and incoherencies implicit in existing arrangements.

The Church has both a divine and a human dimension. In its human dimension it is a political association and so has structures, traditions of behaviour, institutions and laws that have been developed over the centuries so as to suit the character and needs of the people in the church. As this character and these needs change, often in response to the wider environment, changes are made that, in turn, bring about further changes.

For at least several generations it was thought that the church did not change. There were many reasons for this; one was a mistaken notion that the church was a perfect society. The Second Vatican Council said differently when it stated that 'the church, embracing sinners in her bosom, is at the same time holy and always in need of being purified' (*Lumen gentium*, 8). Current crises in the church also point to a need for change.

Since the Council there has been profound liturgical change and a great diversification of ministries in the church. Each of these has affected how we live and act in the church and the relationships between different groups in the church. These are changes in the ways in which we constitute ourselves as a people. Further changes are ahead of us as we deal, for instance, with the decline in the number of clergy.

What Strauss and Oakeshott offer us are ways of thinking about this change and the activity of bringing it about. For Strauss the activity is governed by discernment of good—both ultimate goods and immediate goods. Oakeshott reminds us that change comes out of what is already there. It is a response not to an abstract idea or to a sudden whim but to a desire to fix what is not working very well. The process is slow and sometimes has to backtrack, but in time we can expect the change to be great and our condition to be better.

References: Leo Strauss, 'What is Political Philosophy?', in What is Political Philosophy? (University of Chicago Press, 1988), 9–55; Michael Oakeshott, 'Political Education', in Rationalism in Politics and Other Essays (Indianapolis: Liberty press, 1991), 56–57.

Integrity in Ministry: A Response

Integrity in Ministry, the draft document setting out ethical standards for Australian Catholic clergy and religious, at one level contains no surprises. The things in it are roughly what clergy and religious have been trying to do and what they have been talking about for years. Fortunately, the drafters have managed to broaden the scope of the code beyond the issue of sexual abuse, which was the stimulus for its development, and to deal somewhat holistically with the life of ministers.

How, then, is it different? It is different from at least remembered Church practice in that it expresses moral norms in terms of publicly stated standards of behaviour to which clergy and religious are to be held publicly accountable. While we are used now to most serious professional bodies having codes of ethics, it is not how the Church has normally acted. What is added is the note of public accountability.

Normally, the Church has dealt with morality either by way of law and commandment or by way of virtue. In either case, failure was for the most part something that a person would work out with authority, either divine or ecclesiastical, either sacramentally or administratively. In this new document accountability is public. It follows a more modern practice that recognises publicity as a sound way of assuring adequate, if minimal, standards of behaviour.

This is why, among other things, the bishops need to be explicitly included in the provisions of the document. At present it is ambiguous because in common parlance the term 'clergy' is used variously—on one hand to distinguish those ordained from those not ordained, hence including the bishops, on the other to refer to the body of priests in relation to its bishop. Although the bishops are clearly included in the standards by implication, in the interests of clarity this ought to be said.

This would have an added effect of removing much of the negative feeling that has been expressed about the document. It would be seen not as an imposition but as an expression of broad accountability of ministers in the Church to the People of God and to the world. This is in keeping with the spirit of the document, which has been developed out of broad consultation and which is still open to further consultation.

Some lacunae will show up. Under stewardship something needs to be said about adherence to civil law, specifically in the areas of tax law, management of property and employment. The same section ought to suggest what is to be done with auditor's reports, which themselves are simply pieces of paper that can easily be hidden.

On the whole, however, the document ought to be seen as a move in the right direction. It should lead to greater professionalism in the Church, which in turn should lead to better ministry and richer lives for ministers.

Reference: National Committee for Professional Standards, *Integrity in Ministry (draft)* (Canberra: Australian Catholic Bishops' Conference and the Australian Conference of Leaders of Religious Institutes, 1997).

Reorganisation in the Church

It has been reported that three Catholic dioceses of New South Wales were undergoing a reorganisation of parishes that would leave some parishes without resident priests. The processes engaged in by each were different, but the material effects were similar.

The contexts surrounding each of the announcements were also varied—sheer necessity, a Paschal Mystery experience for the Church and increased ministry of the laity. Each of these is valid, and between them they form a fuller picture of what appears to be happening in the Church.

In many respects, the announcements were not surprising. We had all noticed the paucity of vocations and the ageing of the clergy. But this ought not blind us to the dramatic nature of these changes. The Church is changing its manner of operation under the pressure of necessities it can no longer control.

Many of us would have thought of the Church as static and unchanging—a point of timeless stability in a difficult age. But this is a conception of the New World. If one travels, for instance, in East England, one sees architectural evidence of a succession of Churches—a Church under the Romans that was destroyed by the pagan Saxons, who were in turn converted by Celtic missionaries; replacement of a Saxon Church by pagan Danes, who were succeeded by Christian Normans. The medieval Church was extremely vigorous and saw the flourishing of both a diocesan and a monastic church. With Henry VIII, the monasteries were destroyed and the dioceses were separated from Rome. Roman Catholicism became public again in England only in the nineteenth century.

Reactions to the present change are various. They range through attempts to go back to the past, 'when we must have been doing it right'; reaction against changes of recent decades, 'which must have been wrong, if we are where we are now'; disappointment and discouragement; determination to develop new zeal for a mission that will bring many new faces into our churches; hopes that at last the Church, though smaller, will develop life and ministries that are truly communal.

None of these makes much sense by itself. The Church is a form of life, and so, in an analogous way, it must go through its periods of growth and decay. It is disappointing when it appears weak. While we always draw on our traditions, simple returns to the past are regressive and rarely effective. Pessimism is a likely indication that we have not read the signs of the times well. Missionary activity will work only when speaker and hearer find common interests. A 'new' Church may well have a longer and more difficult birth than we anticipate. And so we must find the reality in each.

Yet life does renew itself, and Jesus sent his Spirit. Each of us can live well by making the best of what our times offer us.

Church Unity: A Role for Australia

Recently in a Catholic parish England, I was startled when a petition in the Prayer of the Faithful prayed for the conversion of England. Afterwards, I told an English colleague that in Australia, while we used to pray for the conversion of Russia, our ecumenical prayer has always been for Christian unity and asked about the English practice. He replied, 'Oh, here we are looking for total submission'.

Fortunately, my colleague's response was meant in jest. Also fortunately, what I had experienced was a relic of past practice, of which the continuation was somewhat eccentric. The incident did, however, point to dramatic differences in the experience of Christian division between Australia and England and, indeed, between different European countries and countries of the New World.

In England, evidence abounds that the reformation was a damaging and hurtful event. In villages one sees houses that incorporate stones from the medieval abbeys and churches that were mined for stone after Henry VIII dissolved the monasteries in 1538. As well, one knows that Anglican parish churches predating the dissolution were once Catholic. From another perspective, any Catholic buildings are less than two hundred years old, having been built since the restoration of the Catholic hierarchy in 1850. These are all signs of the damaging and lasting impact of the reformation on persons and communities.

In Australia, our experience is quite different. Our nation was formed long after the reformation, so that, although we inherited some of its consequences, we did not experience the reformation itself. Generally, the churches of any denomination were built by that denomination itself. Although we did see a degree of sectarian strife, pre-existing communities were never ruptured by the split.

This should put us in a singularly good position to work towards Christian unity. Our experience is not ignorant of the divisions among Christians, as it is for the exclusively Catholic nations of Europe. We have felt the division and we know that it is scandalous. On the other hand, we have not suffered in the way in which the peoples of those European nations that experienced the reformation suffered. Nor do the signs of that suffering surround us. We ought to be freer in our movements towards unity.

Work towards unity proceeds on different levels. For many years Christian theologians have laboured over doctrinal questions in an endeavour to find common understandings and formulations among the churches. At the international level, church leaders meet and their actions bring about growing recognition of each other. Communion, however, is not something abstract. It can exist only among worshipers and communities, and so is found primarily at a local level.

In Australia as in much of the New World, we have an opportunity at the levels of parish and diocese to lead the way in establishing greater commonality of thought, action and feeling with other Christians. Such commonality will be an essential element of eventual full communion.

Good Popes and Bad Popes

On 16 October 1998 we celebrate the twentieth anniversary of the election of Pope John Paul II as pope. He is only about the tenth pope to reign this long, whereas about six times that number have reigned for less than two years.

Whether it is because of the approaching anniversary or the coming of the new millennium or perhaps some other reason is hard to say, but a number of books on the papacy both scholarly and popular are being published around this time.

One popular work just arriving in Australia is *Lives of the Popes* edited by Michael J Walsh. It is written by nine English historians and sets out in chronological fashion brief biographies of all the popes. It is richly illustrated by art spanning the two millennia. Interesting things show up as the popes are displayed in this kind of historical relief.

First, one realises that the papacy has not developed in a simple and straightforward way from the words that Jesus said to Peter to the present. Its power and influence have waxed and waned. Often, it has had to bend to historical circumstances. Even Innocent III (1198–1216), who is credited with having set the papacy on course to becoming a European power, did this not so much as an end in itself, but in order to protect the rights of the papacy from secular rulers.

Second, one begins to appreciate the enormous range of qualities expected in a pope whom history is going to judge as having been a good pope. He needs to be a saintly person, a wise pastor, an astute theologian, a skilful administrator, and an accomplished politician.

These qualities seem to have come together in Gregory I (590–604), whom we remember as Gregory the Great, a good man and a good pope. In Celestine V (1294), however, we find a truly saintly man who was completely incompetent as pope and who, recognising this, freely abdicated. Conversely, in Alexander VI (1492–1503) we confront a man who led a profligate life, yet is judged as having successfully managed the interests of the papacy. At the bottom of the scale is John XII (955–964), who was both a bad man and a bad pope.

In our own time, we have seen a progression from Pius XII (1939–1958), a recluse who spoke infrequently, to the present pope, who speaks often and who has made full use of the possibilities and speed of modern forms of communication. In between fit John XXIII (1958–1963), who, although elected as a caretaker pope, earned great respect for his simplicity and goodwill and set the Church on a new course by convoking the Second Vatican Council, and Paul VI (1963–1978), who saw it through.

In terms of human history, the papacy is an ancient institution that has adjusted to meet different times and circumstances. Perhaps, the current interest is in ensuring that further change will be for the good.

References: Michael J Walsh (ed), Lives of the Popes (London: Salamander Books Ltd, 1998). See also Eamon Duffy, Saints and Sinners: A History of the Popes (Yale: Yale University Press, 1997), and JND Kelly, The Oxford Dictionary of Popes (Oxford: Oxford University Press, 1996).

Perspectives on the Church

In an article in *America* magazine, Archbishop Rembert G Weakland OSB, Bishop of Milwaukee, shared his reflections on his diocese as he prepared for an *ad limina* visit to the Holy See. The article is thoughtful and pastoral, and, although he speaks only of his own diocese, much of what he says applies readily to those local immigrant and English speaking churches of countries in the New World that share a liberal political tradition. Australia is among these.

First the Archbishop notes the social diversity of the contemporary local church. In Australia fifty years ago, most Catholics would have appeared to be working class and of Irish descent. While their descendants have found their way into university education and the professions, more recent immigrants, whether Mediterranean or South-East Asian, are generally not so well off.

He then notes three groups of baptised persons who have left the Church. The followers of Archbishop Lefebvre had thought that the Church would not change. Others have left the Church because they were angry or disillusioned with how it has dealt with issues such as remarriage and the role of women. The larger group, however, has just drifted away, believing without much thought that the Church is irrelevant.

Of those who remain in the Church, Archbishop Weakland recognises four groups.

A small but strong group follows Tridentine usage in the liturgy and seeks to bring up children with what they see as solid pre-Vatican II values.

'Papal maximalists' are rather vocal and pride themselves on loyalty to the Pope. He points out that often this loyalty is rather selective both in terms of specific doctrines and of which popes are listened to. Behind their thinking is fear that the Church be overwhelmed by modern culture.

'Restless innovators' look for constant change and, disillusioned with the slow implementation of Vatican II, eagerly await Vatican III. They tend to be uneasy with authority in the Church, expecting more democratic ways. Their fear is that the Church might become callous.

Finally, Archbishop Weakland says that the largest group in his diocese is those who take the middle ground. They are not necessarily up with the latest disputes in the Church but are concerned that they can be members of vital local parishes and that that their children be well-inducted into the Church. Their fear is that before long there will not be ministers in the Church to do these things.

This picture is not too different from what is found is most Australian dioceses. It presents us with some problems. How do we find communion in the midst of such diversity? How do we as Church offer something vigorous and relevant to those who have drifted away? Can we find a new identity that relies not on conflict and difference but which takes up, purifies and makes holy our own culture?

Reference: Rembert G Weakland, 'Reflections for Rome', in *America*, 178/13 (18 April 1998): 8–13.

The Pope and the Roman Curia

In another essay in this volume I wrote about Pope John Paul II's encyclical, *Fides et Ratio*, and showed how encouraging he was of scholarship in philosophy and the sciences and how open he was to their respective projects. Several commentators have agreed that they were glad that the pope had written such a document while others have gone on to ask, have others in the Roman Curia read it?

The simple answer is that of course many of them have read it. That, however, is not what these people were meaning. They were referring to the contrast between the hope that they felt in response to the pope's letter and the sense of repression they have felt in recent years in response to the activism of the Congregation for the Doctrine of the Faith (CDF), of which then Cardinal Ratzinger, now Pope Benedict XVI, was Prefect. If, indeed, the Congregation works for and with the pope, how can these be reconciled? Two things can be said.

First, the congregations of the Roman Curia are at the service of the pope in his ministry as primate of the universal Church, but they are not always in step with him. The story is told of how, on being made pontiff, Pope John XXIII went to the CDF and examined his own file. He found that he was in some ways suspect, but, as Pope, he was able to amend the file to say that he had been cleared. Later, however, that did not stop the Curia imposing unapproved changes in the letter he wrote to convoke the Council.

Second, the CDF is engaged in ensuring that what is taught about the faith is true thereby ensuring that order and discipline pertain in the Church. Since classical times, philosophers have been very conscious of the extreme difficulties of balancing the activities of holding power and of furthering truth. At the very beginning of philosophy, the Athenian assembly executed one of its own, Socrates, who refused to refrain from being truthful. In religion, the issues are more complex, but it remains true that to balance power and truth requires gifts of great wisdom and prudence.

During his pontificate, Pope John Paul II put enormous energy into travelling and into speaking to the peoples of the world. In doing so, he used his considerable gifts in communicating with large audiences. In addition, he taught vigorously, especially in the extraordinary number of encyclicals he wrote. It is unlikely that he had a great deal of time to work on the Curia. As well, that he first learnt about government and politics in Poland during the second quarter of this century could hardly have prepared him for the intricacies of Roman bureaucracy. What we can thank him for is his serious teaching and the way he at times engaged with us. Prominent in the former is the encouragement that his encyclical offers.

Mischief in the Vatican

At the end of the Synod of Oceania a few years ago, a moment of public controversy arose in Australia about conflict between the messages that seemed to be coming from the series of meetings being held in Rome involving the pope, the Bishops of Oceania and various curial officials. It can be traced for the most part in articles by Chris McGillion in the *Sydney Morning Herald*.

On 15 December 1998, he wrote enthusiastically about the straightforward and positive nature of the Bishops' interventions in the Synod. On the 16th, he reported on reproofs of Australian Catholic life said to be found in the *Statement of Conclusions* of the Interdicasterial Meeting held just before the Synod. On the 17th, he examined the contrast in what we were hearing from these two meetings. On the 18th, he reported on a statement to the press by Cardinal Clancy, just returned from Rome, saying that the media coverage was confused and ill-informed and giving some insight into the status of the various meetings and statements. Left out of this tracing is the media frenzy of the day and night of the 15th, when the negative impact of the Statement was much in the news.

When one reads the *Statement of Conclusions*, one wonders what all the fuss was about. The now familiar items of reproof are there, but they are a very small part of a rather long document. What happened?

On December 14, the first Monday after the Synod, the Vatican Press Office released a number of documents on its web-site. The first was a communiqué announcing the nature of the *Statement of Conclusions* and saying that it would be posted immediately on the web-site of the Australian Bishop's Conference. This was timed for midday in Rome and 10 pm in Canberra.

In Australia, the *Statement* appeared on the web-site on December 19, but a printed version marked 'strictly embargoed until 10 pm, 14th December' had previously been faxed to various destinations, including, one assumes, some media representatives.

In Rome, later on the 14th, the full text of the *Statement* was, in fact, put on the Vatican web-site. Also that day, now the next morning Canberra-time, a press release was posted by the Vatican Press Office purporting to summarise the Statement. This 'summary' is overwhelmingly negative in its content, as what it does is list the sections of the document and, where possible, quote a negative kind of comment. This press release, it seems, is the likely source of the general press reaction.

Something is gravely wrong in this. The Vatican, through its Press Release has seriously misled the Australian Press and through it the Catholic community and the general public. Why it might do this is hard to explain but would be worthy of careful investigation. It is not, however, without precedent and raises serious questions about how the Curia views the work of evangelisation.

Tactics Unacceptable to Most Australians

In the 'Letter from the Australian Bishops to the Catholic People of Australia' of 14 April 1999, the bishops set out to deal with issues that surfaced in the course of three different meetings during the bishops' recent visit to Rome and with the aftermath of those meetings in Australia. The letter is of singular importance, because it expresses the united stance of the bishops on some topics of current difficulty.

In paragraph 11, the bishops said, 'Some groups have initiated a deliberate and intrusive surveillance of clergy and liturgical celebrations. While Catholics have a right to be heard, such tactics are not acceptable to most Australians. Instead, we encourage constructive dialogue that builds harmony.'

By 17 April, Paul Brazier was quoted in the *Herald* as saying the statement was a cheap slur and that he was unaware that the bishops had taken a poll to ascertain what is acceptable to Australians. It seems timely, therefore, to examine what is unacceptable about the condemned practice.

Aristotle described the practice well in his discussion of how tyrants preserve their power. He said:

> A tyrant . . . should employ spies, like the female detectives at Syracuse, and the eavesdroppers whom Hiero was in the habit of sending to any place of resort or meeting; for the fear of informers prevents people from speaking their minds, and if they do, they are more easily found out. Another art of the tyrant is to sow quarrels among the citizens; friends should be embroiled with friends, the people with the notables, and the rich with one another (Politics V, 11).

The practices thus described are un-Australian because they directly undermine our democratic and liberal way of doing things. Fundamental freedoms of speech, assembly and action are at the heart of Australian life, and difficulties and conflicts are worked out in the context of these freedoms. In the Church, differences between pastoral judgement and the letter of the liturgical law can also be resolved in the context of freedom and discussion. The practices under consideration, however, work on fear and uncertainty, so that while, ironically, their use depends on the freedoms our society offers, their exercise destroys those very same freedoms.

The practices are also unchristian, because again they undermine what it is to be a church. The Church is a communion, and this communion is expressed most strongly in the Eucharist but also in other liturgical celebrations. For people to attend liturgical gatherings for reasons so at odds with the very nature of those gatherings is to disrupt communion and, indeed, to put themselves outside communion.

This does not mean that differences will not arise in the Church nor that they will not be the cause of difficulty. We have, however, ways of working out disagreements, and these are modelled for us in the Acts of the Apostles.

Reference: Aristotle, *Politics* V, 11 (1313b11–19), in *The Complete Works of Aristotle*, edited by Jonathan Barnes (Princeton University Press, 1984), vol 2, 2085.

Who Are Our Teachers?

In a letter to *The Catholic Weekly* (21/3/99), Bishop John Heaps took issue with a reference to 'The meeting . . . between the Church in Australia and the primary collaborators of the Roman Pontiff' in the concluding paragraphs of the *Statement of Conclusions* from the meeting between a group of Australian bishops and the heads of various curial bodies held before the Synod of Oceania.

What he took issue with was the implication that the members of the Roman Curia are the 'primary collaborators of the Roman Pontiff'. What is wrong with this is that it is untruthful and flies in the face of Church teaching that the teaching authority of the Church is vested in the College of Bishops in union with the Bishop of Rome. If the term is to be used at all, it must be applied to all bishops but particularly to the bishops of the local churches (*Lumen Gentium*, 22–23).

On Holy Thursday of the same year, 1999, on *Australia Talks Back*, Archbishop Pell disagreed with a caller who restated and expanded Bishops Heaps' criticism. He said that the heads of the Congregations are, in fact, bishops, so that they fall within the scope of the term 'primary collaborators'.

In putting this argument, Archbishop Pell did not bring to light two essential points. First, the use of the term was exclusive. The curial bishops were called 'primary collaborators'; the Australian bishops, and by implication the bishops of the world, were excluded.

Second, he did not advert to the fact that curial bishops are titular bishops. As their titles indicate, bishops are all bishops of somewhere, but titular bishops are bishops of places that either no longer exist or have ceased to be significant. More importantly they are bishops without flocks as their 'dioceses' may be such as are covered by the sands of the North African deserts. They are bishops in the abstract, whose proper role is service to the pastor of the universal church. In earlier times, they were deacons and even cardinal-deacons.

A church, on the other hand, is a very concrete thing. It is a gathering of people. It 'exists in local communities and is made real as a liturgical, above all a Eucharistic, assembly' (*Catechism* #752). Its leaders are bishops, who together with the Bishop of Rome are all 'vicars and ambassadors of Christ' (U*t unum sint* # 95). As Australians, therefore, we look first to our own bishops for guidance and leadership, which are nevertheless exercised in dialogue with their flocks and in union with the whole Church.

The use of this new term is clearly a bid by the Curia for more power than it already has. The Holy See usually gives authority to its documents by numerous footnotes. Since often most references are to its own statements, it is important to object to this new term so that it does not gain authority through being said many times.

'Sorry': A First for the Church

When Pope John Paul II, acting as Primate of the whole Church, acknowledged and sought forgiveness for the past wrongs of the Church, we were witnessing an historic event. It was mirrored here in Australia by a *Statement of Repentance* issued by the Bishops' Conference, which acknowledged failure in important areas and asked for forgiveness. Never before has the Magisterium of the Church performed such an act.

These formal and public acts were preceded by two documents that gave rise to them. In the Apostolic Letter, *Tertio millennio adveniente*, introducing the Jubilee of the new millennium, Pope John Paul II indicated that the Church ought to purify its own memories in respect of the past and in so doing give example to individuals and civil societies. More recently, The International Theological Commission published its study, *Memory and Reconciliation: The Church and the Faults of the Past*, of how this purification might be made and of what it would mean.

This document will be of great interest to us all, because of the care and depth of thought it brings to the Pope's most laudable initiative. For Australians, it may help us understand why an apology to the Aboriginal peoples is appropriate, what it would mean and what it could do.

The primary goal of an apology of this kind is the healing of memories. Memories can be very long, so that, well after the deaths of participants, the effects of events can be felt as a legacy of the past. Easy witness to this is found in the trouble spots of the world where bitterness is still a response to violence done centuries ago. In the Church, disunity springs from the beginning of the second millennium.

The study faces the issue of responsibility for actions of past generations by distinguishing between subjective and objective responsibility. Subjective responsibility refers to the condition of individual consciences and ceases with the death of the individual. Objective responsibility, however, rests in the moral value of an act itself, so that responsibility for evil can outlive those who did it. Such responsibility remains a burden because it lies in the memories of the descendants of those first involved. It is an even greater burden when material effects of those actions are still to be found in the lives of those most affected.

The effect of purification of memory is to eliminate 'from personal and collective conscience all forms of resentment or violence left by the inheritance of the past'. The past does not disappear, but it can take on a different quality 'having a new and different effect on the present'. The acknowledgment of past offences can change relationships in the present. 'The memory of division and opposition [can be] purified and substituted by a reconciled memory'.

In getting on with the future, we must address the past so as to heal the present.

Doctrinal Examination: Procedures

A recent article in *The Catholic Weekly* (30/4/00), written by Western Australian, David Kehoe, and circulated by the American agency, Catholic News Service (CNS), reported on new procedures adopted by the Australian Catholic Bishops' Conference for examining the orthodoxy of theologians, when their orthodoxy is brought into question.

While, except for one irrelevance, the report could be said to have been materially fair because it mainly quoted the document published by the bishops and statements by two church-spokesmen, formally it was quite misleading. It was misleading because it presented the procedures, which it called rules, as a fresh opportunity for the faithful to make complaints against theologians. It even linked the Bishops' Statement inappropriately to the controversies surrounding the end of the Synod of Oceania at the end of 1998.

The nature and purpose of the new procedures contained in the Bishops' Statement, 'Statement of Policy: The Examination of Theological Orthodoxy' (*The Australasian Catholic Record* 77/1 (January 2000): 85–95), are quite otherwise. The procedures are a product of many years of discussion between theologians and bishops and the work of several years of drafting. Their purpose is to ensure that when the orthodoxy of a theologian is called into question, that theologian is dealt with fairly. As the document itself says, 'A theologian has the right to have his or her good name and academic reputation respected, and to just procedures in the resolution of any concerns about his or her orthodoxy'.

Although the detail of the procedures is important, the way in which they work for justice can be seen from three provisions. Firstly, although it is the bishop's role to make determinations in matters of orthodoxy, the procedures ensure that this is not done without proper consultation of experts in the field under consideration. Secondly, should the bishop think that there are grounds on which to proceed, he must give a copy of the expert opinions to the theologian. Thirdly, in those situations where an examination stems from a complaint, the examination will proceed only if the complaint is in writing, contains the complainant's name and gives reasons why a particular public statement of the theologian is not in conformity with Church teaching.

Disputes about orthodoxy are not new to the Church, as the Acts of the Apostles attests. In fact, it has often been through disputes, such as in the early Councils, that Catholic doctrine has been determined. In the continuing development of Christian understanding and practice, bishops and theologians are meant to work collaboratively. While theologians continue to explore the meaning of Catholic Faith and to explain it in language and categories appropriate to the time, bishops are responsible for the teaching of that Faith, both for its propagation and for its purity.

Bishops and theologians have complementary roles, and the January Statement affirms those roles. It will, indeed, protect both orthodoxy and justice.

Thoughts on Authority in the Church

Authority I will define as 'power legitimated'. Of power, I will give two definitions. In the primary sense, power is 'the energy of a group brought to bear'; in a secondary sense, it is 'the ability of an individual or group to subsume the role of coordinating the energies of the whole group'.

Each of these definitions calls for detailed discussion, which I will keep for another time. The theory behind them, however, is that power arises in groups of people when their energies are so focussed that they are able to act in concert to achieve things. In order for this to happen, someone must necessarily, even if only informally and for a short time, act to coordinate this energy and its application to action. If a group is to act other than spontaneously, this coordinating power must be given legitimation, which gives the group some stability.

Different authorities will be legitimated in different ways, which will often be complex. At different times, for instance, political authority has been legitimated in terms of allegiance to the nation or of primitive contract or of divine right or of natural law or of the common good. Generally, however, these different elements of legitimation are interwoven with one another.

This kind of ground for legitimation tends to show up most readily where law is in operation. More informal situations, however, show another order of legitimation, which is the response of those who are coordinated to the speech and action of the one who would coordinate them. This is a matter of the character and qualities of a leader and of the way in which a group of people desiring to act will naturally respond to the person they judge best able to plot the right course of action and to hold the group together.

In the normal course, both of these orders of legitimation will be operative to some degree. In an enduring institution, good leadership depends on a healthy measure of both.

In the Church, the coordinating power of bishops is legitimated sacramentally and juridically. These two do not necessarily always stand comfortably together. It was an important act of the Second Vatican Council to re-establish the centrality of the sacrament of ordination as a source of legitimate episcopal authority. For a long time, juridical legitimation had reigned supreme, which is something that tends to happen in strongly centralised organisations.

It is wrong to think, however, that these are all that is involved in the legitimation of episcopal authority. That other less formal order of legitimation in which people react to the speech and action of a bishop remains important. In the Church, the formal order of legitimation is so strong that authority is unlikely to disappear altogether, but without vibrant informal legitimation it will become either insipid or violent. This is why it is important that we hear our bishops speak and speak well.

Troubled Times in the Church

As Catholics, we have had to bear with revelations of sexual abuse of religious women in Africa by priests and in other places. Some of the stories were horrific and will come out by way of serious reports on the issue by qualified visiting religious.

The scandal will have to do not so much with the fact that sexual activity has taken place but with the kind of coercion exercised by certain priests. Typically, when young women wishing to join local diocesan congregations have approached local priests for the necessary approval, they have found the price of such approval to be sexual favours. The deeper scandal is that the hierarchy and Roman authorities have done little to stop the abuse, although that may be about to change.

In Australia, we have suffered our own deep embarrassment in relation to publicity about sexual abuse of children by clergy. Again, the deeper dimensions of the scandal relate to the ways in which bishops or superiors simply moved men on to other places when their misdeeds became known. Yet to emerge fully is the fact that in some cases the men had been ordained by bishops against the strong recommendations to the contrary by seminary staff.

These are abuses of power, which are inevitable whenever power is used ruthlessly, secretively and absolutely. The Australian bishops have begun to respond with the procedures laid out in *Towards Healing* and with efforts to establish professional standards for bishops, clergy and religious as spelt out in *Integrity in Ministry*. At the NSW Police Royal Commission they received both condemnation for failure to act in particular cases and praise for their early attempts to grapple with the issue.

Until Rome itself changes and until that change is echoed around the world, we can expect scandals to continue to erupt. They will not necessarily have to do with sex. There are lots of other vices that can be symptomatic of underlying malaise. The Vatican itself has already had its own financial scandals.

In South America, there is serious concern about particular bishops who have collaborated with oppressive and evil regimes and about at least one bishop who has publicly justified the murder of civilians by the regime. At stake here is the whole issue of the appointment of bishops and the expectation of many that they will be chosen as pastors capable of service to particular peoples and in particular times.

We should hope that all of these revelations are part of a process of purification of the Church. Then our pain could be seen as something of a Paschal experience and could motivate us to turn more closely to the Gospel. We ought to pray that the whole Church experience such conversion.

'Secrets' Problem in the Church

The complaint, voiced by Cardinal Clancy on radio 2BL in Sydney that a group in the Australian Church had exercised 'undue influence in forming opinions and convictions' in the Roman Curia prior to the Synod in 1998 deserves serious consideration.

He was referring, of course, to the practice of delation, an act according to which individuals or groups take complaints directly and secretly to higher levels of authority in the Church without entering into discussion at the levels at which their concerns arise. It is an activity that the famous French theologian, Yves Congar, called 'a disease which is specifically French' but which most Australian bishops will tell us has spread to our culture also.

The practice of delation stands in stark contrast to the spirit of the Gospel. Jesus' admonition in Matthew 18:15–18 was always to resort first to brotherly admonition when it seemed that someone had done something wrong and only then to bring others into the discussion. One would expect that where Christian life is flourishing most problems could be sorted out in this way.

In the case of more difficult issues, Paul and Barnabus showed the way in Acts 15, when, prompted by disagreements about how Jewish law might apply to gentile Christians, they went to Jerusalem to meet with the elders there and to discuss the issue. A solution was found that was both just and charitable, and their manner of proceeding strengthened the Christian community.

Delation can only be a poor source of information. As Cardinal Clancy said, 'I came away feeling that our brethren in Rome didn't fully understand the situation in real life as we have it here'. It was Machiavelli who most clearly proposed a political rationalism whereby those in power could stand at a distance and use occult information to manipulate the actions of others. A more realistic theory would recognise that leaders can be effective only when they know the people they lead and that this can come about only through personal contact and open dialogue.

In some respects delation is to a hierarchical society what the leaking of documents is to a democratic society. The information is rarely complete and one never knows what are the real motives behind its dissemination. Nor can its recipients question and assess the veracity of the disseminator. It is, however, information with a purpose and a purpose related often to disruption and usually to short term goals. In a hierarchical society, however, it can be stopped.

It is often hard for those in authority to know what to do with the letters of delators. Bishops, particularly, can find them difficult because their own role is one of ensuring unity in catholicity. One suspects that many of these letters end up in rubbish bins. Others end up in archives from where they will, one day, provide curious reading for historians.

Did the Butler Do it?

The reign of Benedict XVI has been marred by disarray in the Curia, brought to a head publicly when secret documents of the Holy See were leaked to the media and eventually by the arrest of the Pope's butler for stealing documents and passing them on. While clearly a very hurtful event for the Pope, the incident of the butler raises very significant issues for the Holy See. Specifically, how will justice be done, and how could the Church be better governed?

It is not just a matter of achieving justice for the butler; it is a matter of delivering justice in the whole situation. Justice for the butler might be found in a full pardon following his full disclosure of everything he knows and a vow of silence ever after. But it is clear that he did not act alone, because documents to which he had no access were also leaked. It is likely that two inquiries have unearthed information about who else was involved, and it is also likely that publication of that information will be damaging to the Holy See. We can only wait and see what happens. The issue is whether the matter will be covered up and dealt with internally or whether wrong-doing and mischief will be put on public display in some form of legal process.

Issues of governance affect the Church not only at the level of the Holy See but also at the levels of dioceses and parishes. They have surfaced most plainly in the difficulties the Church has had in responding to the sexual abuse crisis. Similarly, they are felt in parishes when a new Parish Priest arrives and in short time radically changes the way in which the community functions.

Let me suggest three ways in which the Church might be reformed. Firstly, those in leadership need to learn to exercise authority rather than to merely assert it. The legal and sacramental basis of authority in the Catholic Church is so strong that those in authority can simply hold their ground. What are needed are leaders who hear and understand the people they lead and who are able to inspire them through prayer, speech and action.

Secondly, much would change in the Church if it made itself subject to the rule of law. The Church does, of course, have a great deal of law, but its lawmakers remain outside it. This is clearest in the case of the Pope who has supreme legislative, executive and judicial power in the Church such that 'there is neither appeal nor recourse against a judgement or a decree of the Roman Pontiff'. (Canon 333, 3)

Thirdly, the Church needs to pay attention to the laws of the countries in which it exists. It might at times argue against what it believes to be bad law, but it does need to conform to the local processes of justice and not see itself as exempt from the law of the land.

THE CHURCH IN THE WORLD

Can the Church Speak Out?

The controversy surrounding the Wik legislation, relating to Native Title in Australian Law, raised again the question of whether the Church has a right to speak out in the political debates of the nation. It is important that we as Church address this issue, not from the point of view of our own theologies, but from the point of view of modern political life. We can begin to do this by examining the objections that were raised to statements by Church leaders.

Some of the objections can be taken as superficial. These include those of objectors who welcome statements with which they agree but who condemn speakers of views contrary to their own. Their arguments are rarely consistent. Another group in this category are those who have a kind of allergic reaction to anyone or anything religious, and so object to all Church statements. These need to be met with strategies other than argument.

There is, however, a more serious objection, which is less often stated but which underpins many objections. It is that the modern state is defined as secular, and that, while such a state does protect the rights of individuals to embrace religion, it has no place for religion itself in the state or in its affairs. This was a common position of the seventeenth century theorists, who worked towards what became the modern European state.

Three arguments will be used against this position.

First, the modern state itself, in which rule is not held by a class of people but in which the state itself is sovereign and politicians are a kind of official, tends to concentrate power to itself in ways that tend to be absolute and that in this century have erupted in places into totalitarianism. While constitutional mechanisms offer some protection, society needs other groups that can stand against the state in defence of human freedom and action. The churches are important among these groups.

Second, the Church has an attitude, which in recent years we have called 'an option for the poor and the marginalised'. It is not a glorification of poverty, but rather the determination to ensure that the needs of the people least able to speak for themselves are heard. This is what Jesus meant when he stated that with the coming of the kingdom the poor would be blessed. Modern society needs a voice such as this lest the least powerful of its members sink into oblivion.

Third, the modern state is not usually able to look to the moral good of the society it governs because of the narrowness of its definition. The churches fulfil a useful role in society by teaching about the moral life. While this may not be what churches are primarily for, it is an important role that they play in society.

Further objections and perhaps the majority relate to how the Church speaks. These will be addressed in another essay.

How Ought the Church Speak in Public Debate?

A previous essay in this volume presented arguments for the right of the Church to speak in debates about public policy, especially when those debates were about issues of concern to the Church. It did this by examining some of the objections raised in response to the strong stance taken by the churches in the Wik debate, relating to Native Title in Australian Law. Other objections related to how the Church spoke. Those we examine now.

The Church can, of course, speak in many ways—the published resolutions of parent's groups, papal encyclicals and addresses, statements by religious communities, reports of serious study by Church committees, opinions of experts who speak as members of the Church. In our context, however, it is statements made by leaders that are at issue. They may be heads of Church organisations like the CEO or welfare organisations, but usually they are the bishops.

The kinds of objections we hear are of a holier than thou attitude, of failure to consider the concerns of one side and even to address the interests of particular Catholics, and of questionable moral authority given the Church's own internal difficulties. Padraic McGuinness, in an article otherwise displaying serious want of thought (*Sydney Morning Herald* 6/12/97), complained that Church leaders 'speak confidently with Divine guidance and authority replacing the need of any secular understanding, study or knowledge'. These objections are serious and call for thought on how the Church speaks.

When a bishop speaks, he does not speak as a representative of members of the Church, because the Church has neither elective nor opinion-gathering mechanisms. He speaks, rather, as a leader and teacher of a people who are the Church. Such a voice is not simply the voice of the person himself, but carries with it the weight of office.

In a democracy the power of a bishop's statement is its claim to be persuasive to a large proportion of the population, namely, the members of the Church. The problem that arises is that if the arguments used are entirely faith-based, they make no sense to those outside the Church, and so a claim of misuse of power can be made. The solution is that bishops have to be well-informed and to use arguments which at least have the potential to be persuasive to the whole electorate when they speak.

In speaking publicly, tone is important, so that if a bishop assumes a kind of deference from a general public that he might find in parts of the Church, he is bound to offend. These matters are delicate and difficult. Leaders of the Church intending to speak publicly ought to take courses that help them adopt a suitable manner, particularly if they are to speak on television.

Finally, a public debate is a public debate. Arguments are expressed, opinions swayed, and votes taken. It is rich human activity and ought to be enjoyed. As a participant in such debate the Church, too, ought to be able to view itself with some humour.

Persuasion in and Out of the Church

Some time ago a very successful businessman told me he liked to give reasons when he told his employees to do things. He said that recently he had told a young man that there were three reasons why he should do something. 'First, it is the right thing to do; second, I said to do it; third, you'll be fired if you don't.'

Something that he did not know at the time, but which he later found out, was that these 'reasons' had already been discussed and written down in the fourth century BC. His own formulation was rather rough, but what he was using was something called by the Greeks, the three modes or ways of persuasion. Aristotle formulated them particularly clearly, though he used a different order.

The first mode is the character of the speaker. We tend to believe people who show good sense (they know what is the case), who are of good character (they will not lie to us) and who have goodwill towards us (they will not disregard our interests). A persuasive speaker has to display each of these in the course of his or her speech.

The second mode concerns the feelings of the audience—sympathy, anger, pity, confidence. People act on their emotions, and so a speaker has to be able to generate those emotions that will move them to believe or to act. This may sometimes be complex. An audience may first have to be provoked and then to be calmed.

The third mode is the argument itself—the way the salient facts are collected and presented in a logical way. In public discourse, the facts and premises used in argument have to be those that are widely known and accepted.

Intelligent persuasion is fundamental to the health of any democracy and of any society in which people are free. Where decisions are made by a free majority, that majority needs to come to a common mind. This can happen only by persuasive speech and writing.

The danger, of course, is that demagoguery and tricks will take over. That is why persuasion has to be intelligent. Matters of importance have to be treated seriously and investigated with the best of the sciences available to us. The art is then to find the persuasive aspects of each matter and to present them effectively.

The Church, which does consider matters seriously, is neither liberal nor a democracy, yet in the Western world it exists in states that are liberal democracies and it consists of people who have learnt to live and who do live in those states. Whenever it wishes to speak to the public of those states, it needs to do so in ways that are effective. Increasingly, it needs also to be more conscious of the same conditions when speaking to those who are in the Church.

References: Aristotle, *The Art of Rhetoric*, I, 1-2; II, 1.

Evangelisation in Liberal Societies

In other essays in this volume I looked at the English liberal political tradition. It is one of the traditions in which we Australians live and in which we sort out many of the issues of living together. In brief, it is a tradition that prizes freedom and which promotes the view that governments or other powers are limited in terms of the restrictions they can impose on citizens.

A question that arises for the Catholic Church, or any of the churches in our time in countries like Australia is this: how do you evangelise a people whose culture is heavily influenced by what we call liberalism or, in another mode, individualism?

Evangelisation is an act of persuasion. It is the process of persuading people to accept the message and person of Jesus Christ and to transform their lives accordingly. Like any act of persuasion in must take into account the character of the people to whom it is directed. Two aspects of that character are worth bringing out.

Firstly, irrespective of how well they do it, people in a liberal society expect to be able to make up their own minds about what they will do and what they will accept. This is one of the reasons why universal education is necessary. It contrasts with medieval feudal life, which could be lived successfully by many without much formal education.

Secondly, by definition, neither a government nor any other authority can impose on a liberal society the goods for which it will act or the ends that it will pursue. These are for the choosing, and any form of unified action will depend on reaching some form of consensus. This brings about a weakness in modern societies because proposal and agreement of goals is a very difficult process, and often we drift to the lowest common denominator, namely, the accumulation of money.

The Church in its evangelisation needs to take these points into account. Firstly, in proposing belief, it needs to recognise that it is addressing people who have been educated in specific ways and to offer them reasons for acceptance that will mean something to them. Authority is not enough, nor is it the case that any publicity is good publicity.

Secondly, it could well exploit the difficulty which modern society has in determining goods by proposing goods of life in attractive ways. This is different from mainly criticising the negative, which tends to grate on the nerves of liberal people. This has been the problem with the "culture of death" program. Despite the worth of its objective concerns, a positive message would be far more likely of success.

There is evidence that our society is looking for goods to pursue. The widespread movements towards reconciliation and towards the acceptance of people's traditions and cultures is evidence of this. Our religious tradition has much to offer, if we are able to bring it out.

When a Joke is Not a Joke

Publication in *The Catholic Weekly* (6/6/99) of details of a letter from Cardinal Clancy to the brewing company, Lion Nathan, manufacturer of Toohey's beer, brought to light action what has been in progress over some months. A number of Catholics and Cardinal Clancy as President of the Australian Conference of Catholic Bishops had objected to an advertisement which had been run on television for Toohey's beer. The action has gone as far as a complaint to the Advertising Standards Board in Australia.

The advertisement is built around a joke that has been in circulation for some time in one form or another. Basically, in questioning a young man in the confessional about an improper liaison, a priest unwittingly gives away the names of some young women, who, it might be thought, could be open to further improper liaisons.

The joke is one of a kind told by Irish Catholics, who are only too well aware of the severity of the confessional as it used to be and who have experience of the closeness of life in a small village. It would more than likely be told after a few beers by people letting down from the stress of daily life. Its humour rests in the incongruity of the idea of a priest giving away such information. That a priest would never do so, both because of the seal of confession and because it would undermine the very pastoral objective of confession itself, is the foundation of the joke.

What Lion Nathan did in running this advertisement was to take this old joke out of a private context, in which it would be understood and then passed over, and put it in the public forum of the television set where it has played night after night indiscriminately to whoever might have turned on a set. This is what is offensive.

The new audience of the joke was hardly likely to understand it, though they might have found something funny in it. Further, it is more than likely to further misunderstanding about the sacrament and the role it plays in the lives of Catholics. For priests, who have been knocked in many ways over the years, it is additionally offensive as it implies a lack of care and also laxity about the seal of the confessional.

The joke needs to be on the other foot. Lion Nathan showed by their response to the Cardinal that they do not understand what we are on about. Let them enjoy our joke when we object to their actions. Let them experience the incongruity of a 'successful' add that drives customers away. It is, fortunately, no longer an age in which Church leaders can impose bans in these sorts of matters, but that need not stop Catholics themselves voluntarily turning to other beer products of other companies—VB, Fosters, Crown, or Coopers. Forget XXXX or Swan, which are produced by Lion Nathan, and which is in any case now not owned by an Australian company.

Accepting an Apology

On June 27, 1999 *The Catholic Weekly* published a letter from Walter Bugno, the Managing Director of Lion Nathan, responding to issues on the question of an advertisement for Toohey's beer and also to Catholics generally who were offended by the advertisement.

The letter contained an argument for the appropriateness of the advertisement in the light of prevailing community attitudes, an assertion that the company could not bow to demands within the Catholic community that the advertisement be withdrawn, and a public apology to those who had been offended.

Mr Bugno and I will, it seems, continue to disagree about the advertisement, but that will become immaterial. I suspect that not all the evidence is in yet, and in any case the advertisement has reached the end of its life. The points of disagreement fall well within the range of matters on which reasonable people can disagree.

What I do take seriously in Mr Bugno's letter is his apology. He is a person who has a senior position in our community and, one assumes, the qualities necessary for exercising that position well, and he has put on public record an apology to those who have been offended. His apology is a significant act, and for my own part I accept it. What other Catholics do will be up to them, and some may, indeed, exact retribution from the company by avoiding its beers.

Advertisements need to be novel in order to attract attention, and it is when we enter into the novel that we are most likely to make mistakes. As I have said in other essays in this volume, it is forgiveness that allows us to relegate mistakes to the past and move on. Usually we end up wiser, and, in this case, Lyon Nathan and its advertisers will be a little more aware of Catholic feeling. Catholics, in turn, should become more aware of some of the issues surrounding protection of things we view as sacred.

The Catholic Church does not constitute a minority either materially in terms of its numbers or formally in terms of its understanding of itself. Catholicity is the 'mark of the Church that emphasises its universality, its inclusiveness, and its openness to truth and value wherever they might be found'. A minority is the opposite, generally constituted by a small number of people associated in virtue of a very focussed range of interests. The Church, then, does not usually enjoy those rather peculiar political advantages that minorities claim at the present time.

Nevertheless, we need to exercise vigilance in protecting the sacred in a society that is increasingly likely to demean it despite its own search for deeper meaning. In this we will find more serious issues to address and more difficult opponents than Toohey's, who are friendly to us and who simply made a mistake. It is in meeting these other situations that we will need to be clever.

Reference: Richard P McBrien, *Catholicism*, new edition (Melbourne: Collins Dove, 1994), 1235.

Thinking About an Injecting Room

Many of Catholic's were surprised a few years back to learn that the State Government and Saint Vincent's Hospital had agreed to trial a safe injecting room for drug users in the heart of Sydney, at Kings Cross. The headline in *The Sydney Morning Herald* ran, 'Nuns to run heroin room'. Within hours journalists were phoning around in an attempt to get a whiff of dissension among more public figures in the Church.

Fortunately, they did not get much to go on. That is how it should have been, not because everyone in the Church should be or will be of the same opinion, but because the issue is notoriously complex and any simple stance would be just that, simple-minded.

The announcement did, however, launch us as Church into the limelight in respect of the discussion around the deep problems associated with drug taking in our society. It may well be an uncomfortable position, because it will demand hard work, careful analysis and clear thinking. To date, we have mostly been in the more comfortable position of being able to say, 'drugs are bad, and that's that', a stance that was not very effective in making our world a better place.

Given the Government's decision to trial this hitherto untried practice, there is good reason that it be at Saint Vincent's. It is in a major drug area of the city; the Sisters have, from the beginning, cared for the least advantaged people; the hospital has ready access to the best medical and social science; it is a strong institution with high intellectual and ethical standards. It is better that it be done in a Catholic hospital than in an institution in which we might question the ability to address ethical issues well.

In taking on this project, however, the hospital and the Sisters have put themselves on the line. They will need to learn a lot in a short time. How do you do this? What associated problems arise, and how can they be dealt with? What procedures need to be in place? What are the specific goals of the project, and how will success be measured? What can be done morally and what cannot?

While we hope for success, the trial may well be a failure, in which case we need not be critical, if the hospital has done its best. What we will expect, however, is a publicly available report at the end, which will address the many aspects of the project in a frank and detailed way. It will be on the basis of that report that the government should decide whether there are any real grounds for the continuing operation of the facility or of any like it.

In Melbourne, the Church is also freshly active with its own inquiry into the drug problem. There we will expect the same conditions of objectivity and frankness in a report that may well help find a way ahead.

Coming to Terms with a Complex Event

The issue in the 1990's of the Sisters of Charity and the drug injecting room did not go away quickly. The then Archbishop of Sydney, Cardinal Clancy, received a letter from the then Cardinal Ratzinger, now Pope Benedict XVI, in Rome instructing the Sisters to withdraw from the injection room trials. Cardinal Clancy's delivery of that ruling to the Sisters, and the Sisters' announcement of compliance constituted an event that drew much reflection and discussion in the Australian Church.

Up until the letter arrived many of us were doing what we could to help the Sisters work through moral and other issues surrounding their agreement with the State Government to trial a safe injection room as a way of healing people caught by addiction in an almost inhuman condition.

That activity ceased, and the questions were not resolved, because the Church's involvement in the numerous practical judgements that would have arisen has ended. The letter from Rome illuminated moral reasoning, since the reasons stated publicly amount to no more than the fact of difference of opinion among experts and the likelihood of scandal among people overseas.

Instead, we then had to deal with the effects of an event, which raised many fresh questions that were more difficult and more demanding of resolution than those that sat with us at the beginning. Among those questions were the following.

How would governments in the world feel confident in entering into agreements with Catholic hospitals for more than basic health care? This question was compounded by the timing of the announcement, which came while the New South Wales State Parliament was debating the legislation.

What would the credibility of the Catholic Church be in the public discussion of difficult moral and social questions that always face our society and that desperately beg careful and compassionate consideration?

What ethical restraints ought to apply to the way in which power is exercised in the Church? What is the relationship between service and power in Scripture, theology, Canon Law and day-to-day practice?

How do Church authorities come to judgement about serious matters and what sort of processes ought to be involved in this? Where and how, for instance, do the Roman congregations or other Church agencies gather their information?

How is the extraordinary role that religious women have played in Australia during the last two hundred years recognised in word and in deed?

These and questions like them emerged afresh and even ten years or more later continue to need to be dealt with seriously at all levels of Church life. Failure to do so will deepen malaise and increase disaffection in the Church. The Conference of Bishops should play a leading role, but all Catholics should also give thought to the character and quality of our life together. Should we be successful, some good may come out of this extremely distressing event.

A Response to David Marr

David Marr's book, *The High Price of Heaven*, would probably have slipped under the waves were it not for his media contacts, who have managed to give him plenty of early air time. The book seemed timed for Christmas, and, although it was difficult to say how long it will receive attention, its attacks on Christianity call for some response.

The thesis of the book is that Christianity has inflicted unjustified pain on many Australians by rejecting pleasure and by using its political power to drag us all into heaven. Since it has a thesis, the book can be evaluated in terms of the success of its arguments, the reliability of its assumptions and the quality of its distinctions.

The arguments are by way of story or narrative. They comprise an inductive argument by example. The stories are of people whom Marr has interviewed or heard speak—Brian Watters, John Howard, Gerard Brennan, Brian Haradine, Philip Jensen, Brian Lucas and others, many of whom Marr has had access to as a reporter. In beautiful language, he carves out their personalities with the incisiveness of a neuro-surgeon but in a way that reveals mainly their weaknesses rather than their character. The argument is, therefore, *ad hominem* and it suffers also because it wanders from topic to topic weakening an already weak inductive argument.

Marr's assumptions are largely libertarian. Any restriction of movement or action by authority is wrong. Pleasure of any kind, though he does not distinguish kinds, is good. This applies particularly to sexual pleasure. The problem with these assumptions is not that they are held but that they are unexamined. They have to do with ethics, but there is little ethical argument in the book. Marr, therefore, writes for the already converted, who may enjoy the book in a graceless kind of way. This is a pity because the issues of freedom, pleasure and sexuality are well worthy of more serious discussion.

The distinctions that Marr most obliterates are those between Christians as Christians, Christians as persons, Christians as church organisations, Christians as particular churches, Christians as church authorities, Christians as believers in particular doctrines. All of these run together so that by the end of the book, (for example, pages 205–208) 'Christians' means simply those who are opposed to Marr's own position, which, by then, he has taken for granted. At no point does he admit how many Australians are Christians.

The Catholic Church, for one, does, no doubt, need to articulate more intelligent and sensitive understandings of sexuality in general and of homosexuality in particular than it has done for some centuries. Although for largely internal reasons this is unlikely in the short term, Marr's writing may have helped had he stayed with the promise of his introduction and final chapter, which, for a few moments, began to describe his own experience and, indeed, pain, as a Sydney Anglican and homosexual.

Ethics in a Liberal World

Elsewhere in this volume I wrote about the virtues proper to liberal society. Now I would like to go further and discuss the possibilities for ethics in such a society.

Again, I will start with Thomas Hobbes (1588–1679), not because his views are generally ones I wish to espouse, in fact, the contrary is true, but because Hobbes articulated clearly what were to be the central concerns of liberal modernity. At the end of his discussion of laws and virtues in *Leviathan*, he wrote the following.

> There be other things tending to the destruction of particular men;
> as drunkenness, and all other parts of intemperance; which may
> therefore also be reckoned amongst those things which the law of
> nature hath forbidden; but are not necessary to be mentioned, nor
> are pertinent enough to this place.

It is immediately obvious that Hobbes' ethical theory is rather sparse, and this is, I believe, true of most liberal doctrine. The reason for this is that his concern is with a political theory that is directed specifically at carving out that public space in which citizens are free to act as they wish provided that they do not injure other citizens. In like fashion, the personal ethics to which is he alludes has mainly to do with preventing harm to oneself.

That the possibilities for publicly sanctioned ethical positions are so limited in a liberal world is often of great concern to Catholics. We ought, however, be aware of the other side of the picture, namely, that liberal society makes available space in which a wide range of ethical views can be freely articulated. While these may have no public normative value they can be accepted privately and, if presented well, can act to persuade wider populations of ways in which they might best live.

It seems to me that the Catholic Church did well in the twentieth century and before in holding coherent positions on a broad range of ethical issues, albeit with some diversity within the Church. It did not do so well, however, in articulating those positions to a liberal world, since it tended to speak authoritatively and as if to an uneducated audience rather than persuasively and to a world in which universal education is the norm.

Liberal political forms are not ends in themselves but are rather evolving attempts to match organisation and government to cultures that prize individual freedoms. The Church began to come to terms with this in the Council. In the twenty-first century, it would do well to learn how to present the riches of its tradition to liberal-minded people. In order to do this, it will need to concentrate less on expanding the range of specific prohibitions that civil societies accept as normative and more on promoting ways of life that are attractive and meaningful to people, in the process bringing ethics and spirituality together.

Possibilities for a Catholic Modernity

In several essays in this volume I have looked at various aspects of modernity and of the liberal culture in which we live. For traditional Catholics, even dabbling in some of the ideas could seem confrontational, and for some the future no doubt seems bleak. There is, however, a great deal of scholarship being directed towards working out some of the issues that I have raised.

One scholar, philosopher and Catholic, Charles Taylor, addressed the issue of how Catholicism might come to terms with modernity a few years ago in a lecture called 'A Catholic Modernity', published in a book by the same name edited by James L Heft.

Taylor tells the story of modernity as a cultural movement that grew out of Christendom. What he tries to do is to make sense of the situation in which we find ourselves living and to suggest some ways in which we might improve that situation.

He invites us to consider some of the successes of modernity. Two will do for now: firstly, the application of human rights to all human beings; secondly, the drive to preserve life and to prevent suffering. That people today are prepared to confront distant political regimes, when human rights are infringed, or to give generously to the alleviation of hunger among peoples with whom otherwise they would never have any dealings is unprecedented in human history.

Taylor sees these developments as a flowering of the Gospel. The universalisation of rights, for instance, echoes Paul's 'there is no distinction between Jew and Greek' (Rom 10:12) and concern for the life and suffering of all human kind fits very well with Jesus' injunctions to love one's neighbour.

The twist is that these developments could not have taken place within the limits of Christendom, that is, of a political society that understood itself as fundamentally Christian. Christian societies and their regimes, for instance, generally found it difficult to accept the rights of non-believers or of people of other beliefs. Taylor sees this not so much as a failing of Christianity as such but as the weakness of political society itself.

The problem that we live with now is that in freeing itself from Christendom, modern society weakened Christianity and came to 'the view that human life is better off without [a] transcendental vision'. In other words, our wonderful sense of justice and our concern for suffering have become founded on ourselves rather than on something beyond ourselves. Such a foundation, he suggests, will ultimately fail.

He points to Christian spirituality as a source of transcendental vision. We can base our concerns for justice and for human well being on the kind of love proposed in the Gospel and on the recognition that every individual is made in the image of God.

People today cry out for spirituality. We need to find a way not to reimpose Christendom but rather to reintroduce them to the transforming presence of God.

Reference: Heft, James L *A Catholic Modernity? Charles Taylor's Marianist Award Lecture* (New York: Oxford University Press, 1999).

Where Will Charity Move Now?

During the next few decades, we as a Church are going to have to face the issue of where we focus our charitable efforts. We do, indeed, at a personal level face this question frequently as we come upon people with different needs, but the question that I am raising is about our collective organisational and institutional efforts.

To raise this question is not to assume that there is a ready answer or even that, if there were, it would solve our problems or that we could easily change our activities and commitments. It is rather to recognise that change is in the offing and that by keeping the question in mind we are more likely to be open to charitable impetus as new conditions of life and situations of need arise.

In our present situation, activities that began in the nineteenth century when small groups of people with minimal resources dedicated their lives to the alleviation of ignorance and sickness have turned into massive institutions, namely, the Catholic school and hospital systems. It is hard to say any longer that either is in the strictest sense a charitable activity, though the activities of both may well be informed by charity. Both have, in fact, become important public institutions with massive government funding.

This is not to say, of course, that we should necessarily cease to be involved in these activities, because there are things other than simple charity that might motivate us. Schools, for instance, are at least partly conducted for religious reasons—to ensure enculturation into the faith and to provide religious education. Our presence in hospitals may enable us to have some impact on the quality of care that is provided generally, but here we seem to be at increasing risk of entering into compromise with power and money.

Actions of the present Commonwealth Government have given clear warning of the dangers of entering into major funding relationships with government of activities that we might regard as essential to Christian life. Mr Abbott's run in with the St Vincent de Paul Society betrayed a belief that the government could coopt charities to do its work. Mr Ruddock's criticism of the South Australian charities that assisted refugees released from Woomera demonstrated profound ignorance of what charity is. Mr Howard's notion of a social coalition seems destined to draw all communal activities under the government's own mantle. It is not clear that another government would be very different.

It may be that we have to think small again. The needs of the twenty-first century are likely to be very different from those of the nineteenth. We may find that those needs are not best met with money or technology, even if these remain in the background. Whatever they are, it seems to me that compassion, that feeling of one human being for the difficulties of another, will be central.

Taking Seriously the Medium in 'Media'

Reports recent meetings of Cardinals in Rome indicate that calls for the Church to use the public media in the propagation of its message, were high on the agenda. The argument is simple. The Church's mission is to reach all men and women. By using the public media, it can reach thousands of people to whom it would otherwise not get the opportunity to speak.

It is not clear to me where this idea originated, though it has been rumbling around the world for several years. The impact of media interest in some of the Pope's world trips has given it momentum. Indeed, the actions and words of the Holy Father on some of these trips, particularly those to places of religious and political strife, were both evangelically significant and of interest to the media at large.

In suggesting that it might 'use' the media, however, the Church needs to take extreme care. The media are a vigorous and necessary institution of a liberal democracy, and a medium through which events and opinions that are of public interest in matters to do with the life of the community are conveyed. The responsibility that this entails is a significant one because all citizens have to make judgements in political matters and decisions in economic matters based on the information that they receive through the media.

The term 'media' is the Latin plural for 'medium'. In English, the cognate, 'media', is partway through a drift from a plural to a singular noun. The media are, in a real sense, a medium and so passive in respect to what they transmit. They are, however, a self-reflective medium and constantly assess what they are doing and how they are being used.

Journalists often use media releases, which by definition carry the interests of their authors. When, however, those working for the better newspapers, radio stations and television networks sense that they are being exploited, they become very active in unearthing the truth, an activity that often takes the form of unmasking those by whom they have been used as a medium. This process can be quite destructive of reputations, but it is both necessary for the health of political society, which relies on opinion, and ethical, when reasonable evidence exists of deception or manipulation.

The Church could easily hide behind a naive argument that runs something like, the media should report the truth; we tell the truth; therefore the media should report what we tell. It is naive because it masks differences in the kinds of truths we tell, in the grounds on which we base our claims, in the capacities of those who speak these truths and in the purposes for which they speak. We need to be truthful not only in our message and in how we tell it but also in the effect that our telling has in those who hear it.

POLITICAL THINKING

Tolerance

Tolerance as a virtue disappeared from public and religious discourse in the West during the late Middle Ages. Societies that were culturally uniform and feudal and that professed a single religion seemed to have no need of it. The Church claimed ultimate authority over individuals and states, and its certainty of having appropriated the truths of revelation left no room for the recognition or acceptance of difference.

Tolerance or toleration (the words are generally used interchangeably) can be defined as the willingness to endure differences in others patiently. It is implied that these differences are significant and that they are things that are not liked. From the fourteenth century tolerance was regarded negatively. To tolerate something disagreeable was seen as weakness or as lax complacency towards evil.

It was the religious wars after the Reformation that brought a change in thinking. The wars between Catholics and Protestants had been so brutal and damaging that it was recognised as a simple necessity that people of different faiths learn to endure one another. In time it was realised that in any society the majority would tend to persecute a minority that differed from it religiously. Religious toleration became part of the modern world despite the reluctance of the mainstream Churches.

In the seventeenth century theorists discussing the rise of the new liberal democracies recognised the importance of tolerance of social and political beliefs. If freedom of speech and liberty in general were to be possible, citizens would have to be tolerant of one another. If value was to be given to the development of the individual, individual differences would have to be tolerated and even welcomed. Tolerance became an essential principle of the modern state. Its companion is political compromise, and both are directed towards peaceful living and the possibility of acting together.

The settlement of the New World broadened the scope of tolerance. The new states, of which Australia is one, were settled by people of many different cultures and involved as well the indigenous peoples of the lands in which they settled. The mono-cultural nation states of Europe could remain tribal in their outlook as is shown by the superior attitudes they took to the peoples they colonised and by their own continued readiness to engage in war with one another. This was not the case, however, in the New World where cultural diversity was a condition of life.

To be an Australian is to be tolerant of differences of culture. To be intolerant of cultural difference would be a failure as an Australian because it would negate one of the very conditions of being Australian—that of being an immigrant people. This is not to say that we have always been very good at it or that we have found it easy. In the early days the English and the Irish found much to spar about. After the Second World War, Mediterranean and Eastern European immigrants found that they had to prove themselves. Through all of this our aboriginal peoples have had difficulty being heard. Today we are still adjusting to the customs of migrants from many different parts of the world including Asia. Despite these difficulties, however, tolerance of cultural difference remains necessarily a fundamental part of being Australian.

Can Democracy Survive in Australia?

A look among the political theorists down through the ages soon shows that democracy as such has rarely been highly favoured. For Plato, it was the least desirable of the legitimate forms of government. Later, Thomas Aquinas argued against democracy on the grounds that it was likely to lead to tyranny. In the eighteenth century, Montesquieu proclaimed that the only democracy that could survive was one that was small enough for the citizens to be on friendly terms with one another, so that they would watch out for each other's interests.

Today we live in democracies, and democracy is virtually unquestioned as the best or, indeed, the only just form of government. It fits our character as persons who prize freedom and equality and who expect to have a say when issues are being decided. We retain the ancient distaste for tyranny but expect, as well, to participate actively in government. How is it that we manage to live in a way that has not been thought possible for most of Western history?

Learning to live in a democracy took some centuries, but much of it centred around the formation of the American Constitution. At the time those opposed to the Constitution pointed out the impossibility of a large democracy being able to function and argued that it would soon turn into a monarchy and then a tyranny. The argument for the Constitution was put by James Madison and others, who wrote newspaper articles that have since come to be known as *The Federalist Papers*.

In paper number ten, Madison admits the problems of democracy. Whenever people are free and able to form their own opinions, they will frequently take up positions based on their passions and interests. When sufficient people are moved in the same way they are likely to form a faction that will attempt to control the lives and interests of all the rest. The stronger the passion, the more likely it is for democracy to be overthrown altogether.

Key to Madison's solution was federation. A system of government in which a central government had certain powers and separate state governments had others would make it impossible for a faction ever to control the whole and so turn the state to its own interests. Even if one part of the Federation were to be dominated by some kind of madness or self-interest, the rest could resist.

The writers of the Australian Constitution learnt from the American experience. Federation was not just a convenience but a way in which to balance the forces active in a democracy. We ought to remember this as we move towards reconsideration of our political forms in a constitutional convention. Efficient management might make simplification attractive, but when lunacy stalks the land, as it does at the moment, it is the complexity of political structures that protects the democracy we prize.

Reference: Alexander Hamilton, James Madison and John Jay, *The Federalist* (Middletown CN: Wesley University Press, 1961), *Federalist no 10, November 22, 1787.*

Why Opinion Polls Do Not Work

From time to time we are confronted with opinion polls that purport to tell us what people really think. Politicians labour under the impact of these polls, which often seem unchallengeable because they are couched in terms of hard data—facts and numbers that have been scientifically collected. It is worth thinking about what might be wrong with this.

Whenever we make an affirmative statement we are proposing an opinion for acceptance by somebody else. We know that the grounds for acceptance of that opinion can have varying strengths, but we rarely reflect on differences of kind in the opinion itself. For our purposes, three kinds of opinion can be distinguished.

The opinion might be one that is clearly held by the person who states it. Alternatively, it might be an opinion that is generally held across the breadth of society or of some group in society. Finally, it might be an opinion that the speaker would not formulate explicitly, but that he or she would assent to if asked either to agree or disagree.

The problem with opinion polls is that they deal in this third sort of opinion and that they then claim that the opinion is of one or other or both of the first kinds of opinion. In other words, they claim that what people affirm or deny when a question is put to them is of the same kind as an opinion they hold themselves or as one which society generally holds. This is wrong, because what people will agree with in this situation has no essential connection and often no connection at all to the kinds of proposals they would actually make themselves, if given the chance. We experience this un-connectedness when we feel dissatisfaction with questions that we are made on occasion to answer.

This is not to say that opinion polls are completely useless. In a democracy is it important for those in government to be in touch with voters, and opinion polls can in some way gauge the temperature of the electorate, but they are not something by which to make decisions.

A further reason stands out. When we elect people to government, we elect them to do the difficult work of government. Rather than us all voting on every issue, we ask a select group to deal seriously with the issues facing the country and to act consistently in our stead. This is one of the modern meanings of republican government. It suggests that these are the people who should be forming new opinions on how to act and who should be persuading us to follow them. This is what we call leadership.

Had Abraham Lincoln followed the opinion polls, he would not have freed the slaves. His popularity would have increased, and he would likely have avoided much bloodshed. He would, however, have been judged very harshly by history.

References: Robert Sokolowski, *Presence and Absence* (Bloomington: Indiana University Press, 1978), 119; Peggy Noonan, *What I Saw at the Revolution* (New York: Ivy Book, 1990), 158–160; This sense of 'republic': see Madison, *Federalist* Paper # 10.

What is the English Tradition of Liberalism?

In a series of lectures in 1998 at Cambridge University, Professor Quentin Skinner identified Thomas Hobbes (1588–1677) as the first person to clearly articulate what has come to be known as the English tradition of liberalism.

This kind of liberalism lies at the heart of political life and structure in the English speaking world. It answers the general question, what is it for me to be free within a civil association? The movement began when people started looking for forms of association that would free them both from the wanton actions of absolute monarchs and from the devastating wars that flowed from religious intolerance following the reformation. It coincided with a cultural development that emphasised the significance of the individual in relation to the community.

The English tradition is distinguished from other traditions in that it is based on a negative thought and in that it relates solely to action within the civil association. It simply states that to be free is to be unconstrained in one's actions. It differs from modern Continental notions that see freedom as some kind of self-actualisation and from classical Greek notions that place freedom in the intellect. It is not concerned with psychological determinations but with public action.

According to Skinner's analysis, Hobbes's theory contains four essential elements. Liberty or freedom exists when (1) there is an agent or a person (2) who has the power to act (3) and is not constrained in acting (4) by any other agency.

According to this definition, a person who through illness is unable to move cannot be said to be unfree. The absence of opportunity, for instance, for work, is not an infringement of freedom, nor for Hobbes can one restrain one's own freedom. Freedom for him has to do with action in a world of powerful agents. Unfreedom comes when one of those agents, whether it be the state, other citizens, or organisations within the state, makes one unable to act in ways that one could otherwise have acted.

A question that quickly arises is what kind of constraint is meant here? For Hobbes the answer is straightforward. It is constraint of the body, that is, of physical movement. This, he says, can take two forms: prevention from moving and compulsion to move in a certain way. In a complex argument he distinguishes this from coercion by law to which we have given implied consent.

Skinner claims that Hobbes's work is foundational to the whole English tradition and that subsequent discussion occurs within the framework he has established. Of course, there is much disagreement, and objections centre mainly on the third element, namely, the nature of the constraint that restricts freedom. It is in consideration of this that liberalism as we know it breaks up into its different kinds with their different expectations of life within a state. These will be the topic of a further reflection.

Differences Within the English Liberal Tradition

In a previous essay in this volume I have looked at Quentin Skinner's analysis of Hobbes's theory of liberty and at the claim that it was foundational to the English liberal tradition. According to Hobbes, liberty or freedom exists only when (1) there is an agent or a person (2) who has the power to act (3) and is not constrained in acting (4) by any other agency.

According to Skinner, important differences in the liberal tradition centre around the question of the kind of constraint that is involved. For Hobbes and what might be called the classical liberal tradition only physical constraint mattered.

The radical constitutionalists of the seventeenth century claimed that constraint could also be applied to the will by means of threats, which they saw as a means of coercion. Sensitivity to coercion remains with us today, which is one of the reasons why governments tend to bring in change by promising rewards rather than by threatening punishment. Besides being psychologically shrewd, this caters to one kind of liberalism that is abroad in the community.

The neo-classical movement extended the notion of constraint to include dependence on the will of somebody else. This movement, which was influential in establishing American political structures, saw equal involvement in government through federalism as the only guarantee of freedom. The rejection of economic dependence on husbands by the women's liberation movement is heir to this view.

Other differences show up. In the classical view, restrictions on liberty are legitimate only if they ensure liberty itself, but a utilitarian sees restrictions as necessary to prevent harm to others. Hence, for instance, while American laws emphasise the right to say almost anything, Australian libel laws seek to ensure that others are not harmed by what might be said.

Divergence in the liberal tradition affects the answer to the question of what kind of government people want. The Kantian tradition, which seeks personal autonomy, is anarchic and rejects the legitimacy of the state altogether. Utilitarians see law as a necessary evil and so seek to minimise the amount without regard to kind. The neo-classical tradition rejects dependence on the will of others and so supports only republican or self-government. The older classical tradition is content with representative government.

In Australia, we live in a liberal tradition and have been educated to do so. Many of the problems we face about government, ethics or human rights, come out of divergence or inconsistency within that tradition. As Catholics, we are also taught by the Church from within a totally different tradition. Matching the two is not easy. On the one hand, traditions tend to be ignorant of one another and therefore unable to converse. On the other hand, while the tradition in which we live may be inadequate, because of our learning and that of those we live with, solutions have to be sought within that tradition.

Facing the Issue of Sovereignty

Following the lead of Cardinal Martini, I have raised the issue of planetary government. Is it time to develop this idea? Is it possible to develop a vision of such government that would win the assent of the peoples of the world?

Many objections will, of course, be raised. The one that I would expect first to hear has to do with national sovereignty. Simply put, Australians claim national sovereignty and, on the basis of that claim, reject the notion that a body outside Australia could have the power to determine Australian affairs.

This argument has been around for some time and has shown up recently in the current Federal Government's response to criticism by the United Nations' committee dealing with human rights. It is also used in discussions about the effects of foreign treaties on Australian law and about the Federal Government's foreign affairs powers.

Sovereignty is a modern idea, and the term is said to have been coined by Bodin (1530–96). It was first used to locate the supreme power in a state and then extended to affirm the integrity of states in relation to one another. Its articulation belongs to a time when rule ceased to be vested in persons in favour of formal structures, now generally defined in constitutions.

The development of modern political forms, what we call the nation state or modern European state, called for great inventiveness. How could democracy be made to last? As peoples began to think of themselves primarily as individuals, how could peace and order be kept? Mechanisms such as separation of powers, federation and political parties have all played their part.

Although the notion of sovereignty has helped both in the maintenance of internal order and in the settling of relations with other states, it does have its limitations. Internally, citizens have had to be protected from governments by the articulation and assertion of rights. Externally, unless treaties can be voluntarily agreed, states stand in a relationship to one another based mainly on force, a condition likely to lead to war.

The objection that uncontrolled loss of external sovereignty would leave us at the mercy of decisions or judgements of bodies foreign to us and in which we have no say is sustainable. This is why it is central to the vision of planetary government that it somehow be democratic. We could, therefore, begin with skills we already have—the skills to live in federated systems of government, the skills to define powers constitutionally.

It is unlikely that we will have full planetary government very soon. Practical leadership for such a venture is unlikely to emerge quickly, although the need will grow. What is more likely first is the development of regional government such as is happening in the European Union. In Australia, we ought to watch this development and perhaps give more attention to the political development of our own region.

Living in a Liberal Society

An easy way to start an argument in more traditional Catholic circles these days is say a few words in praise of the fact that we live in a liberal society. One can then withdraw and listen to exclamations of concern about moral decadence, to dissertations on the paucity of religious education in schools, and to passionate proclamations on all sorts of subjects. When it all dies down, one will probably find somebody sitting quietly in a corner, who is happy to say that he or she is glad of the freedoms of a liberal society. The irony of the situation is that the conversation could not have taken place in a public arena in other than a liberal society.

Obviously, there is great confusion here, and one needs to draw a number of distinctions before the situation can be clarified. It seems to me that the first distinction is between generic kinds of liberalism which I will call political, epistemological and moral. We might wish to add religious because of its importance to us.

I take political liberalism to be fundamental. In practical terms, it is a political doctrine that articulates basic human freedoms such as freedom of movement, freedom of association and freedom of speech. It calls generally for democratic government, because, even if these freedoms are praised in monarchies and oligarchies, there they are limited and kept for the few. The English liberal tradition protects these freedoms by restricting the right of governments or other agents or persons in society to impede or restrict citizens' rights of movement and action.

Epistemological liberalism is more difficult to define, I believe, because it is derived from political liberalism. If people are free to speak, it is necessary that we respect what they say, even if we do not agree with it. Positive theories suggest that truth will come out if people, especially academics and journalists, are free to research what they will and to say what they conclude. Truth will emerge from disagreement and conflict. Problems arise, however, when people assume that because every person's view is respected, every person's view is true, at least for them. Such a position quickly slips into relativism, which, in effect, says that nothing is true and that people can believe whatever they will.

Moral liberalism works similarly. The liberal virtue is tolerance, which respects difference and insists that we allow people room to live according to their own customs. What limits tolerance are the demands of public order. A nest of concerns grow out of this. The most extreme is moral relativism. More interesting are the questions of whether and how different moralities might exist side by side in one society and of how these might relate to the limited moral norms that a political society itself might adopt as a whole.

Virtue in a Liberal Society

One of the common criticisms of liberal society is that it is society without morals. Such a claim could mean many things. At its extreme, it could mean that liberal society fostered no moral principles at all. This could hardly be true, because a society without any morals at all would surely collapse. People would have no way of dealing consistently with one another.

At another extreme, the claim might mean that liberal society, whether or not it promotes moral principles at all, simply does not promote the principles I, or my community, wish it to promote or believe that it should promote. A simpler claim is that it just does not promote a sufficient range of moral principles.

I intend to look at these issues in a future essay, but first it is worth considering what moral principles might be fostered by a liberal society as such. A fruitful way of doing this is to ask what virtues properly belong to liberal society.

I tried this some time ago by asking some children from a state primary school what they learnt at school. They told me that they learnt to respect one another and to allow one another to be different (tolerance). They were also able to say something about kindness and about helping each other (and not just friends) in the face of difficulties. These are all virtues that allow people to live successfully together while, at the same time, allowing people to be different.

In Chapters 14 and 15 of his book, *Leviathan*, which was the first serious work on how a liberal society might be put together, Thomas Hobbes outlined some of the moral virtues of such a society. He presented them as laws of nature following upon what he called the fundamental law of nature, 'That every man ought to endeavour peace, as far as he has hope of obtaining it'. I will mention just four.

Gratitude, says Hobbes, is necessary so that people will be encouraged to do good to one another by the response they regularly receive.

Mutual accommodation allows for peaceful living among people of different mind and feeling.

Forgiveness ensures that people will not stay at odds with one another simply through fear of retribution.

Hobbes omits a name for the fourth virtue, but he says that its opposite is pride. Its import is that each person should acknowledge every other person as an equal.

Hobbes puts these and other virtues forward as 'laws of nature, dictating peace, for a means of conservation of men in multitudes'. He admits that what he has outlined concerns only life in society. This is a clue to how liberal doctrine works. Its goal is harmonious living among people whose differences might lead them to strife.

Other virtues, like temperance, are important in life but are, according to Hobbes, matters for particular persons.

Problems with a Liberal Society

In several essays in this volume I have been discussing different aspects of liberal society. The fundamental reason for doing this has been that it is the kind of society in which we live, so that, if we are to work for its betterment or, indeed, for its evangelisation, we need to understand it. This is not necessarily easy, particularly for many older Catholics, who, in their civic education and public lives, learnt to prize the freedoms that this kind of society offered but who, in their religious education and private lives, often found reasons for rejecting the kind of society that provided these freedoms.

Liberal society, as we live it, does, however, have its problems, as does any actual society. I will mention just four, which are in various ways interconnected.

Firstly, liberal society offers ready opportunities for the strong to succeed in pursuit of their own interests to a far greater degree than the weak. Although this is in a general sense an ancient problem, it takes on new forms and calls for new solutions in a liberal society.

Secondly, built as it is on individuals, liberal society does not readily recognise natural communities. This has, for instance, placed enormous stress on the family in its various senses. Life can also be difficult for each member of such a society because the notion of a radically independent individual is in some respects a fiction and a recipe for loneliness.

Thirdly, it appears that many people have found liberty a burden and have sought ways to fulfil their desires without having to stand alone. According to Michael Oakeshott, the Marxist proletariat or some aspects of political parties work in this way. 'The people' attempt to have their way, not by acting independently but by being told what to think by a leader.

Fourthly, many fail in the concomitant responsibility of freedom, namely, to exercise freedom well or, in other words, to generate a morality that not only makes claims for individuality and freedom but also explores the exercise of freedom in relation to other persons and to the world as a whole. The conduct of the feminist movement in recent decades seems to be an example. That women would be liberated was in large part inevitable as liberal ideas penetrated more deeply into the particularities of life. That the movement has been so violent and that it has had so much difficulty in shifting its focus beyond its own immediate claims for liberty is puzzling.

The broad moral dispositions of a society and the political forms that support them are not static. Nor, apart from revolution, do they change suddenly and drastically. They change by way of the absorption of new ideas and by amendment of existing practices. Understanding the problems of the way we live is the first step in our attempts to be participants in its slow evolution.

POLITICAL ANALYSIS AND COMMENTARY

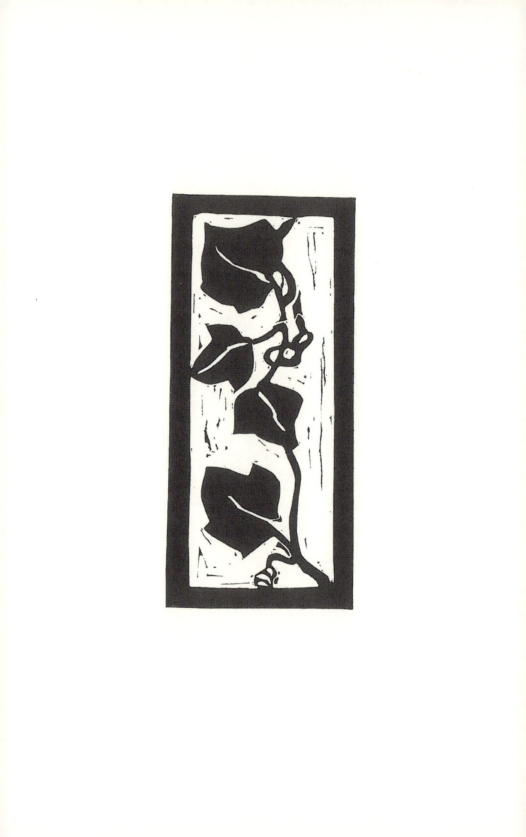

Political Issues for Any Lifetime

In his biography of Paul Keating, John Edwards notes with approval Keating's recognition that economic management is key to successful government. He later speaks of Australia as 'a country where economic policy [is] more important than any other'. What an appalling state of affairs! Although the nation needs to be economically healthy for many other things to happen well, that the economy have or be thought to have this pre-eminence in political affairs should give rise to serious concern.

Politics is about relationships—relationships between groups of people in the country; relationships between this country and other countries. It is about identity—who we are and how we think about ourselves. It is about activity— the kinds of things we do and the ways we do them.

The then Prime Minister, John Howard, seemed even more dogged in his insistence that the business of his job is mainly economic. This may be one of the reasons why he has been unable as Prime Minister to say that the Federal Government is sorry for the suffering that the stolen generations have undergone. He was asked not to impute guilt but simply, on behalf of the nation, to express sorrow. His stated concern has been that this might lead to some kind of liability. His position has been that he will do far more significant things to help the Aboriginal peoples. These, one can assume, will be announced in the next budget.

If economic management does predominate in federal politics, it is probably because of the fiscal imbalance between the states and the commonwealth. The federal government has taxation powers far in excess of its duties, and uses them to control what are really state concerns like health and education through the control of funds. This was not envisaged in our present Constitution, and is something that should be examined when a constitutional convention eventually gets off the ground.

In the meantime we ought to encourage the Prime Minister and the whole of government to engage thoughtfully in debate about the significant political issues of the second half of the nineties. These are the issues of Aboriginal reconciliation and constitutional reform.

We live in an exciting time when the Aboriginal peoples have recovered their political voice and are ready to establish their place in the nation. The multiple issues that this raises are matters of relationship and identity, in which understanding gained through listening and symbolic acts are of utmost importance.

It may or may not be accidental, but it is certainly appropriate that at the same time we are moving towards constitutional discussions that will not be about whether we retain the monarchy or not, but about whether the constitution as we have it fits the character of the people we are today.

References: John Edwards, *Keating: The Inside Story* (Penguin, 1996), 126, 179

Power, Taxation and Government

The exercise of power is necessary in any group of people, because what it does is draw together the energies of many individuals and enable them to be focussed on a common enterprise. When this happens effectively the combined energies of a people are able to achieve far more than would have been possible with the simple sum of their individual efforts.

Power, however, carries with it its own problems. One of these is its tendency to centralise. This seems to be natural to power itself—as power increases the individual or group exercising it is able to extend its influence even further in terms of both the number of people coming under its control and the range of the activities it coordinates. Centralisation coincides often also with the desires of those exercising power.

Excessive centralisation is an abuse of power even when it happens legally. Its exercise is no longer an exercise in coordination, which releases the unified energies of a group, but becomes an exercise of control and domination, which sees the real energies of the group wither and fade. It also allows various forms of violence to develop.

One of the most effective ways of limiting the centralising tendency of power is to have other centres of power. In Australia, we do this by having three levels of government and by having two houses of parliament at the state and federal levels. While this may sometimes seem inefficient, it assures that power does not become completely centralised in one place and that energy moves around the nation.

During the heady days of the first Keating government, senior ministers advocated both the abolition of the Senate and the suppression of the States in favour of enlarged local government areas. Their arguments proposed more efficient government, which they seemed to envisage as some form of economic management. Shock at the kind of power Keating was able to wield after winning the election that he was not expected to win silenced much of that advocacy, although the ideas linger on.

Now we are faced with a new crisis. The recent High Court decision has intensified a problem that already existed, namely, the fiscal imbalance between federal and state governments. We already live in a situation in which power has been over-centralised in the Federal Government because of their excessive taxation powers. Further, the political process has been perverted by one arm of government trying to control the activities of the other through financial constraints.

Tax reform is needed, but it needs to go much further than mumblings about a GST. Two principles are paramount. First, each of the levels of government should collect the taxes it spends. Second, each should collect the kinds of tax that are appropriate to its responsibilities. Broadly, the federal government should rely on transaction taxes and excise, state governments on income tax, and local government on land and property taxes.

Wik: Why is it so Difficult?

Ideally a legislative solution to the issues raised by the Wik and Mabo, legal decisions of Native Title in the Australian High Court would be both elegant and simple. Ideally it would seem that the Federal Government, if its motives are good and if it engages skilful legislators, should be easily able to put in place legislation that would enable peaceful coexistence to the parties concerned.

Three groups of people—pastoralists, indigenous peoples, miners—have rights of usage to the same blocks of land. The rights are specific. Pastoral leases grant rights to use land and water for specific pastoral activities such as raising sheep and cattle. Native title by common law grants the right to hunt, gather and pass over the land. Further rights may have been recognised in legislation. Mining leases grant rights to extract minerals from land and to engage in the activities necessary for doing this.

None of these rights is by its nature exclusive. In addition, the rights apply in the vast empty spaces of inland Australia, where, it would seem, there ought to be room for everybody concerned. A clever piece of legislation would enable all these rights and the further interests and concerns they generate to be respected. We might hope for something like the Strata Title Act of NSW, which, as those who have lived under it know, enables people to live peaceably in a mix of private and common property even if alongside difficult neighbours.

The difficulty of the situation precipitated by the Wik decision is that it is not a fresh beginning. It takes place in the context of history, current practices and prior law. The law is a mix of common law interpreted by the courts and of existing statute law. There are competing jurisdictions—law in respect of land is generally a state issue and varies state by state; the Commonwealth has the power to pass laws in respect of particular races of people and has, in this case, chosen to become involved.

This is why Michael Oakeshott insists that political change comes by way of amendment of what already exists and that it consists in attempting to correct the tensions and incoherencies implicit in existing arrangements. In this sense, an ideal world does not exist. Development of new legislation is affected by what is already in place.

The discussions at this time are themselves complex. They involve rights, which must be fought for; interests, which are properly subject to negotiation; and concerns, which need to be addressed by all parties. These differences tend to become confused, especially when one party or other believes they may gain advantage out of the confusion. As well, legislation is passed in the adversarial context of parliament.

The fundamental issue is of using and managing land fairly and well. It involves personal, cultural, economic, environmental and religious values. We should seek to ensure that all are respected.

References: Michael Oakeshott, 'Political Education', in *Rationalism in Politics and Other Essays* (Indianapolis: Liberty press, 1991), 56–57.

A Jubilee for the Year 2000?

A while back some 60,000 people attended a demonstration in Birmingham, England. It was organised by the Jubilee 2000 Coalition, a loose federation of aid agencies, churches and trade unions, and was timed to coincide with a meeting of the leaders of the G8 nations. Its aim was to persuade the world's richest nations to forgive the debt of the world's poorest nations.

Their suggestion is that the millennium year be declared a year of jubilee in which these debts owed mainly to governments be forgiven. The idea comes from the ancient Jewish tradition, well-attested in the Old Testament, of declaring a jubilee every fifty years when all borrowings, especially of land, were returned to their owners.

The issues surrounding third world debt are, of course, notoriously difficult, especially when you get down the practicalities of finding a solution that will work in the long term. Jubilee 2000's suggestion is, however, carefully thought out. It does not propose simple abolition of all debt, but rather takes into account the specific situations in which the poorest nations find themselves and also the chances of some good being done. In many respects, it amounts to speeding up the already existing relief programs of the International Monetary Fund.

Although problems exist right through the developing world, Jubilee 2000 has focused on Africa, where the problems of human suffering seem greatest. Photographs of people in the grip of malnutrition and disfiguring diseases are very distressing, but the myriad of figures that have been produced are also quite graphic. Mozambique, for instance, spends six times as much servicing foreign debt as it spends on health. Somalia has accumulated 36 times more foreign debt that it earns in foreign currency from exports each year.

While there are many causes of poverty, much of the debt stems from Western initiative. In the 1970s banks were flooded with money from the oil producing countries. They in turn persuaded developing nations to invest in projects that were often unworkable. The 1980s saw policies of high interest rates, and by the 1990s many economies had collapsed.

The organisers of Jubilee 2000 have said over and over again that their proposal is not a matter of charity but a matter of justice. One can both agree with and dispute this claim. It is surely first a matter of love. Justice in our world seems fairly straight-forward—if you take out a loan, you pay it back with interest. It takes love to see the dimensions of the misery in which fellow human beings live. Once that has been seen, rather more subtle forms of justice emerge.

Forgiveness of debt will not solve the situation of poorer countries, but it will surely help. As well, and for the West at not that great a cost, it would have supreme symbolic value of a sign, both to them and to us, that we care.

Understanding the Third World

Discussions about the problems of third world poverty and proposals about how development might best take place are often undermined by two unwarranted assumptions. One has to do with property; the other has to do with political form.

We in the first world live with the notion that property is a radically personal thing. What we often do not realise is that this notion became explicit only in the seventeenth century with John Locke. While Locke recognised limits on how much property an individual might own, he proposed that, in its fluid form, namely, money, it could justifiably be accumulated without limit.

A contrasting view from our own intellectual and political tradition can be seen in the medieval view of property. This is well put by Aquinas, who argued for the appropriateness of private property on the grounds that it motivates people to care for property but who also insisted that its use be for the general good of a community. In such an arrangement a noble might own great holdings but was morally and politically bound to use them for the welfare of the people associated with the land.

In many third world countries today, notions of property are more communal than our own, and that needs to be respected.

The second assumption is that all third world countries ought to become liberal democracies with market economies, just like us. This assumption takes on particular vehemence in American foreign policy which often proposes solutions amounting to states becoming American style democracies. They never add that this will involve learning to deal with the attendant internal violence and moral diversity.

For reasons of history, tradition, geography and character, many countries not at the forefront of Western civilisation live under alternative political forms. External attempts to make them change are highly questionable. Before suggesting political development, one has to ask questions like, How do the people want to live? Before deciding what they can do, one has to ask, How have they learnt to live?

The movement towards globalisation pressures all nations to become the same. While it is enabled in large part by new communication technologies and while it is often praised as a beginning of new world unity, its drive seems to come from economics and therefore from the possibility of gain by the world's strongest economic players. Dealing with this movement, even in the first world, is going to require social and political development that at present is lagging well behind the economic impetus.

In the third world, globalisation, unless it takes on a moral tone, is even more problematic. The relative weakness of these nations means that they are likely to be treated merely as economic resources. Worse, however, is the pressure to become the same and thereby not only to lose their traditions and cultures but also to venture into political forms for which they have no learning.

Dealing with *One Nation*

For some time, I have thought that I ought to make some response to the statements and positions of the One Nation Party, a political party in Australia which had a large following in some parts of the country in the 1990's.

It is clear to me that I am not the only one who has found it difficult. For a time our political leaders seemed stymied. Early demonstrations tended to be rather ugly events. News reporters ran in every direction at once. Cartoonists could barely get past 'one notion'. Serious news commentary was slow to catch up.

It seems to me that both the early success of One Nation and the difficulty of responding to it have something to do with the nature of opinion and its use.

Political life runs on opinion. Hard though it is to tie down, public opinion is the stuff of government, particularly in a democracy. Governments are elected and act in response to the opinions of those who elected them, although they also have a role in developing and moving those opinions along, especially in response to new situations.

Opinion can be defined as 'judgement resting on grounds insufficient for complete demonstration' (*OED*). Its contrary is science or knowledge. It is part of the human condition that most of what we hold lacks the certainty for which we long.

There are, however, many different kinds and grades of opinion. Common opinion is held by many in a society and may for long periods go unchallenged. Professional, for instance, legal or medical opinion carries the weight of an expert called upon to address a question. Vulgar or base opinion is held unreflectively. It is more a response to past irritations than judgement that is weighed and considered.

Pauline Hanson, the leader and founder, had a political knack. She was able to identify and to state those base opinions that sit unreflected upon around the country. This, of course, drew a response because she seemed to be saying what many people believe. There was, however, nothing there. These opinions remained unthoughtful and carried with them only the irritation that was instrumental in their formation.

Thoughtful people laboured over what Ms Hanson says. Eventually they showed that her facts were wrong and that her arguments did not hold up. But by then she had moved on and was stating a new opinion, which had again generated both affirmation and outrage.

This has happened before. In ancient Greece, people, who came to be called sophists, wandered from city to city making statements that brought them quick acclaim but which on careful analysis were shown to be hollow. They were not fit to govern but caused great difficulty for those who did govern because of the way in which they distorted public opinion.

What eventually sank the sophists was inconsistency. What they said at one moment conflicted with what they said at another and people saw this. This is what eventually sank One Nation. The inconsistency was not deliberate but lay embryonic in the unreflectiveness of the opinion the party peddled.

Economic and Political Goods

In the week after an election, the campaign for which was run mainly on issues of taxation and economics, it is worth reflecting on what it might mean for our life as a society. For the most part, the campaign was one of the most boring many of us have experienced.

It may well be that the major political leaders were in tacit agreement that in the light of the rise of the One Nation party, the intellectual climate of the nation was too confused to risk discussions about deeper and broader issues. It may also be that it was necessary in this election to concentrate on economic issues, because of the conditions of the moment.

Economics, which has to do with the life of business and of money, is essential to the operation of any society beyond primitive village communities. Most of the things that we would like to do depend in some way on a sound economy. Before we can do them we have to be assured of food and housing and time and those extra resources that take us beyond mere necessity. In a world as complex as ours has become, maintaining a healthy economy is no easy task.

Robert Sokolowski, however, offers us a timely reminder. He says:

> The economic good must be seen as primarily a condition for other goods; as such it does not define the human good. If its pressures obliterate other human goods, serious social crises result. A society unified only by economic contracts is not a political society, and does not see the human good.

The good that Sokolowski is proposing can be called the political good. But there is a problem with the word. In our time, we tend to associate it with how things get done, something that political science studies. We also use it pejoratively. To call someone political is to imply quite other than good. In older usage, 'political' was more akin to 'moral' and related to questions like, what are the goods that this society can best pursue? or how would we like to live?

Political goods have to do with encouraging human excellence, with allowing people right across society to act in meaningful ways, with promoting social harmony. Presumed is some sense of freedom and opportunity and of elevation above mere necessity.

There are clear signs that we have got some of this wrong. When current economic necessity says that a large proportion of our youth have to be unemployed, we know that economic good has obliterated more important goods like the induction of the young into society and the provision of opportunity for them to be fully active members of society.

Similarly, when enormous disparity of income ensures that some in society are the movers and shakers and that others are simply the working poor, we can be sure that crisis is ahead of us, even if economic arguments seem to justify the situation.

Reference: Robert Sokolowski, *Ethical and Political Life* (Course notes, The Catholic University of America).

Imagining the Republic

One of the difficulties in coming to terms with discussion in the lead up to the referendum in Australia on the republic in the 1990's was imagining what such a republic would be like.

Reactions to this difficulty ranged from fear at initiating any change at all to optimism that a radically different and much better system of government can be found. Confusion was increased by the many meanings and flavours of the word 'republic'. On one hand, 'republic' has often been a word on the lips of revolutionaries; on the other, it has stood for a form of government that is above board and free from tyranny and petty intrigue.

Aristotle gives us some sage advice on how to go about constitutional change when he says, 'what is needed is the introduction of a system which the people involved will be easily persuaded to accept and will easily be able to bring in, starting from the system they actually have' (*Politics* IV, 1).

In other words, in order to imagine a republic, we need simply to start with where we are now. Change will come from amending what we already have to correct things we feel are inadequate. To act otherwise would, indeed, be to engage in revolution, and as Hannah Arendt points out in her book, *On Revolution*, revolutions are rarely successful.

On the other hand, not to change at all will leave us in a condition of growing incoherence. Contrary to the situation of a century ago, allegiance to a British crown no longer has any great significance for many Australians and particularly not for the younger generations. Not to change fairly soon will lead us into confusion about who we are as a nation.

One temptation is to imagine the republic in terms of that republic best known to us, the United States of America. To do so is fallacious because the character and history of that people is significantly different from our own. One can admire the energy of the American people in labouring through such processes as the recent impeachment trial, but it is unlikely that Australians would have much interest in following suit.

Similarly, discussion revolved around the question of how a head of state might be selected. The arguments for popular election seem to be based on two premises - first, distrust of politicians; second, the radicalisation of democracy. To the first, one must point out that a popular election would give us only another politician. People of the calibre of our best Governor Generals would surely not stand. To the second, it must be shown that democracy is fragile and that only the complex structures of modern states have allowed them to survive for very long. As well, the institution of a new base of political power would commit us to years of dispute.

Simpler change at some stage will signal achievement of national maturity, perhaps early in the twenty-first century.

References: Aristotle, *The Politics* IV, 1 (1289a2–3), translated by TA Sinclair and Trevor J Saunders (London: Penguin, 1981): 237. Hannah Arendt, *On Revolution* (New York: Viking Press, 1965).

When Forgiveness Fails

The fracas that followed the release of a prisoner after twenty-five years in jail for murdering a young girl shows, like similar cases before it, what can happen when forgiveness seems impossible. Normally, forgiveness can rectify mistakes and enable people to act again in relation to one another. The vicious murder of a young child, however, could be said to go beyond ordinary human forgiveness, which relates to the kind of trespassing that is an everyday occurrence.

What do we do when forgiveness fails? Two major possibilities face us. We can exact vengeance, which is the exact opposite of forgiveness, or we can accept its alternative, which is punishment. Another possibility is simply to walk away, to abandon the society in which we live.

The problem with vengeance is that it arises simply as a re-enactment of the original transgression so that nobody escapes from the consequences of the first misdeed. Everybody remains caught up in a chain reaction, which multiplies the damage to individual lives and to society itself. Although a somewhat natural reaction, vengeance makes things only worse, as we see, for instance, in so many war torn places around the globe today.

Punishment acts as an alternative to both forgiveness and vengeance. Like forgiveness it attempts to put an end to an unsatisfactory state of affairs that would roll on endlessly unless some action were taken. In this sense, it provides retribution that somehow counters the original offence and allows the cycle to end. It must, therefore, be expected that, if the punishment is completed and a judgement can be made that the original offence is not likely to be repeated, an offender will be able to act in society again.

In the present case, the man in question has completed the punishment that was judged to be appropriate. It has also been determined by a long and diligent process that he is likely be able to live successfully in society. Even further, continuing checks on his progress have been put in place. Under these conditions, to harass him in the way that has occurred is an act of serious injustice and action that ought to be opposed. Should we not feel great concern for the man himself, we should at least oppose actions that will turn our society into one in which ignorant and thoughtless people meter out 'justice' that relates only to their own passions.

It is not surprising that those most hurt by the crime should seem bent on vengeance, but that is something that we can simply regret and leave. We admire, however, in another situation, a father of another murdered girl, who went so far as to meet and forgive some of those who killed his own daughter. That was heroic.

What we must deplore are the third rate media outlets, journalists and politicians who have championed vengeance not from hurt but for their own interests.

Reference: Hannah Arendt, *The Human Condition* (Chicago: The University of Chicago Press, 1958), 236–243.

Evaluating our Relationship with the USA

Relationships between states cannot be called friendships, though they may be called friendly. They are, in fact, alliances, in which utility plays a large part, although history and culture are important. An old rule ran that in looking for allies one first determined who were one's enemies and then chose from among those left. Broadly speaking, however, states form alliances for three main reasons—defence, cultural exchange and trade.

A decision by the Clinton administration to impose punitive tariffs on Australian lamb rightly brought howls of protest from farmers and politicians in Australia. Among the protests was a suggestion that Australia ought re-evaluate its relationship with the United States. This is something that we ought to do, lamb or no lamb.

Australia's close relationship with the USA began only with the Second World War, when Japan entered the war, and Britain, in the midst of its own troubles, was unable to assist in our defence. The USA was largely responsible for the defeat of the Japanese. On other scores, we speak the same language, and both countries are liberal democracies, though of quite different kinds. In our recent past the Australian prime minister called the relationship 'still by any measure the most important relationship that Australia has'. Such an extraordinary claim ought to be examined under the three categories cited above.

The USA was justifiably a key player in Australian defence planning for several decades, particularly during the so-called Cold War. The situation, however, that gave rise to this, cannot be said to exist today. External strife is more likely to come to Australia from disruption in militarily small nations to our north. Australia is better to place its trust in the United Nations. The US, on the other hand, seems bent on military adventures and is more likely to generate for Australia enemies that it otherwise would not have had.

There can be no doubt that American culture has enormous impact in Australia. Intelligent Americans, themselves, tend to regret this and criticise us and Europe for taking on their culture and then complaining about its problems.

Historically, the USA has put its trade interests above even its political principles. It is arguable that Cuba would not have turned communist had the USA changed its exploitative attitudes and practices in respect to that country. In terms of free trade and globalisation, the USA usually seems to want them when they are in its interests but not otherwise. It is part of the American character to be competitive and tough.

None of this is to suggest that Australia and the USA should not be on friendly terms; they should. But perhaps we rely on them too much. It is arguable that the alliance is more important to the USA than it is to Australia, because in its jostling with the UN, the USA invariably looks to Australia and similar countries for public support. We ought to think about that.

Laws and Jones: Tragedy in the Making

The revelations some years back of the deal between the Australian Banking Association and agents of the Sydney based radio talk-back broadcaster John Laws raised a number of issues. Among them are the following.

If the matter is as simple as it first sounded, namely, 'I am bad-mouthing you, and I will change what I say, if you pay me', it is not much other than what the movies used to call a protection racket. This is a matter for the police and the courts to examine and is best left to them.

Certainly involved in the incident is deliberate concealment of boundaries between advertising and editorial comment. Given the implicit claim by Laws to be a significant commentator on current affairs, this is also a serious matter and ought to be examined by appropriate bodies such as the Australian Broadcasting Authority and various ethics committees associated with the media. For the latter, the incident constitutes a significant challenge to the claim that the media can be self-regulating.

A third issue underlies the problems now apparent to most people. The incident reveals what some of us have long suspected, namely, that this kind of talk-back radio amounts to widely heard discussion of serious public issues, done in a way that does not seriously engage those issues yet purports to be serious. The appearance of seriousness comes through things such as Laws' deep voice and communication skills and that of another Sydney radio announcer, Alan Jones', passion and forthrightness.

Current scrutiny of this 'industry' has arisen because the opinion of one man seems to have changed in exchange for money. My concern is that that is only symptomatic of the quality of opinion that has existed in this forum for some time. Clues to this come in the words of the men themselves. Recently in defence of himself, Laws said, 'I'm an entertainer, there isn't a hook for ethics'. While in a public brawl with Laws, Jones said, 'I'm paid to provide opinions and that's what I do'. In neither case does truth-seeking seem to have been an issue.

It may turn out in this case that there has been legally recognisable corruption. This will relate somehow to the payment of money. We can only await the outcome. But a far more worrying form of corruption has been present in these 'shows' for some time, and that is intellectual corruption. The opinions generated and stated are often empty. They are gauged to excite and titillate rather than to further serious thinking about the conditions of our living together. Commitment to truth-seeking and wisdom are lost.

The tragedy in all of this is that anybody listens. Thomas Cahill tells us that preoccupation with frivolous thought was both sign and cause of the collapse of the Roman Empire. A civilisation at its peak, on the other hand, is energetic and vigorous in its pursuit of the best knowledge attainable.

Reference: This essay followed exposure by the ABC by *Media Watch* in 1999 of a radical change of opinion by John Laws of radio and the suggestion that he was receiving undisclosed payments related to the change. Subsequently, Australian Broadcasting Authority held an inquiry and published *Commercial Radio Inquiry: Report of the Australian Broadcasting Authority hearing into 2UE Sydney* (Commonwealth of Australia: Sydney, February 2000).

Should we be Part of Oceania?

While the Australian Church was preparing for the Synod of Oceania, the editor of *The Catholic Weekly* inserted a box on the front page titled, 'What is Oceania, where is it?'. She thought, with good reason, that given all the talk about the Synod of Oceania she ought to inform us about the term 'Oceania' and about the region to which we belong. Not long afterwards, the Prime Minister used the term in one of his speeches.

The term 'Oceania' has been used within the Church since the first missionaries penetrated the vast Pacific Ocean and took up residence on its many islands not long after European settlement of Australia. It does, however, name a well-defined geographical and, I will argue, political region of the world.

Oceania includes Australia, New Zealand, Papua New Guinea, the Solomons, Vanuatu, Fiji, Tonga, Samoa, Kiribati, and several other nations, in all some twelve states and twelve dependencies. They have in common that they are all composed of islands on which most people live near the sea, that they all have indigenous peoples and that all were significantly affected by European culture and settlement during the nineteenth century.

Australia thought of itself for a long time as a part of Britain. It was a long way away, but trust in the Empire, the sight of pink splashed right around the globe and traditional allegiance convinced us that this was a good way to be. Later, after the Second World War, we became the best little brother of the United States. More recently, Paul Keating tried to persuade us to move into Asia, whether or not the Asians themselves thought this a good thing.

All through this time, we failed to look at a map to see where we are, namely, firmly on the edge of that area of the world called Oceania. In a way, we knew where we were but probably thought that the region was too unimportant. We were better to run with the big players like Britain or the USA.

Now the game is different. Trade will be taken care of through global treaties in respect of free trade. Cultural exchange is ensured by modern liberties and electronic communications. With the end of the Cold War defence needs to be looked at in a new light.

Australia ought to put its trust in the United Nations and in whatever that organisation develops into. Enduring peace will be ensured not by national or regional militaristic cultures but by a developing world-wide ethic that military action against neighbours or citizens is untenable and of concern to the whole world community. This ethic will be best nurtured and managed in the only world-wide political organisation—the United Nations.

Should we take this direction, the states of Oceania, each of which has a vote in the UN and shares similar concerns to our own, will be important allies.

How Should a Monarchist Vote?

When I was a young boy, I used often holiday with my grandmother. I was very fond of her, even though she was rather straight-laced, and though she had a brittleness about her that terrified some of my siblings.

On one of these visits during our morning cup of tea and chat about serious matters, I said to her, 'Nan, I think we should get a new flag and a new national anthem'.

There was stunned silence. In my youthfulness, I had not realised the significance of my by now dead grandfather having risen from citizen soldier to high rank through two world wars. Nor had I realised that Nan's invitation to dinner on the Britannia had meant more than a fun night out.

Aunt Mary was promptly rung, and a dinner was arranged during which I was to be inducted into the marvels of the Empire. I wondered what it would be like.

The dinner was extraordinary—best china, best crystal, best food and best fizzy drink, though Nan and Mary drank something else. Neither the Empire nor the flag nor the anthem were mentioned, but I left feeling that the Empire must be a very elegant and gracious thing, whatever it might have been.

That was over forty years ago. I still respect my grandmother's allegiance and her pride at having been born in the age of Queen Victoria, but there are many Australians who were born even after me. The desire to relinquish the current relationship with the United Kingdom, which sees the Queen of England as Head of State of Australia, is strong.

Determined action, chance and compromise have brought us to a moment when we are to vote on whether to remain as we are or to relinquish this particular form of relationship and to make the Head of State of Australia an Australian.

The proposed change is fairly benign. It is much less radical than other forms being proposed by members of the community and will, therefore, be easier to adapt to and less dangerous overall. If we vote for this change, a new preamble will be needed. The one proposed is not outstandingly inspiring, but it is adequate, and something truly inspiring could be written only in more exciting times.

The republic will come soon, even if not at this referendum. A monarchist, then, would do well to vote 'yes' to both questions, because what that will bring about will be closer to what we now live than what is likely to come later. Should further change prove necessary, it can await its time.

Such a vote can be made with the elegance and grace of a world that I only glimpsed. I am sure that the present Queen will accept it in this way. Except for a few old rugby players, the English people themselves seem generally surprised that we have not made this move earlier.

Will Mr Howard's Stratagem Work?

A stratagem is a trick or device used in war against an enemy or in politics against an opponent. In politics, it takes the form of a pattern of action that seems to be fair and above board but which from the start loads the odds against the opponent.

When Mr Howard, the then Prime Minister, held a convention and referendum in the 1990's, the activity constituted an elaborate and expensive stratagem in that they appeared to give the people a choice about a most significant change of political form while at the same time robbing that act of choice of its essential structure. Mr Howard, nevertheless, quickly went on air to say that the people had made their choice, so that the issue could be put aside.

Choice depends on deliberation and is the selection of means with which to achieve an end, in this case the most appropriate form of government for Australia at the beginning of the twenty-first century. There are usually several ways or means in which an end or goal can be achieved, and deliberation is the process of weighing and considering those means both absolutely and in relation to one another. Only if this process is done well can choice be effective.

By demanding that the constitutional convention come up with a final model of a republic in one sitting and by putting only that model to the people, Mr Howard robbed the people of the opportunity to deliberate on alternative means to achieving the form of government that would best suit them. In so doing, he undermined the very possibility of the choice that he says the people have made. Some people could clearly cope with this, but a large number have done what people normally do when they are squeezed into a corner. They have said 'no'.

The question will not, however, go away. Sentiment is too strong and will grow as one generation replaces another. Further, the monarchy is already undermined by the very fact of a referendum and by the strong option for a republic that was expressed in that referendum. One thing that monarchists and Mr Howard forgot during the campaign is that the monarchy is not just an abstract structure but constitutional rule by a human person. The queen now finds herself in the untenable position of a monarch without significant support, though with her customary grace we can rely on her to give us time to sort ourselves out.

What is ahead of us, therefore, is a long and complicated process whereby all the possible options for change are reviewed, considered in turn and then either short-listed or discarded. This cannot happen in one convention but will require several conventions, plebiscites and referenda so that we can all deliberate on the various options that face us before making a choice.

Execution of such a process will require a new federal government with a fresh attitude to the people of Australia.

Corruption in the Olympic movement

The second of the nine fundamental principles of The Olympic Charter, which governs the International Olympic Committee (IOC) and all bodies that belong to the Olympic Movement by reason of having agreed to this Charter and of having been recognised by the IOC, runs as follows:

> Olympism is a philosophy of life, exalting and combining in a balanced whole the qualities of body, will and mind. Blending sport with culture and education, Olympism seeks to create a way of life based on the joy found in effort, the educational value of good example and respect for universal fundamental ethical principles.

During the last few years this Fundamental Principle has taken a battering, and it is not over yet. The first spate of scandals in the 1990's had to do with IOC members taking more by way of gifts and benefits than was allowed by the rules. This was cleaned up by sacking a few Africans, by rewriting the rules, this done by a committee led by then head of the IOC, Mr Samaranch, the man who put many of them in place, and by, we are told, a $225 million advertising program, which was meant to convince us all that the Movement has cleaned itself up.

What has been dealt with so far, however, amounts only to surface issues and symptoms. The corruption of individual members of the IOC flowed, it can be argued, out of the general moral condition of the IOC itself. The basis of this condition is that the IOC sees itself as 'the supreme Authority' in a movement that is 'universal and permanent' and covering six continents. It holds, in fact, absolute power and is answerable to no one but itself.

The more serious ethical condition of the Olympic Movement is the facility that the IOC and its subsidiaries such as the AOC have developed to pervert modern governments. We have seen this in Australia in such things as the speed with which the NSW Government had to sign the hitherto unstudied contract after it was announced that Sydney had won the games; as the very structure of SOCOG, which reduced its accountability and transparency to the dismay of two Auditors General; as the curious financial arrangements which saw the AOC guaranteed $100 million, in part, for relinquishing rights to 90% of the profits of a games now in financial difficulty.

In a modern liberal state, a primary function of government is to adjudicate fairness among its citizens, each of whom competes for economic and other advantages. One of the tools of assuring that this happens is transparency. The Olympic Committees have shown themselves to be well-oiled machines that can undermine both this transparency and government's role in the adjudication of fairness.

Activity of this sort is to a liberal democracy what treason was to a sovereign monarchy. Each acts to destroy the very nature of governance.

What Makes the News?

In an article in *The Sydney Morning Herald* in early 2000, called 'Covering Christianity: Media's Muted Voice', Chris McGillion contrasted the importance that religion and specifically Christian religion plays in the lives of most people in the West with the scant attention given to religion by the media in all its forms. He quoted the conclusion of another author, 'that the most important aspect of life is virtually exiled from public discourse throughout the English-speaking world'.

McGillion was mainly concerned with serious public discussion of the issues and values that underlie our culture and with how critical examination of them or lack of it affects its continued growth or decline. These are important issues. A similar contrast, however, can be made about what makes the news.

A case in point is the Jubilee 2000 celebration held at Stadium Australia on the Olympic site on 17 March 2000 and reported in *The Catholic Weekly* on 26 March. It brought together tens of thousands of school children in a total crowd of 93,742 for a display of mass movement, colour and technical wizardry in ceremonies that included a richly symbolic act of reconciliation with Aboriginal peoples. Nor was it lacking in dignitaries, since the governor general, the prime minister and the premier of the state of NSW were all there.

This event did receive some media coverage but not much. I was aware of brief glimpses of the crowd on two television news sessions. There were, no doubt, other reports, but the amount of reporting of such a large and colourful event seems to have been minimal. *The Herald* did reasonably well with a large picture and a column on page three.

What else did *The Herald* report on 18 Saturday 2000? It contained, of course, a lot of material of national and international interest. Of things that were good, it gave serious coverage to the queen's visit and, indeed, to the pope's impending visit to the Holy Land. The front page, however, led with further detailed scrutiny of the Pratt affair, for which, as Gerard Henderson argued in *The Herald* on the following Tuesday, there were no real grounds for invasion of privacy by the press. At the bottom of the front page continued the extraordinarily detailed coverage of the Moran family conflict in court.

Journalists and editors make judgements about what is of interest when they put news reports together. To some extent they reflect the interests of the community, but they also significantly form and develop those interests.

Had a five year old child sunk its teeth into the Achilles tendon of a policeman at the Jubilee celebration, that would have created more media interest, especially if it had been caught on camera. But of what real interest, apart from a morbid kind of entertainment, would it have been?

McGillion is right. Our society and its media need to become a lot more serious and a lot more clever.

The Moral Condition of the Current Government

Two objections are likely to arise when the moral condition of the current Commonwealth Government is questioned. Firstly, moral judgements are not applicable to governments. Secondly, even if they are, the current Government seems more moral than most.

The first objection betrays a view that would put politics outside morals. This was what Machiavelli did. It is not just a matter of whether political actions are done well or badly or that in a democracy we have often to accept deficiencies arising out of compromise and bungling. Rather, it has to do with whether we accept that there are moral dimensions to the action in which governments become involved.

The second objection betrays a rather narrow view of morality which sees it as comprised of a list of prohibitions that relate to what we might call licentious forms of life.

Morality is more embracing than is implied by the first objection and more complex than is implied by the second. One aspect of its complexity is the role of moral feeling, or what some philosophers call sentiment, in moral judgement and action.

A particular moral feeling of great importance is sympathy or 'the ability to share in another person's feelings and concerns, with the accompanying delight in their joys and grief at their sorrows'. David Hume made it a central plank in his theory of justice, and, however we might judge other aspects of Hume's moral theory, here he seemed to have it right, because unless we are able to read and to appreciate other people's feelings, there is little likelihood that we will act well in their regard.

That this is what the present government lacks, can be seen from its dealings with people in three distinct cases.

Mr Howard's inability to address the issue of reconciliation adequately showed not that his Government was unwilling to work to improve the welfare of Aboriginals but that he had little sympathy for their responses to the hurts that have touched their lives.

The Taxation Department's recent attempts to use the electoral rolls illegally and to sell information relating to ABN numbers shows not only a readiness to flout the law but also insensitivity to how Australians might feel about the inappropriate use of personal information to which the Government has privileged access.

In statements about refugees, Mr Ruddock has shown no sign of awareness of what it might feel like to live in detention behind barbed wire without significant rights and subject to an insensitive and inefficient bureaucracy.

These issues are complex and will always be difficult to resolve, but the current Government will always act badly because it lacks feeling for the people it governs.

The irony in all of this is that Adam Smith, to whom this Government would seem to owe much, saw a morality based on sympathy as fundamental and prior to his economic theory.

GM—What Scientists Cannot Know

The announcement of the decision of a federal parliamentary committee to clear the way for the introduction of genetically modified crops in Australia was reported with a strange rider. It said that the decision was subject to the committee receiving scientifically based objections to the safety of the program within a certain period.

There are significant problems with this approach. At heart, it relies on what we do not know in order to make judgements about what is the case or decisions about what we should do. In an extreme form it becomes the argument, we do not know of any ill effects, therefore, there are not any. Since ancient times it has been known as the fallacy of the 'argumentum ad ignorantiam' or the argument from ignorance.

This is the argument that tobacco companies have used to insist that tobacco smoking is safe. In a certain sense of the term 'scientific', namely, the identification of causal relationships, there is, I believe, still no scientific evidence that establishes that smoking is injurious to health. There is, however, another kind of scientific evidence based on the analysis of the occurrence of illness in thousands of people that shows after four centuries that smoking is indeed dangerous.

An area of serious concern with genetically modified crops has to do with an assumption behind claims of their safety that is philosophical rather than scientific. The assumption is that the replacement of one piece of genetic code with another will affect only the specific function addressed by that code and that after this change the overall genetic structure of the organism will remain stable.

Such an assumption makes sense within a mechanistic view of the universe. Such a view conceives things as a mix of particles and forces. Theoretically, any of the particles or larger units can be replaced much as we might replace components in a computer or in any machine.

It is questionable, however, whether this view is valid, especially when it is applied to organic beings, which in normal experience show themselves to act as a whole so that the whole organism is likely to react to a small change in some part of it.

The movement towards holistic medicine speaks to this concern. We have learnt that medical specialisation that looks at only a small part of the human being often tends to be ignorant of the broader causes of ill health.

'Scientific' claims of the safety of genetically modified crops are currently based on what scientists do not know. The drive to introduce these crops is based on many things, but not on necessity. Australia with its isolation is well-placed to wait and see what complications arise decades after the introduction of these crops. In the meantime, our food products could well be of premium value among those in the world who for whatever reason wish to avoid eating genetically modified crops.

Just Return it All to Sender

About a month ago, I received in the mail an 'Australian Lifestyle Survey'. It came from Australia Post and promised me the opportunity to win a BMW 316i. It also suggested that I would welcome this initiative of Australia Post to find out what I wanted from my post.

These surveys were distributed to letter boxes, and I assume that they have been or will be distributed around much of the country. I also expect that most sensible people will have thrown them in the recycling bin. Some, who feel that they would like a BMW, may have returned the questionnaire. A few, like myself, wondering what a lifestyle might consist of, might have read the document with mild interest.

On the face of it, the survey is fairly innocuous. It contains questions about leisure activities and purchasing patterns. On the other hand, it does seek information that we do not usually make available to others, for instance, personal financial information and medical information.

What is objectionable, however, in my view is that the survey collects responses to one hundred and twenty questions, which together generate a very specific profile of each respondent. That profile indicates the person's usual means of collecting information, patterns of spending and range of interests. In other words, it allows detailed analysis of how individuals and even neighbourhoods are likely to react to different marketing programs.

Much of this information is, of course, already gathered in data bases around the country. The difference is that in other cases privacy is secured by law. The history of credit card purchases, for instance, would be a very powerful marketing tool, but the law protects that information. We are required to give much information about ourselves to governments, but, again, the law limits the use of that information to the specific purposes for which it was sought.

The survey is conducted by Geospend, which on its website at www.auspost. com.au/geospend/ describes itself as 'the market and data analysis division of Australia Post and a leader in the market analysis industry'. It avoids the provisions of the privacy laws by insisting that the survey is optional, which indeed it is, and by undertaking not to pass on personal information to other agencies if a box at the end of the survey is ticked.

It seems to me that serious issues of personal freedom are raised when a government agency goes to this length to assemble and maintain information about individuals and when it contracts to other agencies to use that information and to match it with information held in the data bases of those agencies. We are put in a situation in which powerful concerns, of which we have no knowledge, are able to influence us strongly because of what they know about us.

It is surprising to me that the liberal media has not thought to look into the matter.

Towards a Vision of Planetary Government

The Archbishop of Milan, Cardinal Carlo Maria Martini, has recently been reported as advocating the development of a planetary system of government. The detail of his proposal is not clear, as it appeared in an essay in the Roman daily newspaper *La Repubblica*, was reported in the American *National Catholic Reporter*, and then noted in the Australian email based Catholic News.

What Cardinal Martini seems to have proposed is 'the creation of a "democratic and planetary" system of government that would transcend the powers of presently existing nation-states'. In some respects, the detail is not important, because we are still at a stage in which the very articulation of the idea is likely to be startling to many people. Yet to happen is the development of a vision of what human life on the planet would be like, if there were some universal form of government.

The Cardinal seems to have approached the issue through a discussion of human rights and specifically through recognition of the damage that is done to people when states collapse into chaos or regimes become oppressive. He suggests that when this happens there needs to be another authority greater than the national government that can act to protect its citizens.

Government has to do with bringing order to human affairs where people interact with each other in the same space. The purpose of this order is human well-being, often expressed in terms of justice. The relevant space is that within which people easily move. Both our understanding of what might constitute human well-being and our perception of the extent of the relevant space have changed dramatically in recent centuries.

There were times in the past when well-being related mainly to the very basic needs of food, which could be farmed, hunted or gathered locally, of shelter and of security, which might have meant as little as protecting an area as far as the eye could see. That is no longer the case. Our needs are complex. We live with machines, whose parts are made elsewhere, and our cities would collapse without them. New forms of transport and communication have brought the peoples of the world into close proximity with each other so that they are confronted by many common problems despite the apparent geographical distances between them.

The idea of planetary government is not completely new. We have recognised international law since at least the eighteenth century, and the very existence of such law raises questions about where it will be enacted and how it will be enforced. The second half of the twentieth century saw the development of the United Nations, a legal entity capable of arbitrating disputes between nations and of promoting good living conditions in member States.

The Cardinal is suggesting that it is time to investigate the possibility of going further, of developing democratic government at the international or planetary level.

Can we be Called a Just Nation?

It seems reasonable that on Social Justice Sunday we should ask ourselves whether, as a nation or as individuals or as part of any other grouping in society, we can be said to act with justice.

It is not an easy question to answer truthfully. A simple 'yes' or 'no' are likely to leave much detail untouched. An Australian way around this is to say, 'Oh, we're doing alright'. This is hardly a thoughtful examination and leaves both the diverse range of human interactions in which we are all engaged and the complexity of justice itself untouched. Dismissal of the question is more than likely a sign of awareness or suspicion of the existence of injustice in our dealings or else simply a sign of weariness with the moral life as a whole. On the other hand, the purpose of raising the question is not to inspire guilt but to motivate serious reflection about how we act in relation to other people and to encourage efforts to make things better.

Four major issues of justice confront us nationally at the present moment: a growing inequality in the distribution of wealth and opportunity in our community; on-going issues surrounding Aboriginal reconciliation, the effects of treatment Aboriginal peoples have received and our attempts to rectify this; our response to the needs of refugees, that is, of people who have fled their own homelands because conditions there are intolerable and have nowhere to go; the Federal Government's reluctance to face international scrutiny of conditions in Australia and of its own track record.

None of these issues allow of easy solution. Nor, for the most part will they be resolved by a few quick actions. Achievement of justice is a constant challenge, and perhaps the greatest fault is not to be involved in attempts to meet that challenge.

One lasting difficulty that surrounds justice is that those who have strength, in our society wealth and influence, have little need to fight for it. For those without these, justice is achieved only with great effort. How the weak are treated is a real measure of how just a society can claim to be.

It is simplistic to say that we are just because we keep the law and because we pay our debts. These are necessary but not sufficient. Beyond keeping the law stand questions both of whether the law is adequate to achieving justice and of whether in particular cases it works. Beyond paying our debts, we have to ask whether, when they have been paid, everybody is able to prosper.

A just nation will wrestle with these issues and its goal will be a society in which everybody is able to live well and in which the advantages and disadvantages of the times are evenly shared and a world in which to the degree possible similar conditions hold.

Concentration Camps in Australia

On October 13, 2000 an article in *The Sydney Morning Herald* suggested that 'refugees arriving by boat on Australian shores are now incarcerated in what amount to concentration camps in Derby, Port Hedland and Woomera'. It is a chilling statement, especially if one reviews the use of concentration camps during the twentieth century.

The author of this statement, Bruce Haigh, is neither a young hot-head nor uninformed. He is a former Australian diplomat and served on the Refugee Review Tribunal for six years up until this year. Given the tenor of his article, written at the beginning of this century, however, he was ideas were out of favour with then Commonwealth Government of Prime Minister Howard.

Refugee detention centres are generally recognised as legitimate institutions, which provide temporary accommodation while steps are taken to resolve questions about peoples' future residence. Although a form of incarceration and although in Australia looking more and more like prisons, detention centres are not prisons in the strict sense, because the detention is administrative rather than correctional. In other words, people are held pending the outcome of a process, not in order to be punished for a crime.

Internment in concentration camps, on the other hand, is generally directed at groups of people on ethnic or political grounds rather than at individuals. It is usually by decree rather than by legal process or trial and for purposes that range from state security in time of war to control of a population through terror. Since such camps operate outside of normal law and without respect for individual rights they readily degenerate into places of cruelty. Even when they do not, history rarely judges them to be legitimate.

The question raised by Haigh's article is, What would turn Australian immigration detention facilities into concentration camps?

Significant information about how detention centres are run is available on the website of the Department of Immigration and Multicultural Affairs (www.immi. gov.au). Among the documents on that site is one titled 'Immigration Detention Standards', which sets out the basic standards of treatment of detainees.

For the most part, there is much to recommend these standards, both in terms of care of refugees and in terms of the qualifications of staff who work in the centres. To understand Haigh or the dismay that has more recently broken out in respect of sexual abuse claims, we must look elsewhere.

It seems to me that there are four areas of concern. First and fundamental is the Government's intention, which, it is becoming clear, is to use the centres as deterrents to would-be asylum seekers rather than as places of care for persons involved in an administrative process. The second is the secrecy surrounding the camps and those that work there, because basic rights are readily lost in such a climate. The third is isolation, which must make even some of the Government's own standards impossible to implement. The fourth is unnecessary delay in processing claims, which can too readily be punitive.

The Making of Good Citizens

A consistent theme during the celebrations of the anniversary of the Snowy Mountains Project, a major hydro-electric scheme of the 1950's in New South Wales, was gratitude at the opportunity that the project had given to people from all parts of the world to settle in Australia and to make good. In interviews, person after person spoke about how grateful they had been that nobody had worried about where they came or about what difficulties might have affected their past. All that mattered was that they work hard. These people have become good citizens, and part of what has made them so is the welcome they received when they first arrived in Australia.

This was not a new experience for Australia. At the beginning of European settlement, many convicts, who had been condemned in Britain as unreformable and as of a bad class, became model citizens when freed and granted land in the new colony. In fact, it is a principle of life that when people who have lived in difficult circumstances are given fresh opportunity they often flourish. If this giving is accompanied by generosity, they remain grateful and maintain allegiance to whoever was generous to them.

It seems to me that this lesson is one that we as a nation and especially our Federal Government need to learn again in relation to asylum seekers and refugees.

Instability and internal war in parts of the world will ensure that Australia will be obliged to accept refugees from different parts of the world for some years to come for reasons both of justice and of international convention. This is happening at present and involves not only those chosen by immigration authorities in distant camps but also those asylum seekers, such as the 'boat people', whose arrival in Australia is unauthorised.

At present we treat these people in the worst possible way, yet we will no doubt expect that those who stay will become the best possible citizens. Granted that a wide ranges of issues and problems, some of them intractable, surround the questions of asylum and refugee status, there still seems to be something fundamentally wrong about the way in which we treat unauthorised entries, even if we judge this only in terms of our own long-term interests.

Practices like long-term mandatory detention, detention of children, granting of only temporary protection visas to proven refugees, placement of detention centres in remote areas so that humanitarian support is not available, long delays, uneven treatment of people with similar cases, installation of high security fences and razor wire and criticism of charities that have supported refugees released into the community all seem designed to ensure that people, whom we will expect to become good citizens, will have nothing to look back on in gratitude.

Many of these measures are simply punitive and attempt to stem the flow of asylum seekers. The government could do better, if it better understood human nature.

Keeping the Charity in Charities

There has been a great deal of media and public interest in a government inquiry into charities. The concern of most charities seems to have been about funding and in particular about how tax law relating to them and their various activities might be changed.

This inquiry follows a more broadly based inquiry into charities by the Industry Commission during 1993–95. Its report, 'Charitable Organisations in Australia', pointed out that in Australia, in contrast to some other countries, one of the major ways in which governments have fulfilled their obligations of care for the disadvantaged in the community has been to support community based organisations through taxation advantages and direct funding.

Historically, most of these organisations were Church-based, and charity was their primary motivation. The 1995 Report, however, preferred the term 'Community Social Welfare Organisations', taking into account both the fact that many present day charities act not out of religious motive but out of humanitarian concern and the fact of the high level of government involvement in these organisations through funding and through controlling legislation.

In the present inquiry, the term, 'charity' has to do with law and legal precedent going back to 1601 that governs the kind of exemptions from taxation to which a recognised charity has right. We should expect proposals for change in an area that has become very complicated. If the government is strong enough, legislative change might follow.

For Christians, a deeper concern sits below these discussions and the change they can be expected to induce. This concern is for the continuance of charity itself, meant in the primary sense of the injunction of Jesus to 'love your neighbour as yourself'. Although charity is to be extended by Christians to all human beings, the Parable of the Good Samaritan points to special care of those who are in any way struck down. This charity is, however, not just a benevolent response to need but an integral part of a Christian's response to God. It has as much to do with the life of the giver as with the need of the receiver.

Charity is exercised by individuals, but each of the Christian churches has also had traditions of charitable associations, such as the St Vincent de Paul Society and many religious orders in the Catholic Church, which can marshal the energies and resources of a large number of people who also act in communion with one another. The issue that these organisations are now facing is whether they become instruments of government as it seeks ways to exercise its social responsibilities more efficiently and effectively or whether they exercise the freedom to preserve a practical form of life that is primarily religious in motivation.

These issues are complex and will for historical reasons engage many charitable organisations in compromise.

The Reincarnations of One Nation

The rise of the One Nation Party in Australia in the 1990's has been a cause of concern for many. This was particularly so when reports emerged that members of the Australia First political party with its links to the League of Rights were joining One Nation. This raised the possibility of a third phase of One Nation's life and of the entry of fascism into the Australian political scene.

In its first phase in the second half of the 1990s, One Nation proposed policies that, on examination, fell apart. I suggested at the time that these policies were political opinions based more on irritation than on judgment and that the leader, Pauline Hanson, had a knack for articulating the irritation experienced around the country. This movement had the potential to be dangerous, if any of its policies were taken seriously.

In its second phase, brought to light during the Western Australian and Queensland elections a little later, One Nation was more transparent. Ms Hanson abandoned policy and acted as a spokesperson for still strong sentiment against government in general, which she simply wanted to get rid of. In the short term, this was dangerous mainly for politicians, particularly on the conservative side of politics, though lack of thought indicated a vacuum waiting to be filled.

The irritation and distress that stand behind these events is understandable. People have been deeply affected by rapid change: globalisation in its wide range of meanings from adaptation to technology to aggressive Americanisation; deregulation of institutions and markets on a wide scale; cultural diversification and its attendant difficulties in communication; reconciliation and its demand that we learn our history anew.

The possibility of this third phase is extremely worrying. Fascism, in its strictly intellectual sense, arises as a response to extreme distress in the face of change. By any account, we, as a nation, are at risk. The rise of fascism sees the accession to power of extreme right wing elements, though remarkably with strong popular support.

From the intellectual point of view, fascism is often bizarre, but Roger Scruton, in his *Dictionary of Political Thought*, suggests a list of features that are often present:

> nationalism; hostility to democracy, to egalitarianism, and to the values of the liberal enlightenment; the cult of the leader, and admiration for his [or her] special qualities; a respect for collective organisation, and a love of the symbols associated with it, such as uniforms, parades and army discipline.

One Nation is not yet fascist, and its National director, Frank Hoff, claims that it will keep 'nitwits' and 'nut-cases' out. That will be difficult, because of One Nation's own confusion and because fascism proceeds by conspiracy and cronyism, and, once in power, its exponents refuse negotiation and exercise absolute control.

We often wonder how so much of the world turned fascist during the first half of the twentieth century. Our wonder is magnified by the consequences of those events. Now is a good moment to recollect ourselves and to ensure that it does not happen again.

If We Go to War with China

If we go to war with China, my share of the fighting will be to deal with sixty-four late middle aged Chinese gentlemen, assuming that in each country the load of war is spread evenly across all age groups and both sexes. It will be helpful, if by then a change of government has seen Australian actor, Paul Hogan, become Foreign Minister and American actor, Arnold Schwarzenegger, become Defence Minister, the latter made possible by our ever closer links with the US.

A war would, of course, happen very differently, and one hopes that no such conflict ever eventuates, but the madness of it is implied in the current Commonwealth Government's response to both United States—China relations and the proposed missile defence system. While the United States and China were facing off over American spy flights and Taiwan, we had our own little arm wrestle on the side. Australia has been one of the very few nations to jump to support the United States' missile defence system, a program that will breach current international treaties limiting an arms race.

What Australia gets for its unqualified support of aggressive American initiatives is not clear. It is hardly security, because the US would be unlikely in its present frame of mind to commit the kinds of forces, namely, ground troops that would be needed in the kinds of conflict in which Australia is most likely to become involved. Trade is also tricky, because there profits rule, and we have already had to take the US to the World Trade Organisation over the sale of lamb.

It is more likely that the Australian Government is in awe of so-called military intelligence and advanced military technology, though these come at a high price and are little talked about.

We are living through a dangerous moment in the US. In a pattern going back at least to the War of 1812, upon the accession to power of the Republican Party after difficult years under a Democratic government, nothing is surer than that the new government will become warlike in its foreign relations and cut taxes. In 1812, this meant a comical war that nobody could afford. Australia would be wise to stand back and let the Bush regime settle in before making any firm commitments.

It is part of the mythology of the United States to need an enemy, and they have been looking around for one since the collapse of the Soviet Union. It is to be hoped that they get over their fascination with China, a nation that is at the moment interested in other things but which will react to aggression however subtle.

The talk of rogue states is hocus-pocus. It is sufficient to cause paranoia in the US but only a flimsy cover for a policy designed to beat a new and major enemy, whenever one is found or generated.

Parliamentary Privilege and its Abuse

Parliamentary privilege is a special liberty given to parliaments to go about their business without intervention from institutions or persons outside parliament. It is a necessary privilege because it allows a parliament to deliberate on matters of public significance without fear or reservation.

This privilege was originally concerned mainly with protection from the monarch. Today, however, it is directed more towards the courts and the possibility of individuals or corporations bringing action against parliamentarians for things said in the parliament. The most obvious case is defamation, but actions such as injunctions also apply. Again, the purpose of this kind of privilege is to enable parliament to do its work.

Wherever we find privileges, rights or powers, we also find the possibility of the abuse of these privileges, rights or powers. The potential for and seriousness of abuse is generally related to the extent of the privilege. In the case of parliamentary privilege, the potential for abuse is very high, because only parliaments themselves—through their privileges committees—can act against parliamentarians.

The most serious form of abuse of parliamentary privilege occurs when parliamentarians voice damaging allegations against individuals on matters that are not germane to the business of the parliament and especially when the allegations are not true or not proven. The seriousness of the abuse lies in the fact that citizens have no recourse.

Australian parliaments have seen serious cases of abuse of privilege in recent years. In the NSW Parliament, allegations made by Deirdre Grusovin and later those by Franca Arena in naming persons they believed to be paedophiles proved to be made on false information, and in each case the Parliament acted. In the former case, Parliament acted well and Mrs Grusovin accepted her punishment graciously. In the latter case, Mrs Arena avoided expulsion from Parliament only because the NSW Liberal Party preferred to follow its own political interests and embarrass the Government of the day rather than to see justice done.

The problem we face in any attempt to fight the abuse of privilege is that parliaments are not likely to write rules or to act in ways that curtail their own liberty unless there is strong public protest. It seems to me that the case of the former Premier of Western Australia, Carmen Lawrence, which was fought on the question of lying to parliament would have been better fought on the basis of damage done to citizens through a parliamentary statement that had nothing to do with the business of parliament.

The action of then Senator Bill Heffernan in naming an Aboriginal person a few years ago under privilege in the Federal Parliament was, in my judgement, an abuse of privilege brought on by a similar misuse of journalistic licence, the imprudent outspokenness of others, and by Senator Heffernan's own passions. We are yet to see how Parliament responds, but the curious assumption in many of these cases has been that one form of abuse can cure another.

Jesus Mary and Joseph—Refugees

'After the wise men had left, the angel of the Lord appeared to Joseph in a dream and said, "Get up, take the child and his mother with you, and escape into Egypt, and stay there until I tell you, because Herod intends to search for the child and do away with him". So Joseph got up and, taking the child and his mother with him, left that night for Egypt, where he stayed until Herod was dead. This was to fulfil what the Lord had spoken through the prophet, "I called my son out of Egypt"' (Matt 2:13–15).

This narrative from Matthew's Gospel tells us a great deal about Jesus, Mary and Joseph as refugees. According to the narrative, Joseph had no choice but to flee from danger. He had good grounds to be certain that Herod would kill the infant Jesus, if he found him. We have no reason to suspect that Joseph wanted to go to Egypt, and, in fact, the story tells of the family's return to Nazareth after the danger was over. It is implied that the family could survive in Egypt, and it is reasonable to assume that this meant that Joseph could find work.

And so it has been in all times. Whenever human beings become convinced that they are in serious danger in their homelands, they move, and it is natural that they do so. They do not ordinarily move by preference, because we are beings who are rooted in the earth and that long for the look and the smell of the places where we were born, even if life is poorer in that place. No, they move from fear, fear of death or of the impossibility of the continuation of family life lived according to custom and religion.

The story in Matthew does not suggest that when Joseph got to Egypt he was told that Egypt was a sovereign state and that it was illegal for him to enter, unless, of course, he had lots of money. Nor does it suggest that the family was locked in a camp, in which they could find neither work nor the opportunity for the activities that normally fill all human lives. Nor does it suggest that they were locked behind chain wire fences cloaked with razor wire not so much to keep them in but to keep others out and to make the environment of the camp harsh.

We in Australia are at risk that future generations of Australians will judge us as having remained silent and turned our backs when our government levied cruel and unusual punishments on people who had fled their homelands in fear. Much of the civilized world already judges us that way, and that is how our government would have it, because it believes that such a reputation will discourage other people from fleeing here.

Lying in Politics: Destruction of Facts

In her landmark essay, 'Truth and Politics', the American political philosopher, Hannah Arendt, remarked wryly that 'when Trotsky learned that he had never played a role in the Russian Revolution, he must have known that his death warrant had been signed'. Her point was that once the Soviet regime had lied in its history books about the fact of Trotsky's not insubstantial role in the revolution, it needed to eliminate him so that his existence would not challenge the lies it had told. He was assassinated on the second attempt in Mexico.

Arendt's concern is that lies about matters of fact have become much more part of political life. It has always been the case that statesmen and diplomats have lied about secrets and intentions, but mostly to enemies. Today, however, we all have to deal with the mass manipulation of fact and opinion through image-making and through the rewriting of history aided by modern communications technologies. The lies are told to all to be believed by all, even the tellers of lies.

Examples abound. When Benjamin Netanyahu said in Melbourne three weeks ago, 'Jerusalem has been a Jewish city for 3000 years', he obliterated all memory of the Babylonians, of the Romans, of Byzantium, of the British, to name just a few. Similarly, his attribution of sole responsibility for violence and terrorism in the Middle East to the Palestinians implied that the twentieth century, at least from the 1917 Balfour Declaration on, had not happened.

The recent Independent Commission Against Corruption (ICAC) investigation into the New South Wales Government's handling of a high school incident in April and of claims about the presence of a gun revealed in the Government's media advisers both a desire for a gun to make the story run and a failure to check whether indeed there was one.

Factual truth has to do with facts and events and comes out of our living together. Unlike rational truth, for instance, the conclusions of geometry, which, if lost, might be rediscovered, factual truth is fragile, because it is about things that might have been otherwise. Once these are irrevocably lost, they cannot be recovered.

Though fragile, factual truth is rather stubborn, because while any witnesses or any records remain, facts can reassert themselves. One of the problems the Soviet Union faced was whether it should attempt to destroy all copies of those issues of journals in which Trotsky had written articles. It is in the recovery of facts such as these that institutions like universities do service to political life, though not as participants.

We are not immune from these kinds of failures in truthfulness in religion. The excesses of the Taliban, for instance, are a predictable outcome of religion that that has lost the ability to subject its claims to rigorous intellectual scrutiny and that has ascended to political power.

The Fragility of the Modern State

The monstrous scale and tragic nature of the terrorist attacks in New York and Washington on September 11 threw into contrast the enormous power and the extreme fragility of the technologically and economically based modern states in which we, particularly in the West, live.

The modern state has been an experiment in stability, and it has in many respects been very successful. Rather than populations having to adjust to changes of conditions and direction at the whim of one prince or baron after another, it is the states themselves that reign supreme according to rules enshrined in constitutions. That such an arrangement might work has meant that these states have had to be extremely powerful. Their power has had to be supported by force exercised by police agencies and the military and founded on technology.

Within states, the extraordinary power of the state has been moderated by instruments such as the separation of the powers of the legislative, judicial and executive branches of government, regular elections and the rule of law. Even so, governments have from time to time attempted to overrule the rights of groups of citizens or aliens.

In relations between states, we have not done so well, and for much of the twentieth century, peace, when it existed, amounted to a state of enmity balanced by force. Attempts to find better means to attain peace, such as the United Nations, have had limited success, often thwarted by the stronger members. Neither friendship nor respect can be said to have bound the world together. National interest has reigned.

At the time of writing, it was not known who had been responsible for the attacks in New York and Washington, but two things were clear. Firstly, our modern states with their dependence on bricks and mortar, machinery and confident economies are extremely vulnerable. Bombs and missiles are not necessary, for these states carry the instruments of their own destruction within them.

Secondly, the attacks were highly symbolic. Horrible as they were, far greater devastation could have been wrought just as easily. Instead, they focussed dramatically on institutions of economic, military and state power. However much we condemn them, they had meaning, and that meaning had something to do with a human response to force whether legal or diplomatic or military or economic or cultural.

The event could be a major turning point in world history at the beginning of the third millennium. Whether or not it is, will depend on how it is handled. We should expect some retribution from the United States, but, should the event lead to policies that rely mainly on force at the expense of efforts to build mutual understanding and respect across the world despite differences, our future is dim. One can fear both that it may be too late and that there may be no leaders who are capable of plotting a course for world peace.

Face to Face with Fortune

Several years ago, fortune entered into Australian political life in the shape of a leaky Indonesian fishing boat and of a rather determined Norwegian ship's captain. In the ordinary course of events, neither the fishing boat nor the captain would have had much impact on Australian life. Even now few of us have any idea how much cargo this particular captain has carried to and from Australia. The boat carrying asylum-seeking refugees could have been just one more in the current wave of boat people stimulated by crises in the Middle East and by the collapse of our relationship with Indonesia.

By chance, the two came together, and their coming together plunged this country into political crisis. It need not have been a crisis except that the Federal Government saw in it opportunity, opportunity both to stop the movement of refugees, with which it had been irritated for some time, and to shore up electoral support in an election year. The Prime Minister, in fact, acted quickly and decisively in taking fortune in his hands.

Our culture has almost lost any sense of the presence of fortune in the world. Unlike ancient peoples, we are not very conscious of chance happenings that bring advantage or disadvantage with them. While some of the reasons for this are religious, our mindset is particularly modern and has much to do with Descartes and Bacon's project of the mastery of nature and Machiavelli's project of the mastery of fortune. We expect to be able to control whatever is around us. We reject the thought that we might have to live with uncertainty.

It was Aristotle who established the reasonableness of chance working in our lives. Chance events, he showed in his *Physics*, are not events that happen without causes. Rather they are caused incidentally by the conjunction of overlapping lines of causality, a little like the intersecting purposes of the Captain of the Tampa and of the sinking refugees. For Aristotle, these kinds of events constantly impinge on our lives, and, in the political sphere, we rely on men and women of prudence to act in the best possible ways.

Machiavelli thought differently. He was aware of fortune and of how cruel it could be, but his advice was to master it, to take every turn as an opportunity and to press it to one's own purposes. He recognised both the strength and the cunning that would be needed, and his advice has shocked new readers for four and a half centuries.

Those who would be Machiavellian ought to listen to another ancient. Boethius in his *Consolation of Philosophy* has Fortune personified say, "Inconstancy is my essence".

For some weeks, extraordinary events overseas and in Australia have impacted upon our lives. All most of us could do was observe and wonder. We could also hope and pray for prudence in the halls of power.

What Kind of Justice?

In his State of the Nation address to both houses of Congress ten days after the September 11 terrorist attacks, the then US President, George Bush, promised that justice would be done. Indeed, there is justice to be done in the aftermath of a great crime, an act, in my view, that would best be called a crime against humanity.

Mr Bush used the term, 'justice', four times, three of them in the same sentence: 'Whether we bring our enemies to justice, or bring justice to our enemies, justice will be done.' Justice stands central to whatever the US or the world might do, just as it is central to all forms of political association. How justice is to be worked out, however, is often difficult and promises to be so in this instance. Much of the difficulty lies in the complexity of justice itself.

At first sight, it would seem that Mr Bush was talking about retributive justice or just punishment, which is distinguished from and in civilised society takes the place of revenge. It is enacted through law and precedent and takes place in courts that are removed from the pressures of daily executive decision and politics.

Closer examination, however, suggests that this is not what Mr Bush was talking about. One brings such justice to criminals not to enemies, and the balance of the speech had more to do with war (mentioned ten times) and terrorists or terrorism (mentioned twenty-five times). If the speech was a declaration of war, Mr Bush will have to work out not only what kind of a war it is and who are the enemy but also the grounds on which such a war is justified and the means by which its engagement will be kept in proportion. Notions of 'collateral damage', for instance, stand contrary to justice.

There are, however, other aspects of justice that are relevant. Mr Bush should have addressed these when he asked and appeared to answer the question, 'Why do they hate us?' Distributive justice pertains to the distribution of goods in a community, and in the age of globalisation, serious attention needs to be paid not simply to inequality but to gross distortion of opportunity to satisfy basic needs and values around the world. Perhaps Mr Bush intends to redress these issues.

Commutative justice is consequent on and deals with due proportion of gain or loss in transactions. The areas of the world and the peoples now likely to find themselves enemies have been dealing with the West for over a century and have not done well.

Finally, there is a sense of what is called universal justice that has to do with happiness and well being in political association. This has not generally been well achieved globally or within states. Its wider achievement would be a great thing, but it will be extremely difficult. It will call for much more than war.

People who Throw their Children into the Sea

'I certainly don't want people of that type in Australia; I really don't,' said then Prime Minister, John Howard, on Melbourne radio 3LO on or around 9 October 2001. The question that has to be raised about this statement is whether it was a racist comment. I mean racist here not in the casual and pejorative sense but in the moral sense that I investigated in an earlier essay.

I am discussing neither the fact of there being a problem about asylum seekers entering Australia by boat nor the question of how great that problem might be compared to what is experienced in Europe and America or in Pakistan and Jordan. Nor am I discussing the government's policy of deterring these people at all costs or even the implementation of that policy. My concern is with public discourse and with the kind of language that our political leaders have used in promoting their policies.

Mr Howard's statement looks racist. It is a dismissive generalisation expressed with some vehemence that characterises a group of people as a type or kind so fundamentally different from us that we would not be prepared to have them in the country.

Mr Howard would not agree with this and would surely point out that he is a fair-minded person and that the statement was made in the context of people who had 'thrown their children into the sea' in order to have them rescued by the Australian navy.

There are problems with Mr Howard's position. Firstly, we know few firm facts about the incident, and for some years it has been government practice to reveal isolated damaging facts about asylum seekers while enforcing a mantle of strict secrecy upon all else to do with them. Secondly, what kind of people does throw its children into the sea? Mr Howard seems to assume wicked people, though it is more likely that they are desperate people. Thirdly, how many of us have enjoyed swimming in warm calm tropical seas close to boats and even in life jackets?

We cannot know Mr Howard's intentions, but rhetorical analysis looks also at intended or likely audiences and at the probable impact of statements on them. Mr Howard's statement is examinable in these terms because it is a sound bite uttered on radio by a politician eager both to argue a policy and to win an imminent election.

We Australians do know who these people are, because they have been daily in the news since the Tampa crisis. They are mainly Afghanis and Iraqis, Moslems, people of darkish skin. In the current climate, many of Mr Howard's listeners are likely to assume that all of these people are of a kind who would 'throw their children into the sea'.

This government has led us into racial prejudice not as an end but as a means, and we are poorer for it.

What is Parliament for?

Australian politics in the second decade of the Twenty-first Century has been
marked by dysfunction in the Australian Parliament. The dysfunction might be
put down to the difficulties of a hung parliament, a parliament in which neither
major party is able to govern in its own right on the basis of a clear majority, but in which government has been put together through agreements with
minor parties or independent members of parliament. This might be seen as
a temporary difficulty that is likely to be experienced occasionally under the
Westminster system of government. There are, however, deeper reasons for the
dysfunction, which are disturbing in the long term.

Neither major party has been able to generate the kind of leadership political
parties and governments need. In the Labor Party's desperation, Kevin Rudd
came too soon to the position of Prime Minister and failed. Julia Gillard has not
been able to win the electorate's sympathy. Post Howard, the Liberal Party has
run through a succession of leaders none of whom have proved adequate. The
critical question is whether this is simply a matter of the moment or of genera-
tional change or whether it is an indicator that our society is lacking competent
people who are willing to run for office.

Part of the problem is the nature of debate in the Australian Parliament. This
has long been recognised as forensic, the rhetoric of the law courts, rather than
deliberative, the rhetoric proper to assemblies. Foreign commentators politely
refer to the Australian Parliament as robust. There are factors that make it worse,
such as the residual bitterness of the Keating-Howard conflict and the televising
of Question Time, which has made Parliament a forum for cheap point-scoring
rather than for serious scrutiny of the actions of Government.

Tony Abbot has led the opposition in an extreme form of oppositional politics that can only be destructive of Parliamentary process. It has seen him reject
policy and law that he would otherwise have supported simply to score political points against the Government. He has also refined a mode of commentary
that extracts and attacks small aspects of government policy in order to oppose.
While he avoids lying, his speech is essentially untruthful. The media rarely un-
ravels this, preferring instead to enjoy the conflict.

Parliament should be more serious than this. It is, indeed, a court in which
significant issues of the day are debated, but the discussion should be serious
and directed to problems faced by the country and to the country's future. The
Parliament's primary purpose, however, is to write good law, and in this it has
failed as laws have become compromised by political manoeuvring.

A bicameral parliament offers the opportunity for laws to be made better
by long and serious discussion that allows the interests of different parts of the
community to be heard. In the end compromise is needed, but it should generate outcomes that most can respect. Politics that is simply oppositional and
obstructive raises the spectre of increasingly poor law.

ABORIGINAL RECONCILIATION

Aboriginal Reconciliation

27 May 2007, marks the fortieth anniversary of the referendum that supported the constitutional amendment that meant that Aboriginal and Torres Straight Islander peoples could vote and be counted in the national census. Objectively and symbolically this established these peoples as full citizens of the state that claimed sovereignty over the land in which they had lived for some 40,000 years.

We ought to be joyful about this referendum–that it took place, that it was won, and that it was won by a yes vote comprising over 90% of voters. It is no longer thinkable that a situation in which these peoples were without full recognition as citizens could be considered just.

It is less than a life-time since this change was made, and the process that it initiated goes on. We are still coming to terms with the full implications of what that vote meant. In modern societies citizenship implies equality—equality before the law, comparable liberty and equality of opportunity. It also implies recognition of persons—their feelings, their identity, and their relationships. Of late we have come to recognise the significance of the cultural and ethnic identity of persons and to value the diversity that it brings to a state.

This week another new initiative begins—the Australian Reconciliation Convention. The Council for Aboriginal Reconciliation, which has prepared for the convention, has as its vision 'A united Australia which respects this land of ours, values the Aboriginal and Torres Straight Islander heritage, and provides justice and equity for all'. Its goal is to bring resolution to outstanding issues by the centenary of Federation in 2001.

The Council envisages a process in which we together explore our history, acknowledge past injustice and discover a common heritage. It further envisages programs to remove disadvantage, acts of reconciliation and renewal of our national identity.

We may have once been blind to the need for reconciliation and ignorant of how best to act in relation to aboriginal peoples. It is a grace of our time that we know that something has to be done, even if some of the detail remains obscure. To reconcile means, after all, to return to friendly relations. To not desire that would be inhuman and unchristian.

This is not to say that the process will not be difficult. We will be learning to do new things. The confusion following Mabo and Wik had not to do with principle but with the inadequacy of existing law and procedure to deal with new situations. Considerable effort is, however, justified both by past neglect and by the goal of a richer national identity.

The process may also for a time be expensive, but given efforts to avoid waste, what is money when the dignity of a people is at stake? What we are seeking is wholeness—wholeness for all Australians individually and as a nation.

The Importance of Our Aboriginality

A few years back in his draft preamble, the then Prime Minister, John Howard, acknowledged the Aboriginal peoples in this way: 'Since time immemorial our land has been inhabited by Aborigines and Torres Strait Islanders, who are honoured for their ancient and continuing cultures.' What he did then, was to place them first in a list of peoples who make up our Commonwealth and express some appreciation of what they bring to it.

Criticism of the draft has said that this is not enough and, in particular, that it is nothing more than acknowledgment of an inescapable historical fact. Many think that the proposed preamble should have rectified past injustice by giving special recognition to Aboriginal peoples. The Constitutional Convention had proposed that they should be called 'custodians' of the land.

What might a preamble to a constitution do? There are two things that it can do. First, it can say who we are; second, it can perform an act.

Mr Howard did not do either of these very well. His act was to 'commit ourselves to this Constitution'. That act stands outside a constitution. The act of constitution itself is the act of enactment, or in this case re-enactment. That should be said.

In saying who we are, he noted the series the peoples who arrived on this continent and listed a collection of values that could belong to any liberal democracy in the world. More is needed.

There is a tendency in the modern world to imagine that all peoples could be the same. The more we live in machine-driven environments, the more this might seem possible. The invention of cyberspace suggests that lives and cultures might be able to exist without any reference to place at all. Yet these are fallacious. As material beings we belong on the earth and from it take our sustenance.

When we ask what is it that makes Australians unlike any other people on earth, a significant part of the answer has to be that it is the place on earth where we live. This is a vast dry continent. It is unlike Britain, where it rains all the time, or America whose land, though vast, is rich and productive.

When European settlers first came to this continent they neither understood it, as is shown by their art, nor knew how to live in it. They were also rather arrogant in pretending that much of it would be better, if it were turned into an English garden.

Now their descendants are finding that to live here one must understand the land in image and in symbol and that that can be best done by learning from its first inhabitants, who have lived here so long and who have lived so close to the earth. In attempting to capture our identity, the preamble must show that to be Australian is to take on aboriginality so as to become more intimately joined to the land.

The Power to Forgive

The Jewish political philosopher, Hannah Arendt, defined the faculty of forgiveness as 'the possibility of redemption from the predicament of irreversibility, that is, of being unable to undo what one has done though one did not, and could not, have known what one was doing'.

Although she credits Jesus of Nazareth as the discoverer of the role of forgiveness in the realm of human affairs, her analysis is political and philosophical rather than religious. As such, her claims are interesting, because we can restate them in the public arena without risk of being told that we are imposing religious beliefs on non-believers.

Arendt's interest in forgiveness lies in its being the remedy to one of the problems of human action. When we act freely and in the light of an understanding or interest of the moment, we act in a truly human way, but we can also make mistakes, and often they hurt other people. Were we not able to be released from the consequences of these mistakes by being forgiven, we would spend our lives 'confined to one single deed from which we could never recover'. In other words, having made our first serious mistake, we would never be effective agents in human affairs again.

In recent years in Australia, the Aboriginal community has shown that it has understood the possibilities for better life for all Australians that lie in forgiveness. Leaders of the calibre of Patrick Dodson and Lowitja O'Donoghue have pointed the way and worked with a broad spectrum of people for Aboriginal reconciliation. They have understood that such reconciliation is not just for Aboriginal peoples but for non-Aboriginal Australians as well. It is in being forgiven for mistakes of the past that we will all find new possibilities for action.

Forgiveness, however, is not a solitary act. Forgiveness 'enacted in solitude or isolation remains without reality and can signify no more than a role played before one's self'. In other words, forgiveness is relational and must be played out between persons. Although it can be offered, it cannot be given without being sought. That is why it is important that we say, 'Sorry', at all levels of national life.

There can be no doubt that Aboriginal peoples have been hurt as a consequence of European settlement in Australia and of subsequent attempts to live alongside those who lived here previously. Hurt experienced by many still living is well documented in *The Stolen Generations*. To say, 'Sorry', does not necessarily attribute malice to those who caused the hurt nor does it imply a continuing personal guilt of their descendants. What it recognises is that damaging mistakes were made, the consequences of which are with us today.

The grace of the present moment is that Aboriginal peoples are seeking reconciliation. Not to accept that grace and so to cooperate in reconciliation, would be to make a mistake that would restrict the scope of action by all future Australians.

Reference: Hannah Arendt, *The Human Condition* (Chicago: The University of Chicago Press, 1958), 236–243.

Aboriginal Reconciliation: What kind of Justice?

On 27 May 2000, the Council of Aboriginal Reconciliation unveiled its declaration of reconciliation. It was an important moment in the process of reconciliation and the culmination of the work of the Council. This moment called for some assessment of how we have gone.

There are pluses and minuses. Much has been done particularly in regard to recognition of Aboriginal peoples and of their history and culture, and many non-Aboriginal people have undergone deep changes of attitude. Further, Aboriginal people themselves have developed prominent voices in the discussion of public affairs, which, in a political society, is a singular good. Other things remain to be done.

Something that seems unlikely to be resolved is the Aboriginal peoples' repeated request that the Commonwealth say sorry for past injuries and the then prime minister, John Howard's stubborn refusal to do so.

One way through this impasse might be to examine competing senses of justice. Aboriginal people are looking for justice because they have been hurt and excluded, and they are seeking reconciliation as a step towards healing. The Prime Minister is insistent that he need not apologise for something done by previous generations.

Philosophers distinguish two basic kinds of justice—distributive justice and commutative justice.

Distributive justice has to do with the various goods and opportunities that are available to the members of a community and with how they are distributed. What I believe Aboriginal people are seeking is fairness in the distribution of these goods—access to all the rights, privileges and opportunities that flow from citizenship.

Commutative justice follows human interaction and has to do with how one action might demand another, such as in a financial transaction. One kind of commutative justice is retributive justice, which applies when damage has been done and retribution or punishment is required.

It seems to me that John Howard was thinking only of retributive justice. The government's conduct in response to the report on the stolen generations bears this out. As this is the justice of punishment and payment, resolving the issues confronting us in this way is likely to be both very expensive and very damaging to all concerned. We, Aboriginal and non-Aboriginal alike, would all be far better off, if we were to concentrate on the demands of distributive justice.

The place that 'Sorry' has in this scheme is that it will enable forgiveness and with forgiveness, healing and mutual respect, all basic goods of human society, which under distributive justice are meant for all. It will also take us all closer to recognising the truth, and this can set us free.

If the Prime Minister cannot say 'Sorry', and perhaps he cannot, our Head of State should, not just as a personal statement, but on behalf of the nation.

Pilgrimage to the Heart

In June 2000 eight Australian heads of churches and eight youth representatives of those churches together with representatives of the National Council of Churches Aboriginal and Islander Commission, support personnel and media representatives will leave the national capital for a week-long pilgrimage to Uluru ('Ayers Rock') at the heart of the Austalian continent. The pilgrimage took a route through New South Wales, and South Australia (Narrandera, Cobar, Wilcannia, Broken Hill, Port Augusta and Coober Pedy) and concluded with a Pentecost Sunday Ceremony of Reconciliation in the Mutitjulu Community at Uluru.

Along the way, the pilgrims met with people from local churches and communities to hear their stories, to share their company and to pray with them. We can expect that much will come out of these meetings in the long term.

While there are many aspects of this pilgrimage that are worthy of exploration, at heart it was an act of religion giving praise to God and asking for salvation, salvation viewed at this moment as freedom from the divisions that afflict our life together. The pilgrimage therefore, took as its theme reconciliation—reconciliation between the Christian churches, reconciliation between the different cultures of the people who live in Australia, reconciliation between indigenous and other Australians.

How many of us have been to Uluru? Probably a significant proportion of Australians visit Uluru at some time during their lives. Why do we go? Each of us ought to ask ourselves this question. Is it because 'it's there'? Or, is it because, in a sense, it is all that appears to be there once one ventures into the flat wilderness of central Australia? Is it because we recognise that in varying senses it is at the heart of our continent?

There was a time when many of us went there to climb the Rock simply to get to the top. It was a challenge. After Uluru was given back to the Anangu People in 1985, they began gently to instruct us in how to view the place differently. Without stopping us from climbing it, they helped us understand and appreciate the ways in which its shade and water foster life and the meaning that has developed through their own long residence in its shadow.

The Pilgrimage to the Heart prompts us all to journey into our own hearts while, at the same time, journeying in spirit to the heart of our great land. As it seeks healing of division it will draw Christian sacredness from the sacredness of the land itself. It may bring some fruit to Jesus' prayer that 'all may be one'.

At the present time, Western culture has but a weak hold on symbols that can give its participants meaning individually and communally. If it is successful, this pilgrimage may well bring unity through a symbolic act of national and religious significance.

Moral Leadership in Australia

It struck me while watching Corroboree 2000 on television on 27 May 2000 and again while walking across the Harbour Bridge the following day that the movement for Aboriginal reconciliation, of which the work of the Council for Aboriginal Reconciliation is part, is providing some of the most significant moral leadership that is to be found in Australia today.

On one hand, this was indicated by the fine character of the Aboriginal leaders in the reconciliation process, who despite their own experience of hardship and disadvantage have been able to act with dignity, strength and concern for others. On the other hand, it was indicated by the presence in the march of such large numbers of young people, who were walking peacefully and publicly for a vision of good in which they believed. These youth, young men and women in their twenties, whose morals are often lamented by their elders, showed that they believed strongly in justice and right for all and that they were prepared to act for what is good.

While morals are, indeed, largely a matter of character and action, we have, too, various intellectual traditions that have tried to give an account of the moral life. Again, the movement of reconciliation is showing real leadership because it is thoughtfully bringing these accounts together. This is demonstrated in the Australian Declaration Towards Reconciliation.

Broadly speaking, moral thinking has devolved into two main languages, the language of virtue and the language of rights. The two are always with us, but if we look to the ancient and medieval West we find predominantly the language of virtue, and if we look to the modern world we find the language of rights. Each of these has its relation to law, but only as something extrinsic to the moral life itself.

The Declaration engages both these languages. It proposes virtue—courage, truthfulness, justice, respect, hope. It claims human rights. What is extraordinary about the Declaration is that it puts them together in a coherent manner, something rarely done, and that in doing so it brings integrity to the life it proposes.

Rights, it says, are not achieved without virtue—courage that enables us to face difficult things; justice that ensures that the rights we claim are not just our own but are those of all Australians; hope that looks to a future and, indeed, to a common future. It is little wonder, then, that the Declaration so easily links rights with responsibilities to others, something that contemporary voices often fail to do.

On the other hand, it implicitly recognises what modernity saw so clearly, namely, that to talk only of virtue left ample opportunity for the strong and apparently virtuous to trample the weak. Bitter experience has taught that, when justice is left only in the hands of 'the just', those who are different or weak are liable to suffer.

Something We Cannot Ignore

The Royal Australian and New Zealand College of Psychiatrists agreed to a position statement on the Stolen Generations in April 1999, which was made more generally available to the public on their website in July of the same year. The statement is careful but unambiguous. In part, it states

> that past practices of state-sanctioned abduction of children from parents and from their culture are cruel and wrong. The psychological trauma involved has life-long mental health consequences and significant inter-generational effects. As a result of this practice, many indigenous Australians suffer severe emotional distress including continuing disruption of family relationships and secondary social, psychological and psychiatric problems have arisen from the disruption of culture and community.

At this stage, I do not want to comment further on the content of the statement itself. That can be read on the web. Rather, what I want to suggest is that no Australian who holds an opinion on the condition of our Aboriginal peoples can afford to ignore this statement. How is it that I can say that?

The statement is authorised by the Council of the professional organisation whose members are the best qualified in our community to make judgements about the damage accruing to people from past and consistent policies and practices. It is not, therefore, the opinion of one perhaps eccentric and over-focussed individual but a considered judgment that is representative of the whole profession.

To ignore the considered judgment of any professional organisation in the area of its competence is to proclaim ignorance as a virtue. To wipe such an opinion aside without careful consideration is to declare oneself to be prejudiced, that is, to have formed one's opinion prior to and irrespective of any examination of the information and advice relevant to the particular issue.

One of the social ills of our time is that many Australians have taken the view that ignorance and prejudice are legitimate conditions of mind. It is a view that was made acceptable by Pauline Hanson and the One Nation movement. It surfaces in the claim that one has the right to one's opinion, which is as good as anybody else's, and in the assertion that nothing will change it.

Opinions come to us easily, as is seen in the case of young children, who pick up and repeat their parents' opinions without any real grasp of what they might mean or any attempt to substantiate them. Intellectual maturity comes to us when we are able to step back from our opinions, to examine them in the light of wider evidence than we first had and then to make a judgment about their validity or invalidity.

A good test of intellectual liveliness, therefore, is to ask oneself whether one's opinions on a range of issues changed and developed during recent years. An answer, 'No', would indicate that one had not thought for some time.

Becoming Clear about Racism

Talk of racism filters through our lives and we have laws against certain forms of it, but what is it? We experience various forms of negative feelings towards other people—dislike, incomprehension, even hatred. Are these what lie at the base of racism, and, if so, do they become such only when directed at people technically of other races?

Raimond Gaita, Professor of Philosophy at the Australian Catholic University, gives an account of racism in his recent book, *A Common Humanity*, which, I believe, removes much of the confusion that sometimes surrounds use of the term, while at the same time showing how radically evil racism is.

Gaita proceeds by way of examination of a number of examples. One is a comment by the Protector of Aborigines in Western Australia at the beginning of the twentieth century, who said that he 'would not hesitate for one moment to separate any half-caste from its Aboriginal mother, no matter how frantic her momentary grief might be at the time. They soon forget their offspring.'

There are many things wrong with this statement, but a clue to its racist nature lies in the generalisation of the last sentence. 'They' refers not just to a few Aboriginal women who may have been so damaged by other trauma that they, like others, could, in fact, have forgotten, but to all Aboriginal women. 'They' also distances these women from 'we', the white women and men who normally would never forget. The fact that the Protector could acknowledge frantic momentary grief but reject its durability shows his belief that the thoughts and feelings of all Aboriginals are of a lesser order than those of white people. His belief is not that individual Aboriginals can be shallow or deep as also white people can be, but that Aboriginals are essentially inferior and lack the potential for the inner life available to white people.

Another aspect of the racism of the Protector lies in his differentiation of mothers and children, which can have been made only on the basis of their faces. A small difference of appearance distinguished for him those who might be 'saved' from those ever incapable of real life.

The statement of the Protector is not a careful one but rather a dismissive generalisation that suggests a radical imperviousness of the beliefs behind it to evidence and to reason. This is what makes racism different from things like ethnic hatred, as when conflict and confusion make peoples enemies for the time being.

Much racism is rationalised on the basis of differences of capacity, physiology and outlook. To be non-racist, we need to be able to respect people whom we might not be able to understand, due to cultural and linguistic differences, as having inner lives as significant as our own. It means treating their understanding of themselves seriously and being grateful for whatever understanding of it we might achieve.

Reference: Gaita, Raimond. *A Common Humanity* (Melbourne: Text Publishing, 1999).

Farewell to Sir William Deane

It was entirely appropriate that Sir William Deane began his last month in office as Governor-General in 2001 by visiting Aboriginal peoples in the Kimberly region of Western Australia. Throughout his term of office he has shown himself to be a model reconciler by his efforts to sit down with and to come to understand Aboriginal peoples. By going to the Kimberly region he went where dispossession and ill treatment are matters not of history but of current memory.

Sir William said at the beginning of his term that his only power as Governor-General would be the power of persuasion. He has used it well to exercise civic leadership of the highest standard. We have seen it in his speeches such as that at Donald Bradman's memorial service, in his presence at difficult moments such as Port Arthur and Childers, in his prayers at Thredbo and in Switzerland, in the unassuming manner of his attendance at significant public functions.

Fundamental to any act of persuasion is the ability to recognise and to respond to the feelings of those with whom one speaks. Sir William has shown this ability in the hardest of situations during his meetings with those least privileged in our country—the homeless and destitute in our cities and Aboriginal peoples throughout the land. He has also shown it in his acceptance of disappointment at how little many Australians have been prepared to move towards reconciliation. He has not pushed too hard too soon, though he has left a legacy that cannot be ignored.

It is fitting though accidental that Sir William's retirement from office coincides with Aboriginal Sunday. It is a good moment to review progress in reconciliation.

It is easy to be overwhelmed by the relentless continuation of Aboriginal poverty and mortality and by dysfunction in Aboriginal communities. These are difficult conditions that could take generations to rectify. The beginning of change, however, is attitudinal, for as Sir William said at Hall's Creek, "the more you see the more you realise that present disadvantage is the product of past oppression".

I believe that there has been significant change in Australia and that it consists in a fundamental change in Australian consciousness. One can no longer speak of being Australian without giving full account of Aboriginality. I will give three instances of this, which are relatively new in our experience, unlike Aboriginal art that has been with us for some time.

When as Australians we attempt to express our identity as we did at the opening and closing ceremonies of the Olympic games, we cannot but acknowledge Aboriginal culture. At significant meetings, it has become commonplace to conduct a welcome ceremony, which is led by or includes Aboriginal people of the place. Liturgically, some Catholic ceremonies are now regularly accompanied by smoking ceremonies.

Thank you, Sir William.

WAR, CONFLICT AND MEMORY

A Silent Monument to War

Anzac Day always reminds me of great uncle Fred. He was really Thomas Frederick Murray, and I have seen his name written in stone on the cenotaph at Manly and in bronze at the War Memorial in Canberra. It is also inscribed at Lone Pine in Gallipoli, though none of us have seen it there. We know him from a photocopy of his war record and a few letters.

The letters are those of a young man travelling aboard ship to the Middle East. They mention food, illness at sea, and something of the boredom of it all once the initial excitement had worn off. He recounts an incident in which he and a mate were able to slip ashore in a native boat while the ship awaited permission to enter the Suez Canal. Later he describes his first impressions of the countryside in Egypt. However, for the most part the letters are short and meant to keep contact and to assure his parents that they need not worry.

His military record tells us that he enlisted at Liverpool with the Fifth Reinforcements of the First Battalion, AIF, on 15 June 1915. His age is recorded as twenty-one and his occupation as electrician. He left Sydney aboard the HMAT Ceramic on 25 June 1915, was taken on strength on 5 August and landed at Gallipoli 7 August. On 10 or 11 August he was killed at Lone Pine.

On 5 September 1915 Fred's parents received a cable saying that he had been wounded at the beginning of August but that other particulars were unavailable. On 20 September his mother, Margaret, wrote to The Hon WM Hughes, on whose campaign she had worked, asking for help in finding out how he was progressing and saying that she was 'almost worried to distraction'. It was not until the end of January 1916 that a letter was sent from England by a soldier who had been with Fred when he died. Fred had been hit in the chest by a hand-thrown bomb that exploded on impact.

There is other information in the file, but it is mostly a story of the confusion that followed Fred's death, of the difficulty of confirming his fate and of the impossibility of ever finding his burial place.

This is a story much like thousands of others. Yet just over eighty years later it still has an impact. The descendants of Fred's brothers and sisters are so numerous that it is probable that nobody knows them all. His generation are now all dead, but of most of them there are stories—stories of lives that were long and eventful; stories of kindness to children growing up; stories of actions at family gatherings; stories of relationships and of what they still mean to people today. Of Fred there is none of this, and the emptiness stands as a silent monument to war.

The Spirit of the Anzacs

On a monument at Gallipoli erected by the Turkish government, the following words of Ataturk, the founder of modern Turkey and himself a Gallipoli veteran, are engraved.

> These heroes that shed their blood and lost their lives . . . You are now lying in the soil of a friendly country. Therefore rest in peace. There is no difference between the Johnnies and the Mehmets to us where they lie side by side here in this country of ours . . . You, the Mothers, who sent their sons from far away countries, wipe away your tears: your sons are now lying in our bosom and are in peace. After having lost their lives on this land they have become our sons as well.

It is dated 1934.

It is characteristic of the Australian way of remembering war that the event, which we celebrate by way of national recognition of the valour and the sacrifice of our service men and women in all wars, was a defeat. This is not the common practice. European nations tend mainly to erect monuments to their victories such as Nelson's column at Trafalgar Square. The United States may have caught something of our spirit with its Vietnam monument, but soon afterwards it invented a new form of war in which only one side was meant to suffer.

It is also characteristic of the Australian spirit that those who suffered in war kept most of the wretchedness of it to themselves. While Anzac Day itself may have been an annual festival of remembering the whole experience in the company of those who understood it, most stories passed on to succeeding generations were about either humorous incidents or acts of daring. Men, who for decades have woken in the night with fearful dreams, have said very little. While we sometimes regret this silence, we must recognise that in taking their dreams to the grave with them, they have ensured that those same dreams did not become the stuff of hate for succeeding generations.

The purpose of war, if, indeed, it has a purpose, is not winning per se. It is that the world be a better place after the war is over. Australians do not value war, nor do we want it, though history shows us that sometimes it seems unavoidable. What we remember is the worst and the best of it—death and destruction; courage and self-giving.

It is reasonable to suggest that the spirit of the Anzacs was a factor in the conditions that enabled Ataturk to say the words cited above only eighteen years after the end of the war. He was able to show the same warmth for his one-time enemies as he showed for his own people.

Reconciliation is always difficult to achieve, and especially so when people have been maimed and killed. Yet the Anzacs and the Turks managed it in a very short time.

Keeping Humanitarian Contacts Clean

The revelations on an Australian television program, *Dateline* (2/2/2000 on SBS), which had been rightly kept from public broadcast until all three Care workers imprisoned in Yugoslavia had been freed from jail and had left the country, carried two surprises. The first, was that the intelligence contract was with the Canadian Government rather than the governments of the United States or the United Kingdom. The second, was how forthright the National Directors of Care Canada and Care Australia, John Watson and Charles Tapp, were in defending the contract.

It was not a surprise to discover that a murky deal involving non-humanitarian work in Yugoslavia by the humanitarian organisation had been done. The discovery that it had and what it was were only a matter of time, and, despite denials at many levels of government and of the aid community, it had always been a possibility.

What appears to have happened is that Care Canada undertook a contract with the Canadian Government to engage in peace monitoring activities in Yugoslavia on behalf of the Organisation for Security and Co-operation in Europe. The detail of the activities is unclear, but it almost surely involved monitoring military operations of some sorts. While not technically a military intelligence operation, the information gathered was almost certainly used by the NATO forces bombing Yugoslavia.

Another program, *Four Corners*, on Australia's ABC television, in February 2000 interviewed Pratt and Wallace and provided further interesting information. The NATO bombing war began six days before their arrest and ended three days after the end of their trial. Among the papers in Pratt's possession were a curriculum vitae, which made it clear that he had the capability of being a military observer, and a situation report, which contained a paragraph about fighting centres in strategically important areas.

Pratt insisted that he was not engaged in gathering military intelligence as such but that what he gathered was important to Care Australia for its humanitarian operation. That is a fair claim but one that is hard to prove in the public forum. It will, however, become a less significant issue now that the three men are free, and we can only hope they and their families will be able to get their lives back together.

The more significant claim, however, which I am prepared to make, is that the Yugoslavian Government, in a time of war, when it suspected that covert operations were directed against it and with the evidence that it had, was justified in suspecting and prosecuting Pratt and by implication his associates for spying.

This is of great moment for Care International, which must now decide whether it wants to remain a humanitarian organisation that can expect free and safe access to people in misery or whether it wants to be a quasi-military peace monitoring organisation, in which case it will be regarded with suspicion in hostile environments.

On the Future of Anzac Day

An eminent persons group was formed a few years back by the Returned Servicemans' League (RSL) to conduct a government-funded review of the way in which we celebrate and regard Anzac Day. The declining number of living veterans of war, it seems, has prompted the review. There are now fewer than thirty World Way I veterans, and the RSL expected that by 2010 there will be only a few World War II veterans still able to march. The assumption behind their concern is that with few veterans to march the day will cease to be celebrated.

The assumption may or may not be valid. It will be invalid if, in fact, children, grandchildren and great-grandchildren of veterans continue to march. It will also be invalid if we face a major war during this decade. It is, however, reasonable to think about how, given current projections, things might change.

Something that should not happen is that Anzac Day become armed services day. It has always been for veterans, most of whom had returned to civilian life. Further, it has always celebrated the sacrifice of soldiers who gave their lives of necessity even if futilely. It has never been a celebration of military might or prowess. Australia has been outstanding on the world scene in so far as its remembrance has been founded on a campaign that was a loss. This has enabled us to respect sacrifice without becoming triumphalistic.

A suggestion that is being mooted is that Anzac Day become Australia Day. It is understandable that some for whom personal experience has made Anzac central to their identity as Australians might think this. The suggestion does, however, depend on a profound misunderstanding of differences between the two days.

Australia Day, whenever we decide to celebrate it, is a day about beginnings and hope and joy. Packed into to it are not so much the past but what we hold for the future, our anticipations and expectations. Anzac is about endings and sadness and respect marked by a note of sombreness. It is not about the future but about past events and actions that we honour while at the same time hoping that their like does not return. Were it to become otherwise, we would risk triumphalism and militarism.

It is unlikely that our future will be free of war of any kind. Whenever there will be wars in which we find ourselves through no fault of our own, there will be sacrifices that we will want to recognise and human lives that we will want to honour without any sense of shame. Part of the meaning of Anzac Day is to remind us that this is how we want to be – not warlike but in the face of war brave and self-giving.

It seems to me then, that we should continue to march and that we should march as civilians, whether we have been to war or not.

REASON TO LAUGH

On Talking to Oneself in Public

From time to time one hears speeches or sees written statements that seem to come from nowhere, to go nowhere and, while they may seem to address someone, to address no one. Although one presumes that any locution is meant for someone and suspects that this particular one may even be meant for oneself, one recognises that something is amiss - speaker and hearer do not meet in any recognisable way.

In the early seventies, Richard B Gregg, made a rhetorical analysis of the speeches of three different protest movements. He began with the usual assumption in such studies that 'when people communicate with each other, they somehow physically or symbolically face toward each other' and that 'if the act of communication is to be successful, there must be a mutual willingness and commitment to interact'.

He found, however, that this analysis did not work. The mix of impossible demands, chanted slogans and a general refusal to make any identification with those, usually authorities, who were apparently being addressed, meant that these speeches did not fall into the classical pattern of persuasive speech.

Gregg's breakthrough was to realise that these speeches were not for the sake of those to whom they were apparently addressed or even for the sake of those who heard them. They were, rather, exercises in self-persuasion even though carried out in public. Their function was to build up the self or the ego of the speaker and of those represented by but not addressed by the speaker.

Thinking that one is being addressed by a speech like this is very confusing. One can only empathise, for instance, with a policeman who was called 'a fascist pig'. He was not to know that, rather than being a statement about his character, this was merely an attempt by the speaker to establish his or her own identity. The insult was a by-product.

One of the problems of this kind of speech is that, while at first hearing it can seem impressive, its effect quickly evaporates when exposed. I saw this happen during a protest rally at Macquarie University in the seventies. During a pause part-way through an impassioned and captivating performance, a labourer on top of the new administration building roared out a short, crude statement ending with '. . . Love'. The speaker had to acknowledge another person and the ego-building performance fell apart.

To ensure that we do not fall into the practice of this kind of ego-building, we, in the Church, often use the language of dialogue. Although the term 'dialogue' is used in numbers of ways and some of them are often a little fuzzy, what it is trying to get at is the fact that constructive speech acts cannot stand alone. A serious interlocutor has to deal fairly with the positions and statements of other persons, even if in disagreement.

Reference: Richard B Gregg, 'The Ego-Function of the Rhetoric of Protest', in *Philosophy and Rhetoric* 4 (Spring, 1971): 71–91.

Roofs that Leak; Some that Don't

In Ireland there is a roof that was constructed over 5000 years ago (around 3200 BC) and that today still keeps the floor dry. It belongs to a tomb of the type known as a passage-grave and is at Newgrange in County Meath near the river Boyne.

The tomb is made of stone and the roof is corbelled, that is, slabs of stone are laid horizontally in such a way that each overlaps the wall below it. Successive layers of roof-stones are also corbelled so that eventually they meet at a capstone. This structure is covered with round boulders that form a monumental cairn.

A feature of the tomb is that groves have been cut in the upper surfaces of the roof-stones so as to carry water that has filtered down through the cairn from roof-stone to roof-stone until it falls beyond the walls of the tomb.

Although no doubt an expensive construction in its time, the success of this building in keeping the elements out for so long provides strong contrast to the experiences of many in the Church today who have had to deal with inadequacies in the construction of modern roof structures.

Institutional buildings like those owned by the Church are generally large and tend to have either flat roofs or very elaborate roofs. Too frequently the flat roofs have internal gutters that flood or are compromised by service ducting, which in time begins to leak. The more elaborate roofs can also be a long-term headache.

The commonness of failure in this area leads one to suggest that it relates to a major failing within the architectural community itself. It involves both practitioners and educators and seems to have two dimensions. One is a failure of principle; the other is a denial of reality.

The principle can be simply stated as 'if it has a hat on, it will stay dry'. Professionals may wish to state this differently, but too often we see roofs that resemble swimming pools with small exit holes in their sides. Questioned about the problems that necessarily arise, architects too often reply, 'It is a question of maintenance'.

The denial is of the existence and properties of water. Although water is catered for by drains and down-pipes, the overriding intent in design is to ensure that these are not seen. They are often hidden behind walls or buried in pillars so that water is made to follow tortuous paths rather than the more easy routes it would naturally follow, and so blockages are frequent.

The church commissions many buildings that are large and complex. While we might not expect and could probably not afford structures of the enduring quality of our stone-age forebears, we do have ground for insisting that our facilities are designed in such a way as to remain leak-free for a long time.

Reference: Claire O'Kelly, *Concise Guide to Newgrange* (Cork: Houston Printers Ltd, 1996).

Rationality in the Modern Age

One of the advantages the motor car has over other forms of transport seems to be that each small unit is under the control of a rational being, who is able to modify the vehicle's progress in accord with observed conditions.

It is interesting to consider how this works on our growing number of three-lane carriageways. Let us consider a freeway in Sydney, New South Wales, say the M4 which runs from one of the suburbs, Strathfield, to the base of the Blue Mountains, out of Sydney, in Penrith.

In mid-afternoon, as traffic builds past moderate levels, most cars are travelling in the right lane. The drivers of these vehicles are important people, and their importance is gauged by the lateness with which they began their drive for an appointment of some note. Most people in this lane drive with a sense of urgency, but there are some exceptions. An aggressive feminist knows that out here no man will pass her, and a man in a big hat is anxiously preparing for a right turn somewhere the other side of the mountains.

The middle lane, though busy, is a little less packed and sometimes travels faster. This is the lane for solid citizens, people of good character who deviate neither right nor left. One tends to find retirees or families with small children, though again there are exceptions. Here also are found people with chiropractic necks, who cannot turn to see what is in the other lanes, and the occasional builder with a dodgy load, who cannot see anything behind him anyway.

The left lane has least traffic. It contains an occasional slow vehicle and some heavy trucks. The boyos weave in and out of this lane as they try to see who can get to Penrith fastest.

There is a reason for avoiding the left hand lane. Either the Road Traffic Authority in New South Wales has not yet learnt how to construct entry ramps to a freeway, or Treasury decided to save money by making most of them too short for traffic to be able to merge smoothly.

Along the motorway large signs warn of hefty fines for anyone who drives in a right hand lane for reasons other than overtaking. Nobody I know has ever heard of anyone receiving one of these fines, even though the signs have been in place for a number of years.

There is good reason for the traffic authority to begin to levy fines for those who drive on the right for reasons other than overtaking or dense traffic. For a start, it would bring in a great deal of revenue. The State Government would be able to keep the Australian Olympic Committee rolling in gravy for many years to come without ever having to go to the trouble of running sporting events.

More importantly, the fear of the blue and red lights would induce drivers to begin to use the roadway in the manner for which it was intended, which shows just how rationality works in the modern age.

Now, Why Didn't I Say that Before?

Many of us from time to time experience mild annoyance when, walking away from an encounter with people, we think of what we should have said. I am told that there is even a name for this experience in French and that it equates to something like 'a thought on the back stairs', an unfortunate place to make one's best response.

There are, no doubt, a number of factors that give rise to this experience. Lack of self-assertion, timidity or poor language skills might be blamed, but most of us probably put it down to slowness of thought. We 'do not think well on our feet'. Philosophers suggest another reason that has to do with the structure of perception itself.

Occasionally in a class, I hold up a solid cube and ask my students how many sides it has. Most answer quickly that it has six, and a few shrewd or suspicious students suspect a trick. I then point out that they could have seen at the most three sides. In fact, without mirrors or other devices we can never see more than three sides of a solid cube from one position or at one time.

When I was a child we used to sing a song that went like this. 'The bear went over the mountain . . . to see what he could see. And what do you think he saw? . . . The other side of the mountain . . . and that is what he saw.' It may seem all very obvious to adults, but that is our loss. Young children have yet to learn to anticipate with confidence something that they cannot see. At the same time, they know that it is very obvious that the bear would indeed see the other side of the mountain.

When something is given to us in perception, it comes as a flowing mixture of directly intuited aspects and of anticipated aspects of the thing. We may address it with all of our senses and over a period of time. When we bring unity to all of this, the act of perceiving is somehow complete. In complex situations this may take considerable time, and the perception can be said to reverberate in us.

Human interactions are often far more complex than physical phenomena. We have to deal with what is said, with what it might have meant to the different people present, with how they might have been feeling, with what was done, with body language, with what had happened before, with events seemingly unconnected. It is when the reverberations stop and the perception comes to term that we are ready to speak, even if it is then too late.

People who respond quickly are often very funny, because they precipitate the incomplete perceptions of others. They do, however, sometimes jump to wrong conclusions, and then we usually wish that they had been slower to speak.

The Long Path to Safety on the Roads

I happen to live not far from the notorious new permanent speed camera on Concord Road in Sydney, which has caught up to 240 people a day. I know a number of them, and some of their stories are funny. The camera is placed at the bottom of gentle hill, at the end of a shopping centre, around a left hand curve.

What is surprising, even when one takes the controversial placement of the camera into consideration, is that people do not notice it. It is an ugly piece of machinery in clear view at the side of the road. It is preceded by two signs, one of which says 'Speed camera in use 24 hours' and the other 'Your speed will be checked'. Such notices are placed only where there are cameras, and fulfil the Road Traffic Authority's (RTA) obligation to give warning about cameras.

I suspect that one of the reasons that people do not read these signs is that they have learnt not to. For some years now, the RTA has used signs with blue lettering on a white background as what we might call promotional signs—signs promoting compliance. 'Speed cameras used in NSW', 'Keep to the left unless overtaking', 'Operation X is now targeting Y'. Our instincts have been trained to ignore them altogether.

The shattering of instinct by placement of the cameras should be a final sign to drivers that speeding is no longer an option. In similar fashion, random breath testing and the criminalisation of drink driving have finally convinced us that drink driving is not an option and in doing so have brought enormous reduction to the road toll. We should be very happy about this.

If any criticism is to be levelled at the RTA, it is that their focus has been too narrow and that there are other practices that are also dangerous that have not been targeted. Chief among these, in my view, is the use of mobile phones in cars.

Research by Charles Spence at the University of Oxford has shown that the danger from using mobile phones while driving approaches that of drink driving. Spence researches 'cross-modal links in human attention' and has found that, when we listen to a mobile phone while driving, our attention is divided between our senses of hearing and sight and that this confuses our sense of direction.

The practices that the RTA has targeted are those that are easily detected by instruments thereby dispensing to some degree with the use of human skills and judgement. While there are good economic grounds for this, there is also in it something of the spirit of an age that is fascinated with instruments and machines. Perhaps policing of our so far minimal laws on the use of mobile phones while driving awaits the invention of yet another machine. A narrowly focused radiation-seeking destructive ray would do.

A Conversation with the Plumber

A recent conversation with a plumber revealed lots of interesting things to me, some of them to do with plumbing itself, but most of them to do with people and with what they perceive and how they react to things.

His experience with dripping taps demonstrated the breadth of human reactions to similar situations. At one extreme, some people notice and react to the slightest drip. He recounted one case in which a person had called him to fix a dripping tap, which, he found, was simply not turned off properly. He turned it off, but the person wanted it 'fixed' anyway.

At the other extreme, some people do not notice dripping taps at all. He cited a case in which he was called to repair a toilet but noticed that a tap was running quite badly due to a broken washer. He pointed this out to the home owner, who said, 'Oh, is it?'

Things can get more complex. In a larger job, he found a set of units in which washers with metal backings were used and in which the hot water temperature was set too high. This caused the hot water taps to start dripping as soon as the metal in the taps cooled down. Again, people reacted differently.

Some did not notice. Others noticed the dripping and were unhappy with it. Others realised what was happening and easily developed habits of turning taps off twice—initially and after the pipes had cooled. Still others understood what was happening but left the taps dripping, while attributing to themselves an inability to turn off taps properly.

What is interesting philosophically about these examples is that they illustrate how differently people perceive things around them and how differently they react to what they perceive. We tend to presume that people see exactly what we see, and then we become puzzled when it becomes obvious that they have not seen something that we regard as obvious. Similarly, we often expect that people will react to things in the same ways that we do. We readily blame people who seem to come up short. We offer surprised praise to people who seem to do something 'exceptional'.

Although we generally presume that what we each perceive is precisely the same, this is not the case. What is amazing is that we are actually able to communicate at all about how we find the world when first seeings are often so different. We work to achieve exactness with words and through careful conversation. When science, on the other hand, wishes to describe the world with precision, it turns away from the senses and uses instruments and applies numbers. This is a powerful and successful technique, but it also leaves out much that is enriched by our personal responses to the world and particularly those things that fall into the realm that we call imagination.

Being on Time

My first degree was in physics, and although much of it is lost to me now, Galileo's physics sticks with me. The time to leave one place is the expected time of arrival at the other place minus the travel time. It could not be simpler, except that few people can manage it.

When I was fifteen, my family moved to the city. I had always walked to mass and was always early. After all, I was the only altar server in our village, and things had to be prepared. In the city, the family travelled to mass by car, all ten of us. I could not understand why we were always late.

One Sunday morning, I stood at the car and watched what happened. Various members of the family in turn appeared at the back door and looked out. Seeing only me, they turned back inside to do something that needed to be done. Eventually, it was clear that we would be late and all managed to emerge at the same time.

On the following Sunday, I again went to the car early and as each person appeared at the back door drew them out. In short time, a critical mass developed and off we went to mass, on time for the first time in ages. Nobody could quite understand why.

Friends do not always cope with punctuality, but there are ways to deal with it. When now close friends first invited me for a formal dinner party, I turned up at exactly 7 pm as requested. I rang the doorbell and was treated through the screen door to the sight of family members running across the hall from bathroom to bedroom in various states of undress. In the twenty or more years since, my invitation to dinner has always been set for thirty minutes after the time set for their other friends.

For those who prefer to be late, there are compensations. In the years that I studied in Washington DC, I took up symphony concert subscription tickets with friends who always drove me to the Kennedy Centre. They were always late. I learnt to stand on the curb at the designated time and to wait without incrimination but also without the anxiety that I had kept them late. We were always surprised that the traffic downtown was busy on a Friday evening, but we made it to the concert stressed and anxious but relieved to be inside the hall as the doors were closed. The concert seemed better for it.

There are, of course, times when being late cannot be avoided. Traffic accidents happen; people get sick; public transport is disrupted; miscalculations can be made. But in the end, normally and for the most part, as Aristotle would say, Galileo was right. The time to leave one place is the expected time of arrival at the other place minus the travel time. The Higgs boson and other remarkable discoveries have nothing on that.

The End of an Adventure

It is over five years since I began writing these essays in *The Catholic Weekly*, and I decided some time ago it would be time for me to take a rest before moving on to other forms of writing. This then, is my last essay.

In these essays, I have tried to reflect as a philosopher and as a Christian. Faith and reason, which John Paul II called 'two wings on which the human spirit rises to the contemplation of truth', have for me not found themselves in conflict, and remain solid guides to the understanding of a reality that is far greater than any of us can fully grasp.

The work of a philosopher is to make distinctions, in other words, to display differences in things. Often these differences are there for all to see and the work of the philosopher is simply to draw attention to something to which otherwise people may not have adverted. This can both bring insight and clarify confusion.

If this sounds a little dry, the philosopher, Michael Oakeshott, captured something of its spirit in the following words.

> Philosophical reflection is recognized here as the adventure of one who seeks to understand in other terms what he already understands and in which the understanding sought is a disclosure of the conditions of the understanding enjoyed and not a substitute for it. Its most appropriate expression is an essay where the character of the utterance (a traveller's tale) matches the character of the engagement, an intellectual adventure which has a course to follow, but no destination.

The life of a Christian consists in identification with the person of Jesus Christ. While this has its personal and mystical dimensions, it has also communal dimensions and calls for engagement with the mission of Jesus, which we find stated in Luke's Gospel (4:18–19) at the beginning of the public ministry in Galilee.

'He has sent me to bring the good news to the poor, to proclaim liberty to captives and to the blind new sight, to set the downtrodden free, to proclaim the Lord's year of favour.' I take it from this that involvement in seeking justice particularly for those who suffer most and who can claim least for themselves is essential to the Christian life. Alternatively, its neglect or lack of concern brings diminishment to that life.

I have tried to keep these two dimensions of my life together as I have written and chosen topics from week to week. My success or otherwise is for others to judge, but as time has gone on they have drawn me more and more into matters of the day. Nevertheless, it has been an adventure.

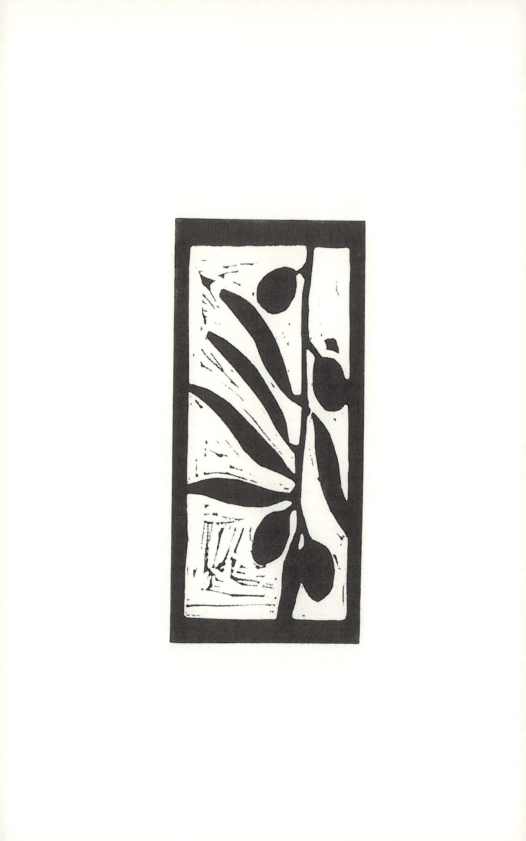

Topical Index

Fundamentalism, 44, 57, 76.
Funeral, 22, 101.

G

GM crops, 174.
God, 1, 8, 18, 20, 22, 23, 24, 26, 27, 28, 32, 33, 34, 35,
40, 43, 45, 46, 49, 51, 52, 53, 54, 55, 56, 57, 58, 71, 94, 99, 111, 139, 180, 197.
Good, 1, 2, 3, 4, 6, 8, 9, 10, 11, 14, 21, 26, 32, 33, 36, 44, 51, 52, 55, 58, 61, 65, 66, 71, 72, 76, 77, 81, 82, 87, 88, 89, 93, 94, 96, 99, 100, 101, 102, 103, 107, 108, 110, 113, 114, 121, 122, 129, 131, 132, 135, 136, 145, 152, 159, 160, 163, 168, 171, 172, 176, 179, 184, 188, 190, 196, 198, 200, 213, 214, 221.
Good Samaritan, 45, 55, 180.
Gospel, 12, 17, 20, 21, 22, 24, 27, 48, 49, 50, 52, 55, 58, 93, 98, 123, 124, 139, 184, 221.
Government, 7, 25, 34, 61, 67, 91, 95, 104, 116, 132, 135, 136, 138, 140, 146, 147, 149, 150, 151, 157, 158, 159, 160, 162, 164, 170, 171, 173, 175, 176, 177, 178, 179, 180, 182, 183, 184, 186, 187, 189, 190, 196, 206, 207, 208, 213.

H

Happiness, 1, 3, 65, 66, 67, 71, 89, 188.
Hell, 37.
Homosexuality, 12, 137.
Hope, 3, 7, 12, 17, 18, 19, 22, 23, 41, 48, 52, 78, 79, 87, 89, 96, 98, 103, 109, 112, 116, 123, 135, 152, 159, 182, 187, 198, 205, 208.

I

Injecting room, 135, 136.
Intellectual virtues, 80.
Intelligence, 80, 182, 207.

J

Joke, 58, 90, 133.
Journalism, 4.
Jubilee 2000, 92, 160, 172.
Justice, 9, 13, 27, 34, 46, 47, 53, 58, 68, 108, 121, 125, 139, 160, 165, 173, 176, 177, 179, 183, 188, 193, 196, 198, 221.

K

Kingdom of God, 26, 50, 52, 58.
Knowing, 4, 14, 20, 57, 58, 71, 72, 76, 87, 96.
Knowledge, 17, 18, 39, 54, 62, 65, 66, 67, 71,

72, 78, 80, 81, 87, 100, 108, 109, 130, 162, 167, 175.

L

Labor Party, the Australian, 190.
Leadership, 36, 61, 104, 119, 122, 125, 147, 150, 190, 198, 201.
Lent, 19, 23, 28, 92.
Liberal society, 7, 91, 118, 131, 132, 138, 145, 151, 152.
Liberal democracy, 131, 171, 181.
Liberal Party of Australia, 183, 190.
Liberalism, 132, 148, 149, 151.
Literacy, 62.
Love, 3, 12, 20, 22, 24, 27, 33, 34, 36, 40, 45, 55, 58, 63, 71, 72, 83, 94, 96, 99, 101, 103, 139, 160, 180, 181, 211.
Luck, 11, 21, 79, 89, 100.
Lying, 79, 183, 185, 190, 206.

M

Magisterium, 39, 44, 47, 120.
Marist, 35, 48, 101.
Marriage, 18, 19, 42, 58, 88, 91, 95, 100, 115.
Meaning, 3, 4, 8, 17, 18, 28, 31, 32, 39, 42, 49, 51, 53, 56, 61, 62, 73, 75, 96, 98, 116, 121, 134, 138, 147, 163, 164, 181, 186, 197, 208.
Media, 4, 31, 57, 117, 137, 141, 165, 167, 172, 175, 180, 183, 190, 197.
Medicine, 6, 56, 67, 174.
Millennium, 52, 56, 67, 92, 114, 120, 160, 186.
Ministry and Integrity, 111, 123.
Modernity, 31, 35, 57, 75, 138, 198.
Morality, 111, 153, 173.
Myth, 53, 54, 93, 98, 182.

N

Neo-classical tradition, 149.

O

One Nation Party, Australia, 162, 163, 181.
Opinion, 7, 12, 37, 61, 78, 91, 121, 124, 130, 135, 136, 141, 146, 147, 162, 167, 181, 185, 199.

P

Parliament, 68, 136, 158, 159, 174, 183, 190.
Parliamentary privilege, 183.
Paschal Mystery, 41, 101, 109, 112.

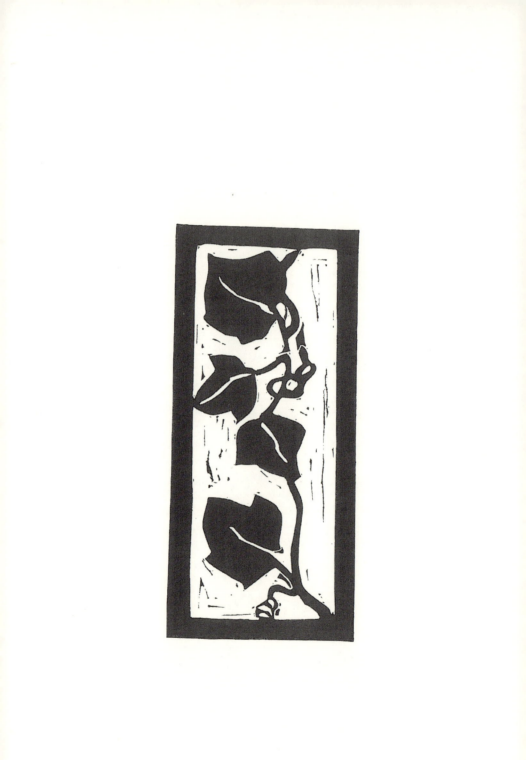

Index of Names